THE FUTURE
OF HISTORY

Essays in the

Vanderbilt University Centennial Symposium

Edited by

C H A R L E S F. D E L Z E L L

V A N D E R B I L T U N I V E R S I T Y P R E S S

Nashville, Tennessee   1977

Library of Congress Cataloging in Publication Data

Centennial Symposium on the Future of History,
  Vanderbilt University, 1975.
  The future of history.

  Includes bibliographical references.
  1. History—Congresses.   I. Delzell, Charles F.   II. Vanderbilt. University,
Nashville. III. Title.
D3.U6C4 1975   900   76–48199
ISBN 0–8265–1205–4

THE FUTURE OF HISTORY

Contents

Preface

This collection of perceptive essays had its origin in the Centennial Symposium on "The Future of History" that was held recently at Vanderbilt University. The advent of the University's second century of classroom instruction in 1975 suggested to some of us who make history our profession that this was an appropriate time to pause and reflect on the nature and scope of present-day historical study and its relationship to other scholarly disciplines; to assess where we are in our understanding of certain regions, periods, and branches of historical study; and to engage in cautious speculation about the paths that Clio may be inclined to pursue in the years that lie just ahead.

For this purpose we invited a number of thoughtful and respected historians to our campus to present a series of public lectures in which they would carefully address themselves to the problem of "the future of history" as they perceive it in their own fields of inquiry, fields which embrace some of the "new" as well as more "traditional" approaches to the discipline. Each participant was free to tackle his assignment in the manner he felt best. Those of us who had the privilege of listening to these scholarly presentations found them instructive and insightful. We hope that this timely publication of the lectures will help to make it possible for the entire historical profession, and many interested laymen as well, to share the observations and reflections of these specialists. All of the participants in the symposium have had an opportunity to revise and footnote their original papers.

Our understanding of the dimensions of history has broadened considerably during the past century or two; it is not unlikely that our conceptions may expand still more in the years ahead. It is sufficient to mention only one or two examples. Historians since the time of Karl Marx have tended to pay closer attention to the possibility that economic factors may have influenced many aspects of history, though most non-Communist historians stop short of making the Marxist theory of class struggle the sole determinant. In 1929 another important and influential school of historiography emerged in France when a loosely organized group of historians began to popularize a sophisticated new "social history" ("history from the bottom up," in contrast to Thomas Carlyle's elitist "history from the top down"). Its proponents, who rejected an ideological point of view, were concerned chiefly with the "structures" of history that endure over a long span of time, and with the social and cultural history of ordinary people. They came to be known as the "Annalistes," from their association with the bimonthly journal that is now entitled *Annales, Économies, Sociétés, Civilisations*. Historians of the caliber of Marc Bloch (in medieval social and economic history), Lucien Febvre (in the field of the French Renaissance), and Fernand Braudel (in the study of the Mediterranean basin in the age of Philip II of Spain) underscored the importance of geography, climate, food, trade patterns, and population shifts—rather than wars, treaties, and dynastic marriages—in shaping history. This school of historiography received encouragement from the VIe Section (Sciences économiques et sociales) of the French École Pratique des Hautes Études. Meanwhile, in England, an analogous movement gathered around the journal, *Past and Present*, founded in 1952 and currently edited by Trevor H. Aston of Corpus Christi College, Oxford. These scholars, in writing their social history, looked especially to census reports, estate financial records, parish registers, and local history rather than to state papers.

In view of this increasingly intimate linkup of history, geography, and the various social sciences, it seemed clear to those of us who planned the Centennial Symposium that the relationship of history to the economic and social sciences was a topic that must be explored. In this task we were fortunate to engage the support of Lawrence Stone, who was trained in both Britain and France and is now Dodge Professor of History and Director of the Shelby Cullom Davis Center of Historical Studies at Princeton University. Stone offered to present a paper that would focus on the interpenetration of "History and the Social Sciences in the Twentieth Century," and that would assess the contributions as well as the dangers that the latter disciplines bring to historiography. His lecture considered such aspects of the "new history" as the history of science, demographic history, the history of social change, the history of mass culture (*mentalités*), urban history, and history of the family. He also noted psychohistory and the new economic history.

Several of the above subtopics were subjects for ensuing lectures. Professor Stephan Thernstrom of Harvard University reflected on the "new urban history," a field which he has done much to cultivate.

Professor Kenneth A. Lockridge of the University of Michigan at Ann Arbor explained the kind of research that is now being undertaken in "historical demography." I. Bernard Cohen, Professor of the History of Science at Harvard University, analyzed "The Many Faces of the History of Science" in a broad-ranging lecture that was subtitled "A Font of Examples for Philosophers, a Scientific Type of History, an Archaeology of Discovery, a Branch of Sociology, a Variant of Intellectual or Social History—OR WHAT?"

Intellectual history, a genre which in the judgment of at least some observers now faces a crisis, was the subject of an attentive reconsideration by Paul K. Conkin, who holds the doctorate from Vanderbilt University and is now Professor of History at the University of Wisconsin at Madison. He entitled his probing essay, "Intellectual History: Past, Present, and Future."

The fruitful opportunities for writing regional and comparative history were in the minds of those who designed the symposium. The history of the American South is a field in which Vanderbilt has shown much scholarly interest, especially since the 1930s and 1940s when the late Professor Frank L. Owsley and his students launched social studies of the "plain folk of the Old South" and other themes. We therefore invited C. Vann Woodward, Sterling Professor of History at Yale University and a former President of the American Historical Association, to examine "The Future of Southern History," which gives every appearance of being one of the most active frontiers of historical scholarship. Woodward's paper touched, of course, upon the Afro-American experience.

Regional history on a still larger geographical and comparative scale, "Latin American History in World Perspective," was carefully examined by Woodrow Borah, Abraham D. Shepard Professor of History at the University of California in Berkeley. Professor John W. Hall, who holds the A. Whitney Griswold chair of history at Yale University, undertook a somewhat parallel assignment in his lecture, "Japanese History in World Perspective." These topics were of special interest to Vanderbilt University's Center for Latin American Studies and its Program of East Asian Studies.

Certain problems of periodization in history provided the framework for two other lectures in the symposium. Lewis W. Spitz, who is William R. Kenan Professor of History at Stanford University, analyzed the rationale for continuing to treat the Renaissance and Reformation as a justifiable "period" of history. Gordon Wright, William H. Bonsall Professor of History at Stanford University and

President of the American Historical Association at the time, reflected on the imprecisions of "Contemporary History in the Contemporary Age."

In a lecture that ably inaugurated the series, Richard W. Leopold, William Smith Professor of History at Northwestern University, offered a number of perceptive observations about the past, present, and future trends in the study of the history of American foreign policy.

The participants in the symposium varied considerably in their approaches to the theme of the lecture series. Several of them were, understandably, reluctant to extrapolate the future from the past and the present. After all, the historian, by definition, is concerned with chronicling and interpreting the human past. Thus all of the participants did what historians generally find themselves most comfortable doing—that is to say, they took stock of the contemporary state of the discipline in their own fields of competence, and they examined with a critical eye some of the new trends in historical methodologies and interpretations. Although it is not easy to reduce to a single statement the wisdom imbedded in these scholarly reflections, one message does seem to recur through most of the essays: the historian should keep his mind open to new methodologies and revisionisms but at the same time preserve a healthy skepticism of pseudosciences, new dogmatisms, and the merely faddish. As Professor Thernstrom observed, "The most thorough mastery of the new techniques is not sufficient to make a good historian, much less a great one." Above and beyond the possible development of technical competence in some of the new methodologies, the historian of tomorrow must continue to nourish his aesthetic and humanistic sensibilities and work harder at refining the skills of writing lucidly and persuasively.

The list of topics that might well have deserved attention in a symposium of this type is, of course, considerably longer than the eleven essays published here. If money, time, and the stamina of our audiences were unlimited, we should have liked to accord special attention to Africa and the Middle East, to continental Asia, to various national histories, to women's history, black history, and numerous other topics. Their absence from this volume is not to be construed as meaning that we regard them as being of little importance. We hope that this cluster of essays will help to inspire similar reflection on the future of these and perhaps other significant fields of history.

As coordinator of the Centennial Symposium and editor of this volume, I wish to thank the members of the Department of History at

Vanderbilt University for their advice, assistance, and faithful participation in the undertaking. I owe a special debt of gratitude to Chancellor Alexander Heard, Executive Vice-Chancellor and Provost James R. Surface, former Provost Nicholas Hobbs, Vice-Chancellor for Alumni Relations John W. Poindexter, and Reba Wilcoxon, Associate to the Chancellor, for their generous support of the symposium and this book.

CHARLES F. DELZELL

April 1976

THE FUTURE OF HISTORY

1

History and the Social Sciences in the Twentieth Century

Lawrence Stone

I. *The Evolution of the Historical Profession*

From the sixteenth to the mid-nineteenth century, history became increasingly popular as a field of research, writing, and education, and from Guicciardini through Ralegh and Clarendon to Gibbon, Voltaire, and Macaulay there appeared some of the most readable and enduring works of narrative history that have ever been written.[1] These books were essential elements in creating the high culture of their time, in the sense that all men of education and sophistication were expected to have read and to have absorbed their contents. At the same time, it was also expected that an educated man would also be familiar, if only in translation, with the great classical historians such as Thucydides, Suetonius, Livy, Plutarch, and Tacitus.

History was widely accepted at this time as an essential part of a gentlemanly education for three main reasons. Firstly, it was believed to be a source of moral instruction, a story which demonstrated how, thanks to the beneficent providence of God, virtue in the end triumphed over vice. This comforting theory was coolly ignored by Machiavelli in *The Prince* in the sixteenth century and savagely satirized by Voltaire in *Candide* in the eighteenth, but neither work seems to have had much effect on public consciousness. There is thus a great gulf between the attitude of past generations to the moral lessons of history and that of our own day, when it is assumed as almost axiomatic that the wicked will flourish and that most men in positions of political power are self-seeking and probably corrupt paranoiacs, and more interested in furthering their own careers than in serving the public good. This is an utterly different perception of

3

the objectives, stature, and achievements of major political actors from that generally prevalent before the mid-nineteenth century.

Secondly, history was a prime source of entertainment, providing a narrative story more gripping, more intriguing, and more meaningful than the long-winded and artificial romances and novels of the day. Sober apparent truth, as elegantly told by historians, was regarded as more interesting than the imaginative constructs of creative writers. Thirdly, history was thought to be an invaluable source of instruction for adolescents, to teach them about the nature of man and the nature of political power. As such, it was required reading for the sons of the elite, who were being trained at home, in academies, or at the universities for future positions of political leadership.

It is possible to obtain an illuminating insight into the nature and scope of history as it was regarded in 1850, just at the end of this long amateur-status phase, and before it developed into a full-fledged profession carried on almost exclusively by full-time experts working in universities. The evidence comes from the inaugural lecture in 1848 of the Regius Professor of History at the University of Oxford, H. H. Vaughan. Vaughan had a tragic and ultimately sterile career and produced little or nothing of permanent value, but he had a vision of what history ought to be which is of considerable historiographical significance today. The key issue every historian should tackle, according to Vaughan, is "a disclosure of the critical changes in the condition of society." It should be noted that the emphasis here is on change, not on static description, and that the nature of change in history is defined neither as recurrent nor periodic, as in the social or natural sciences, but as critical and, therefore, presumably unique. The subject matter of history Vaughan described in the broadest of terms, ranging far into popular, social, and cultural history in a way that would win the approval of the newest of the "new" historians of today: "There are institutions, laws, customs, tastes, traditions, beliefs, convictions, magistracies, festivals, pastimes, and ceremonies, and other such elements of social organization which are both in thought and in fact distinguishable from the condition of a national unity." Vaughan's definition of the content of history thus went far beyond the political evolution of the nation state, to embrace the widest possible range of sociocultural phenomena. Indeed, he went out of his way to express considerable skepticism about the writing of history exclusively in institutional terms, on the ground that such an approach provides a very misleading guide to change over time. Institutions, he wrote, "preserve their name, but they change their qualities, or, maintaining the type of their original structure, they exercise new powers altogether. Under such conditions alone are they truly, actively and healthily permanent."[2] This is the very same point made by Walter Bagehot in his classic study of the English constitution published less than twenty years later.[3]

The qualities of a good historian, according to Vaughan, are three: the first is the "principle of attraction to the facts"—in other words, a passionate curiosity about the past, and an infinite capacity for taking pains in the delving into musty archives to find them. The second is "instincts of expectations more or less definite"—in other words, a preconceived hunch to be tested against the factual record. This is a position normal enough for the social or natural scientist, but one which was for a century to follow to be anathema to the professional historian. The third is the "habits of rapid recognition"—the intuitive gift of picking out the significant detail in a chaotic mass of documentation.

If Vaughan can be regarded as at all typical in his interpretation of the historian's function as seen in the middle of the nineteenth century, and there is some reason to think that he was, then the subject embraced a vast range of human experience—political, religious, intellectual, social, ritualistic and cultural—and was to be studied by a combination of prior theoretical formulations and the closest attention to the record evidence about the concrete and the particular circumstances. This is why the work of the nineteenth-century scholars like Burckhardt are still so extraordinarily fresh and exciting to students a century after they were written. Historians at that time were still inspired by endless curiosity, and the range of their interests was limitless. This is what makes them so immediately attractive to us today.

Between 1870 and 1930, history developed into an independent professional discipline in its own right. Separate history departments were created at the universities, Ph.D. programs for the training and accreditation of future professionals were instituted, professional associations were formed. Meanwhile, the prime subject matter of history, under the influence of the bourgeois liberal nationalism of the age, was defined as the administrative and constitutional evolution of the nation state and the diplomatic and military relationships between those states. National record offices were set up, and the basic documents relating to these issues were calendared and made available to scholars free of charge. The problems, the methods, and the sources were thus all well established by 1900, and the crowning monument to this great development of the profession was the massive volumes of the *Cambridge Modern History*.

From these volumes it is clear that the professional evolution of history and the definition of its purpose had made enormous strides but that the gains had only been achieved at a considerable cost. That all-embracing sweep of subject matter, which had been so generously embraced by H. H. Vaughan and others in the middle of the century, had now been severely whittled down, partly because of deliberate choice by the historians, and partly as a result of professions organized within departmental structures, which now laid claims to their own share of the study of man in the past and the present. These included both the social sciences—anthropology, sociology, psychology, economics, human geography, and demography—and also specialized historical subdisciplines such as the history of law, the history of art, the history of education, and economic history. Secondly, the theory of historicism was triumphant, and it was seriously believed that all that was needed to establish Truth was to cleave faithfully to the facts gleaned from the archives. History was value-free.

The results were both good and bad. The good included the development of narrative political history as a highly professional skill, firmly based on archival research, conforming to the highest standards of scholarly erudition, and dependent on the formulation of special techniques in palaeography and diplomatics for testing reliability and meaning of documentary sources. As a profession, history had come of age and had successfully mapped out the main outlines of the political, military, constitutional, and diplomatic evolution of the major Western powers over the last one thousand years.

On the other hand, as has been seen, the range of questions asked and of methods used had undeniably been severely narrowed. As a result the next generation, the historians of the early twentieth century, can be seen in retrospect to have fallen into two groups, the vast majority belonging to the first category. These were scholars content to elaborate on the problems and techniques established by 1900 and to describe in ever more minute detail discrete events, mainly political or administrative, without showing much desire to relate these events to anything else or to render them meaningful to more than a handful of fellow workers in that one highly specialized vineyard. The pages of the journals published by the official national organizations, and representing the views and interests of the professional elite, such as the *American Historical Review,* or the *English Historical Review,* or the *Revue Historique,* were from 1920 to the 1950s almost entirely devoted to such material, the scrapings and shavings of historical antiquarianism, the publication of documents merely because they had never been published before, and the rehashing over and over again of the same tired old questions. More specialized journals, such as the *Annales Historiques de la Révolution Française*, became even more myopic in their interests. Historians were no longer addressing the educated public: they were talking to a small handful of their professional colleagues.

Both social scientists and the general literate public, therefore, began rightly to accuse the historians of being narrowly devoted to the brute fact—especially to the unique fact—to the exclusion of all theory; of neglecting the irrational, as if Freud or Nietzsche had never lived, so that the men they wrote about were not only wholly rational, but also rational in certain very limited ways—*homo economicus* or *homo politicus* or *homo theologicus*, for example; of harboring very naive views about historical objectivity and value-free history; of underestimating the importance, if only as limiting possible options, of material economic conditions, as if Marx had never lived; of having little serious understanding of the significance or mechanisms of social structure and social mobility; of being content with a two-dimensional analysis of politics without probing the underlying forces; and of concentrating upon the activities of tiny elites and neglecting the masses below them.

The second, very small, group of historians, who were reacting somewhat extravagantly to the ever narrower empiricism of their colleagues, went to the other extreme and became macrotheorists, either visionaries with global models of human evolution, like Spengler or Toynbee, or men working at a lower level of theoretical generalization, like Turner or Beard. What bound them together was a contempt for most of their professional colleagues who were content to spend their lives on one tiny fragment of the vast mosaic which was supposed eventually to form the factual basis of definitive political history.

These two groups, the fact seekers and the macrotheorists, have been brilliantly described by Professor Emmanuel Le Roy Ladurie as the truffle hunters and the parachutists: the first grub about with their noses in the dirt, searching for some minute and precious fact; the second float down from the clouds, surveying the whole panorama of the countryside, but from too great a height to see anything in detail very clearly.

Meanwhile, the social scientists were also splitting up into two rather similar groups, the survey researchers and experimentalists on the one hand, and the model builders on the other. If one wished to be unkind, one could define the former as persons who say, "We don't know whether what we find is particularly significant, but at least it is true," and the latter as persons who say, "We don't know whether what we allege is true, but at least it is significant." It was the former who tended to predominate in the vast and spreading social science empires in American universities.

Unfortunately, neither group had—or has—much interest in or respect for historical evidence and methods. They did not recognize the relevance of history to their work, nor did they admit the possibility that every individual and every institution is profoundly influenced by its unique past. They despised the qualitative description of sets of unique events which characterized much of the old history, partly since such empirical particularism made impossible any comparative model building, or even the development of medium-range general hypotheses, and partly since the methods employed failed to provide scientifically verifiable evidence. As a result, skepticism regarding the historical approach was common in political science, anthropology, psychology, and many of the other social sciences. Thus history was dismissed as irrelevant by most economists and sociologists, with a few very striking exceptions, like Joseph Schumpeter and Max Weber.[4] Many, especially the sociologists, cut themselves off still further from the historians by writing in an almost consciously antiliterary style, obscure, turgid, repetitive, flatulent, studded either with meaningless jargon and neologisms or with over-sophisticated algebraic formulae and impenetrable statistical tables. As Liam Hudson has pointed out, "in the entrenched sciences, it is possible to transmit truth in prose that is as crabbed as it is evasive. But where foundations are shakier, style not merely limits what we find it natural to express, it is, in important respects, the very essence of that expression."[5] This vice has been especially prevalent in American sociology, although there were and are some very distinguished exceptions like Robert K. Merton and C. Wright Mills, while many anthropologists wrote and write like angels. The prose of the most influential American sociologist, Talcott Parsons, is almost impenetrable to all but the *aficionados*, and this is a vice that now shows signs of spreading to France and Italy.

Neither group of social scientists had much serious interest in either the facts of change or explanations of change. For the anthropologist, time was fixed at the moment his field notes were taken, and he probably had little interest in, and certainly no way of investigating, whether the phenomena he discovered were of ancient origin or merely of very recent development within the last generation.

Psychology found itself trapped by unverifiable Freudian assumptions about timeless centrality and universality of certain human experiences in childhood. Freud postulated an endlessly repetitive drama involving birth traumas, weaning traumas, toilet-training traumas, shame and guilt over infantile-childish sexuality, and Oedipal conflict with parents—an inevitable cycle which we now know to be historically, and probably also theoretically, untrue. These are culture-bound assumptions, which may have been correct for some sick members of European bourgeois society of the late nineteenth century but which do not apply to most persons from most classes in most earlier and even later periods of time. Another flourishing school of psychologists were the experimental behaviorists, collecting ultimately trivial data about observable responses, and their modification under stress, in human beings or rats.

Sociology was also trapped in a wholly static vision of society, partly by its devotion to the survey research technique, and partly by its wholesale adoption of functionalist theory. Indeed, all social sciences were to some extent afflicted with the disease of functionalism. According to this theory, all behavior patterns and institutions must have some functional utility for the maintenance of the social system—and if this function is not apparent, there is promptly invented a "latent function," visible only to the expert eye. There are three reasons why the historian must reject functionalist theory if carried to its extreme limits (as it often is). Firstly, all societies contain within them vestigial institutions, even less useful for system maintenance than an appendix in an individual but which survive simply because they have taken on a quasi-independent institutional life of their own, which enable them to survive the overwhelming evidence of their social dysfunction. The early sixteenth-century church, or the early eighteenth-century university, or the late twentieth-century prison are cases in point. Similarly, the values of all individuals are molded and fixed in their childhood and adolescence, and if they happen to be living in times of rapid change, the inherited baggage of values they carry over with them from their youth is no longer functional and conducive to system maintenance. Indeed, it is more likely to lead to acute intergenerational tension, protest, and even revolution. Any given society is thus saddled with dysfunctional institutions and dysfunctional values.

Secondly, many societies find themselves attacked by new and powerful ideologies which threaten to shatter their whole social, political, and cultural frameworks. Early Christianity in the late Roman Empire, Calvinism in the late sixteenth century, and Marxist-

Leninism in the twentieth century are examples. Thirdly, and most important of all, man is much more than a rational, system-maintaining being, and there are therefore many aspects of his society, his culture, and his institutions which lack functional utility. Man is among other things a playful animal—*homo ludens*—a seeker after pleasure, a lover of aesthetic enjoyment, a player of games, and for these purposes he devises a wide array of institutions and structures, like Las Vegas and Disneyland, football stadiums and ski slopes, bars and dance halls, gardens, art museums and theaters, which are basically for fun and not function—unless fun is to be defined as a system-maintaining, and therefore functional, criterion. He is also a creature whose life is ordered and given meaning by a series of symbols and rituals, by no means all of which have functional significance, as Victor Turner, Clifford Geertz, and other anthropologists are now busy telling us. They are profoundly illuminating about the deeper levels of meaning in the society but do not necessarily display function.

Finally, both linguistic revolutionaries like Noam Chomsky and symbolic anthropologists like Claude Lévi-Strauss have suggested that vast areas of speech and ritual have no functional utility at all but are indicators of underlying processes of thought which govern behavior, often in wholly irrational ways. Even if one discounts much of what is exaggerated in their hypotheses, they have nonetheless dealt functionalism a severe, perhaps a mortal, blow. If history, along with the social sciences, could at last rid itself of this perniciously simple-minded straitjacket of interpretation, they would all be freer to explore new and more sophisticated avenues of explanation of the vagaries of human behavior.

The result of these trends in both history and the social sciences in the period 1870 to 1930 was that the two moved further and further away from each other. History became more and more myopic and inward-turned, and social science became more and more ahistorical. The result was the breakup of the study of man in the past and the present into small fragments defined, and heavily defended, by professional departmental boundaries. The objection to such a fragmentation is the obvious one, that the solution to an important problem involving real people cannot normally be solved within any one, or even several, of these artificially constructed academic boundaries. The historians were increasingly cut off by the new disciplines from an ever-wider range of human experience, a situation despairingly described by Carl Bridenbaugh in 1965 as "a mounting tendency to abandon history to the social scientists, who are even more culturally deprived than we are."[6] The social scientists, on the other hand, were locked in by their total ignorance of, or interest in, the past; by their neglect of the effects of historical conditioning upon any existing situation, set of beliefs, or institutional arrangements; by their lack of interest in the processes of change and by their lack of any theoretical models to get at this problem of change; by their tendency to write crabbed and knotty prose; by their growing obsession either with experimental or survey quantification, often applied mindlessly to the most trivial problems, or with overarching macrotheory. Pleas by historically minded sociologists like R. K. Merton for mutual cooperation in the solution of middle-range problems went largely unheard, both by historians and by social scientists.

About 1930 the tide in the historical profession began to turn, and for the next thirty years or so, a civil war raged between the "new" and the "old" historians, especially fierce in France, but also spreading to England and America, which were the two other main centers of historical scholarship at the time. The war began with the launching in France in 1929 of the new historical review, *Annales d'Histoire: Économique et Sociale* (later to be retitled *Annales, Économies, Sociétés, Civilisations),* and the almost simultaneous launching of the *Economic History Review* in England (which in its early days embraced the whole range of social as well as economic history).[7] The battle was long and fierce, and some idea of its intensity can be gleaned from the title, style, and content of Lucien Febvre's book, *Combats pour l'histoire*.[8] By 1960 the "new historians," with their social science orientation, had captured the imagination and the passionate loyalty of the most talented of the young; and by 1976 in France, and to some extent in America, they have themselves become the power elite in control of academic patronage and are infiltrating at last into such bastions of orthodoxy as the Sorbonne and Harvard.

In England, *Past and Present*, a journal with similar ambitions and objectives as *Annales*, began a sudden upward trajectory of popular success in 1960, to become by the end of the decade its nearest rival in the world. It has exerted greater influence, perhaps, in America than in England, for although some members of its editorial board were well entrenched at Oxford, Cambridge, and London, and many now hold chairs, they were and are very far from capturing the critical levers of academic power and prestige in these major seats of English learning. It is not without significance that two members of the editorial board have since moved to the United States. In America, the flood of periodicals founded there in the 1960s tells its own tale of the triumph of the new movement, while their titles indicate the way the wind has been blowing: *Comparative Studies in Society and History; Journal of Interdisciplinary History; Journal of Social History; Computers and the Humanities; Historical Methods Newsletter; The History of Childhood Quarterly: the Journal of Psycho-History;* and *The Family in Historical Perspective Newsletter.*

Meanwhile, in the social sciences there were some slight, but in retrospect largely abortive, movements back towards history. In political science, Gabriel A. Almond in 1964 claimed that "students of comparative politics, having turned away from history and towards sociological, anthropological and psychological theories and methods, may now be at the point of turning to history again. But if they do so, they will bring with them the questions, concepts and methods acquired in their prodigal sojourns."[9] In sociology there seemed to be signs of a similar turning back to history, the most notable evidence being the rush of translations into English in the 1950s and 1960s, for the first time, of perhaps the greatest of all historical sociologists, Max Weber. The translation of Weber probably did more to influence the writing of history in the 1960s than any other single influence from the social sciences, particularly since he offered an alternative to vulgar Marxist economic determinism, which was by then falling into historical disrepute; to Marxist theories of class, which were by then appearing to be largely inapplicable to premodern societies; and to vulgar Marxist theories of changes in the means of production as the prime generating force for change in other aspects of society. From Weber historians learned that institutional, ideological, and cultural factors were not mere superstructures, a proposition whose validity had become more and more doubtful as research progressed. The translation of Weber, and also a renewed interest in both the early Marx and in Émile Durkheim, were immensely stimulating to historians who could neither understand the language of the acknowledged doyen of current American sociology, Talcott Parsons, nor could fruitfully use for their own purposes what little they could grasp of his structuralist theories. They therefore turned back with relief to these classics of the nineteenth and early twentieth centuries.

Among the economists there was also a renewed interest in history, if only in order to gather more concrete data with which to test their theories. The result was an explosion of economic history, organized in very different ways, with significantly different results, in the different countries. In America, economic historians were mostly attached to economics departments rather than to history departments. This gave them a strong theoretical and statistical orientation with which to interpret and analyze their data. On the other hand, when American economics became concerned with macro-econometrics, the economic historians dutifully followed down this theoretically fascinating but historically rather sterile road, with somewhat mixed results. In France, economic historians were attached to history departments and were primarily concerned with data gathering, with the assembly of long-run time series of quantitative information about prices, wages, money, rent, output per capita, capital investment, overseas trade, and other key economic variables. The most distinguished, like Henri Sée or Ernest Labrousse, used this data to reinterpret big historical problems, but others, like the traditional political historians they so much despised, were more concerned with the accumulation of concrete data rather than with the development of interpretative models. In England, by some mysterious quirk of administrative history, economic historians tended to belong neither to history departments nor to economics departments but to set themselves up in wholly independent, and inevitably very small, economic history departments. Some members of these departments came out of economics, but most of them were trained as historians and followed the normal empirical methods of inquiry which seem to be deeply ingrained in English culture. Despite some brilliant early successes and a massive output of very high quality scholarly work, it seems likely that the administrative, and therefore ultimately the intellectual, isolation of English economic historians both from noneconomic historians and from professional economists may in the long run lead to introversion and sterility. The pages of the *Economic History Review* today show clear signs of a growth of this inward-looking trend.

The most influential social science to turn to history to test its theories and expand its data base was demography, and the astonishing successes of historical demography over the last decades, the result of a fruitful intercourse between professional demographers and professional historians, will be discussed later. The social science which has most recently begun to show interest in both the past and in change over time is anthropology, where the static studies of men like Bronislaw Malinowski and Radcliffe Brown are being replaced by more sophisticated and more historically rooted work by men like Edward Evans-Pritchard, or more recently, the newest symbolic anthropology of scholars like Mary Douglas, Victor Turner, and Clifford Geertz. It is only in the last five years, beginning with Keith V. Thomas's *Religion and the Decline of Magic: Studies in Popular Beliefs in Sixteenth and Seventeenth-Century England* (London: Weidenfeld &

Nicolson, 1971), that anthropology has begun to have a major impact upon the historical profession, particularly in the development of studies of popular religion (for example, magic and witchcraft) or symbolic social rituals (for example, coronation and funerary cere- monies, public festivities and group displays) or folklore and forms and meanings of popular culture. Whereas economics had most influ- ence on history in the 1930s, sociology in the 1950s, and demography in the 1960s, it is these newer kinds of anthropology which are attract- ing most attention from some of the younger historians today.

The climactic years of the conversion of historians to an interest in the social sciences and of high hopes that the social scientists would themselves turn back to history came in the late 1960s. Evidence for this assertion is not hard to find. There is the admission at long last into the pages of at least two of the major official journals, the *American Historical Review* and the *Revue Historique*, of articles which clearly show evidence of the methods and problems of social science–influenced historians (the *English Historical Review* has so far maintained its traditional sectarian exclusiveness). The second piece of evidence is the invasion of American history departments by missionaries from the great French school of historians known loosely as the *"Annales* school" (from their in-house journal), or the "VIe Section School" (from their institutional affiliation with the VIe Sec- tion of the École Pratique des Hautes Études in Paris).[10] Beginning with an exchange visitor program set up by the Princeton University History Department in 1968, the trickle has now grown to a flood, and the American historical profession is now becoming very familiar with the personalities and the works of this remarkably talented and innovative school of historical research. The third piece of evidence is the transformation of the subject matter of the sessions at the annual convention of the American Historical Association. Today a casual glance at the program gives the impression that hardly any work is in progress in America which is not concerned with the subject matter of the oppressed and inarticulate—slaves, the poor, or women—with problems such as social structure and mobility, the family and sex, crime and deviance, popular culture and witchcraft, and which is not using social science theories taken from psychology or sociology or anthropology and social science methodology like quantification. The first impression is on closer inspection not wholly an accurate one, but the change from 1965 to 1975 is startling.

Excluding sessions on teaching methods, there were 84 sessions at the American Historical Association convention in Atlanta in December 1975. No fewer than 12 of these 84 were concerned with Women (8), the Family (3), and Sex (1), to say nothing of 6 workshops on Women's History. The session on Sex included such somewhat esoteric subjects as "Buggery and the British Navy during the Napoleonic Wars"—not, one would have thought, among the more historically significant aspects of that period of European crisis and upheaval. The dangers of fashionable faddishness were very clear in the contents of the sessions at this convention.

The final accolade for the new movement was given in 1966 when the *Times Literary Supplement* devoted three whole issues to "New Ways in History." The articles were full of hope about the prospective new historical millennium, which was, it seemed, just around the corner, as soon as the old-fashioned historians could be eased out of their chairs by retirement or death—or perhaps even by a conversion experience to the New Light. For example, Edward Shils, who spends half his life in Chicago and half in Cambridge, England, wrote optimistically:

We are seeing in the United States the first signs of an amalgamation of history and the social sciences, at a time in which scholars have ceased to regard it as legitimate to confine themselves within the boundary of their own society, and historians are beginning to free themselves from the bonds of historicism. The outcome, which we can see at present only in a very incipient state, is a scholarly comparative social science and a comparative history. It is the beginning of a true "science humaine."[11]

The ambition, so well described by Shils, is a noble one and not to be dismissed with a sneer. It is to reunite history with all the social sciences and the humanities, and to create once again a single field for the study of all aspects of human experience in the past and the present: to go back, in fact, to 1850, but with all the expertise accumulated in the last 125 years in a wide variety of different disciplines.

II. *The Influence of the Social Sciences*

Having described the external evidence of the civil war and the successful triumph of the revolutionaries within the profession of history from 1930 to 1975, it is time to define more precisely what it was that the social sciences contributed to the new movement. In the first place, they forced historians to make their hitherto unspoken and indeed unconscious assumptions and presuppositions more explicit and precise. The latter were told that the idea that they had no such assumptions was mere self-deceiving nonsense. Human thought, after all, "before it is squeezed into its Sunday best, for purposes of publication, is a nebulous and intuitive affair: in place of logic there brews a stew of hunch and partial insight, half-submerged."[12] The social scientists demanded that it be brought to the surface and exposed to view. Historians were now asked to explain just what set of assumptions and just what causal model of change they were using —things which most of them had tended to avoid like the plague. They were also prodded into defining their terms more carefully. Historians have always made use of general concepts of considerable vagueness, like "feudalism" or "capitalism" or "middle class" or "bureaucracy" or "court" or "power" or "revolution," without explaining very clearly just what it is they mean by them. This fuzziness has often led to confusion, and it is now clear, for example, that the two most ferocious and lengthy debates in English historiography since the Second World War, over the rise or decline of the gentry in the sixteenth and early seventeenth centuries, and its relation, if any, to the English Revolution, and the rising or falling standard of living of the working class in the late eighteenth and early nineteenth centuries, were caused, in large part at any rate, by the failure of all parties to define their terms with sufficient clarity. As a result, on many occasions the protagonists were talking past each other instead of confronting the issues directly. The same is also true of the great debate over the social origins of the French Revolution, which has raged for the last twenty years or more.

The third contribution of the social sciences has been to refine research strategies and to help define problems and issues. In particular, they have pointed to the need for systematic comparisons over time and space, so as to isolate the particular and the unique from the general; for the adoption of scientific sampling techniques; and for the use of another standard group with which to compare that under scrutiny, so as to avoid drawing fallacious conclusions from isolated examples. They have also pointed to some repetitive patterns of, and possible explanations for, such phenomena as witchcraft, millenarian movements, and "great revolutions."

Their fourth major contribution is in methodology, in the testing of commonsense assumptions and literary statements by quantitative data wherever this is possible to procure. Quantification, when used with discretion and common sense, has many advantages over the older methods of historical verification. In the first place, it uses as ammunition apparently precise testable data, which have to be either confirmed or rejected on logical and scientific grounds, instead of strings of selective quotations from favorable sources. As Dr. Samuel

Johnson remarked in 1783: "That, Sir, is the good of counting. It brings everything to a certainty which before floated in the mind indefinitely."[13] An argument over the reliability of the sources and the propriety of the statistical manipulation is necessarily conducted on a higher intellectual level than a mere battle of rhetorical wits or an exchange of contradictory quotations, and this in itself is a great historiographic advance. The result may make much duller reading, but it sheds more light while generating—usually—less heat.

Secondly, whatever its positive merits, quantification has even more powerful negative ones. It can often totally destroy unfounded hypotheses based on purely literary evidence and supported because of national or personal prejudice. To give but two examples, theories about the beneficent results of early Spanish colonization of Mexico collapsed utterly when it was discovered by the demographic quantifiers that the Indian population fell from about 25 million to about 2 million in less than fifty years after Hernando Cortes had first landed. Secondly, the theory that rapid geographical mobility was a special characteristic of the open frontier areas in late nineteenth-century America was destroyed by the discovery of similar patterns of constant movement in the eastern city of Boston.

Thirdly, quantification brings out into the open assumptions that must, if words mean anything at all, be behind the traditional historians' use of such adjectives as "more," "less," "greater," "smaller," "increasing," "decreasing," etc. Such words cannot be used at all unless the author has some unstated quantitative figures to support them floating somewhere at the back of his mind. Quantification forces him to tell his reader what they are, and how they are arrived at. Fourthly, quantification helps the historian to clarify his argument, for the simple reason that trying to express ideas in mathematical terms can be one of the most effective cures for muddled thinking that has yet been invented. But it can also be a means of evading thought, and it should also be noted that quantification in history has very great, and growing, dangers and drawbacks, which will be examined in detail toward the end of this paper.

The fifth and last contribution of the social sciences to history has been to provide hypotheses to be tested against the evidence of the past. Today, therefore, we all make use, when it suits us, of such notions as the revolution of rising expectations, the disenchantment of the world, the role of charisma in politics, the value of "thick description" as a way of interpreting culture, the critical importance of a shift from a patrimonial to a modern bureaucracy, the alienation of the intellectuals, the identity crisis of the adolescent, the differences between status and class, the stem and the nuclear family, etc., which are all theories borrowed from other social scientific disciplines.

One of the most notable examples of the consequences both of accepting social scientific determinants on human possibilities and of adopting a comparative perspective which transcends national boundaries is Fernand Braudel's *The Mediterranean and the Mediterranean World in the Age of Philip II*. First published in French in 1949, revised and enlarged in 1966, and finally published in English in 1972–73, by Harper & Row, this is one of the most influential single works of history to have appeared since the Second World War. It is significant for two reasons. Firstly, it stresses very heavily geography, ecology, and demography as the constraining factors which set strict limits on all human action. Secondly, it frees itself entirely of any national perspective and ranges around the Mediterranean basin, seeing the great clash of Ottoman Islam and Latin Christianity that culminated in the battle of Lepanto in 1571 as a global whole, without any attempt to take sides. Compared with the vast inexorable tides of malaria, timber cutting, soil erosion, demographic growth and decline, bullion transfers, or price revolution, the actions of emperors like Philip II are made to seem of only marginal importance in the evolution of the societies that developed around the great inland sea. This is deterministic, fatalistic history which is alien to both liberal believers in free will and progress and Marxist believers in sociological evolution based on changes in the modes of production. Neither group is happy with this pragmatic pessimism based on the iron limitations of Malthusianism and ecology. Viewed from this perspective, that dazzling urban phenomenon the Italian Renaissance looks like a cultural luxury that the agricultural and technological resources of the area simply could not sustain. This is not to argue that the Braudel model is either true or false but merely to point out the radical shift of historical perspective involved in such borrowings from the social sciences.

At this point some comment is necessary on how historians ought to approach the mysterious and manifold disciplines of their social scientific colleagues. For the historian to get what he wants for his own purposes out of the social sciences, it is not necessary for him to undertake a lengthy and intensive training in one or more of them. The proper attitude of the historian to any social science should not be one of awe at the arcane jargon, the high level of theoretical generalization, and the complex algebraic formulae. He should enter the field merely as a seeker after a specific idea or piece of information. He cannot attempt to master the field, and he should not be intimidated by that most idiotic of proverbs that a little knowledge is a dangerous thing. After all, if the proverb were true and we took it seriously, we should be obliged immediately to abandon high school and undergraduate education altogether, since it is all, by definition, superficial.

There is nothing wrong with poking about in a social science to try to find some formula, some hypothesis, some model, some method which has immediate relevance to one's own work, and which seems to help one to understand one's data better and to arrange and interpret them in a more meaningful way. Of course it is of critical importance to choose the appropriate theory or method rather than the wrong one, and this choice is not made easy by the fact that no social science today has any one True Model, that all are in a highly primitive and almost chaotic state. Indeed, at this moment, some of them, notably economics, sociology, and psychology, seem to be on the verge of intellectual disintegration and collapse. On the other hand, this leaves the historian free to pick and choose what suits him best. He can borrow from Marxist, or Weberian, or Parsonian sociology; from social, or cultural, or symbolic anthropology; from classical, or Keynsian, or neo-Marxist economics; from Freudian, or Eriksonian, or Jungian psychology. The best the historian can do is to select what seems to him to be most immediately illuminating and helpful; to regard any formula, model, hypothesis, paradigm, or method as a good deal less than gospel truth; to stick to the firm conviction that *any* monocausal unilinear theory to explain a major historical event is bound to be untrue; and not to be overawed by methodological sophistication, especially in quantification: in fact, to use all the common sense he can muster to compensate for his technical ignorance.

This is, admittedly, a dangerous procedure. Every social science is a rapidly moving frontier, and it is only too easy for the hurried invader from another discipline to pick up a set of ideas or tools which are already outdated. To ignore the contributions of the social sciences is clearly fatal; to master them all, or even any one, is clearly impossible. The most the historian can usually hope to achieve is the somewhat superficial overview of the enthusiastic undergraduate interested in the field. This is usually enough, and indeed, because of the proliferation and the growing specialization of disciplines dealing with man, it is the most that can be hoped for. But the historian should advance gingerly in these areas and never forget the limitations imposed by his relative ignorance. It is an ignorance inescapably dictated by the enormous growth of knowledge, and its fragmentation into specialized watertight disciplines.

III. *"The New History"*

The "new history" that has emerged from this great upheaval in
the profession over the last forty years has the following characteristics that distinguish it from what went before. Firstly, it organizes its
material in a new way; books are written in an analytical, not a
narrative, arrangement, and it is no coincidence that almost all of what
are regarded as the outstanding historical works of the last quarter of a
century have been analytical rather than narrative. Secondly, it asks
new questions; why did things happen the way they did and what
were the consequences, rather than the old questions of what and
how. It is to solve these new questions that the historian is obliged to
adopt an analytical organization of his material. Thirdly, it is concerned with new problems, primarily in three areas, all of them
concerned with the relationship between man and society in the past.
The first is the material basis of human existence, the limitations
imposed by demography, human geography and ecology (a particular
interest of the French), the levels of technology, the modes of
economic production and distribution, capital accumulation, and
economic growth. The second is the huge and still expanding field of
social history. This covers the study of the functions, composition,
and organization of a whole range of institutions below the level of
those of the nation-state, institutions for the unequal distribution of
wealth, power, and status; institutions for socialization and education, such as the family, the school, and the university; institutions for
social control, such as the family, the police, the prisons, and the
asylums; institutions for work, such as business firms, monopolies,
and trade unions; institutions for local government, such as town
meetings, churchwardens, and urban political machines; and institutions for culture and leisure, such as museums, art galleries, publishing houses, the book trade, festivals, and organized sports.

Beyond social institutions, there is an intense interest in social
processes: in social, geographic, and occupational mobility, both
between groups and among individuals within groups, and changing
patterns of distribution of the three key variables: wealth, power, and
status. Efforts are being made to investigate such mobility—or lack of
it—in terms of group conflict or cooperation. This leads on to a search
for the social roots of political or ideological movements, both among
the elite leaders and the mass following, for example of seventeenth-century Puritans, or eighteenth-century religious or political radicals, or nineteenth-century liberals, or twentieth-century fascists.[14]

The third main area of activity, and one that is rapidly growing in importance, is a new kind of cultural-social history. This takes the form of intensive studies of the effects on mass opinion of changing communications, through printing, literacy, and the smuggling of censored literature; of the links of high culture to its social and political matrix; of the two-way interaction between high and popular culture; and, last but by no means least, the culture of the semiliterate masses as an independent field of study in its own right, not merely as an important part of the growing field of labor history.

The fourth characteristic of the "new history" is its new subject matter, namely the masses rather than the tiny elite of one, or at most two, percent whose doings and writings have hitherto made up the stuff of history. There has been a deliberate attempt to break away from this ancient fascination with the hereditary holders of political and religious power, the monopolizers of the bulk of capital wealth, and the exclusive consumers of high culture. In his "Elegy Written in a Country Churchyard," Thomas Gray observed:

> Let not . . . grandeur hear with a disdainful smile,
> The short and simple annals of the poor.

Until very recently historians have indeed looked upon the poor with a "disdainful smile," and concentrated most of their attention on kings and presidents, nobles and bishops, generals and politicians. In the last few decades this situation has changed dramatically, and some of the major works of history have been devoted to the inarticulate masses, whose annals have turned out, on inspection, to be certainly short but far from simple. The work of scholars like Eugene Genovese on American slaves; of E. P. Thompson and E. J. Hobsbawm on the English working class; of Marc Bloch, Georges Lefebvre, Georges Duby, Pierre Goubert, and Emmanuel Le Roy Ladurie on the French peasantry are generally acknowledged to be major classics of their generation. The challenge, which at any rate for the sixteenth century onward is being more or less successfully overcome, is how to find ways of reconstructing not only the economic and social experience, but also the mind set, the values, and the world view of people who have left behind them no written record of their personal thoughts and feelings: in other words, 99 percent of all the human race who ever lived before 1940. The impetus for this radical shift of subject matter undoubtedly came from anthropology and sociology, but the techniques for probing into such obscure areas of past experience have been and are still being developed on their own by a number of highly imaginative and dedicated historians who have been obliged to discover new source materials with which to work.

As a result of all these developments, there have been at least six major fields of historical inquiry which have been and still are in their heroic phase of primary exploration and rapid development, whose practitioners enjoy the same excitement as the natural scientists in pushing back year by year the frontiers of factual knowledge and theoretical comprehension. They are fields in the first explosive stage of knowledge accumulation and hypothesis formation.

One of the six is the history of science, both as an internal self-contained story of the exchange of ideas between a handful of men of genius and as a reflection of the shifting culture and society of the times. T. S. Kuhn's concept of the scientific paradigm and how it changes and R. K. Merton's work on the sociology of the scientific profession have together revolutionized the field.

The second is demographic history which has developed as a result of a recognition by modern demographers of the critical role of population size, growth, and age composition in determining so many aspects of life in the twentieth century. The result has been a massive attack on the demographic records of the past, mostly census materials and parish registers of baptisms, marriages, and burials, the full fruits of which are only just now beginning to be gathered. But already it is clear that at least since the sixteenth century northwestern Europe and North America have experienced a unique pattern of very late marriage and relatively low fertility. It is also apparent that there have been marked changes in population size and trends in the past, and in both mortality and fertility rates, which have combined to form a kind of homeostatic pattern. This does not destroy the hypothesis of a fundamental demographic transition in the nineteenth century from high birthrates and high deathrates to low birthrates and low deathrates, but it significantly modifies its impact and undermines earlier assumptions about a uniform premodern demographic world.[15]

The third is the history of social change, the study of the interaction of the individual and the society around him. This has involved the identification of social status groups and social classes, and the analyses of social institutions, structures, values, and patterns of individual and group social mobility.

The fourth is the history of mass culture—of *mentalités* (that untranslatable but invaluable French word). Drawing heavily on anthropological ideas for inspiration, this new field has already for the sixteenth and seventeenth centuries produced such striking works as those of R. Mandrou on popular beliefs, N. Z. Davis on rituals and festivals, K. V. Thomas on magic, E. Eisenstein on the effects of the invention of printing and consequent literacy, and whole shelves of books and articles on witchcraft; for the eighteenth century it has produced studies of de-Christianization by Michel Vovelle, and of the spread of the low culture of the Enlightenment by Robert Darnton; and for the nineteenth century, the emerging political culture of the working class has been explored by E. P. Thompson for England and Maurice Agulhon and Charles Tilly for France.

The fifth is urban history, a field that still seems to be a subject in search of a problem, inasmuch as it is only vaguely defined by the fact that it includes everything that happens in cities. At present it is primarily quantitative in methodology and concerns itself with urban geography and ecology, urban religion and social values, urban sociology and demography, urban politics and administration. [16]

Finally, there is the history of the family, which is also currently in an explosive but still incoherent phase of development. This embraces not only the demographic limits which constrain family life but also kinship ties, family and household structures, marriage arrangements and conventions and their economic and social causes and consequences, changing sex roles and their differentiation over time, changing attitudes toward and practice of sexual relations, and changes in the affective ties binding husband and wife, and parents and children.

These six fields only cover what seem at present to be the most promising areas of new inquiry. But there are at least three other candidates for inclusion. New forms of political history, dependent on computerized studies both of legislative roll-call decision making and the correlation of popular voting behavior with social and cultural variables, have so far made only rather tentative, although hopeful, starts. Both are enormously time-consuming, and the rewards are very slow in coming in. Moreover, the second, which depends on linking precinct or ward voting to ethnic, religious, economic, and other variables revealed in nineteenth-century census data, is open to the "ecological fallacy," which is by no means easy to solve. One cannot readily tie statistical information about the characteristics of a group living in a geographical area to the specific political behavior on a certain occasion of a particular, but unknown, set of individuals in that area. [17] The new political history has therefore only just gotten off the ground, despite the massive and expensive data bank now accumulated by the Inter-University Consortium for Political Research at Ann Arbor.

Psychohistory is now making increasingly insistent claims to be a legitimate field in its own right. This can take two forms, of which the first is the study of individuals, of the influence of infantile and childish experience on the psychological makeup, and therefore the behavior and actions, of adult intellectual or political leaders in the past. This involves probing into what is usually a highly obscure period in the life of even the best documented of men and women, as well as making certain theoretical assumptions about the linkage of childhood experience to adult behavior. It is a striking, and disheartening, fact that the most distinguished work in this area is still one of the oldest, Erik H. Erikson's *Young Man Luther: A Study in Psychoanalysis and History* (New York: W. W. Norton, 1958). The second form of psychohistory takes the form of a study of the psychology of particular groups, two of the most influential books of this type being Philippe Ariès, *Centuries of Childhood: A Social History of Family Life* (New York: Knopf, 1962), and Stanley M. Elkins, *Slavery: A Problem in American Institutional and Intellectual Life*, 2d ed. (Chicago: University of Chicago Press, 1968), dealing respectively with children and slaves.[18] As will be seen later in this essay, however, there are strong indications that psychohistory is developing along dogmatically ahistorical lines, based on unproven social science assumptions about human nature, which are wholly independent of the influence of historically based cultural conditioning.

Whether one should still include economic history as one of the fields still in the explosive stage of development is a very open question. Undoubtedly the heroic first phase took place between about 1910 and 1950, dominated by such scholars as Frederic C. Lane, Thomas C. Cochran, and John U. Nef in America; M. M. Postan, J. H. Clapham, and T. S. Ashton in England; and Marc Bloch and Henri Sée in France. These men, and others equally distinguished of their generation, are now all either retired or dead, and the professional journals and books give the impression that most of the current generation are concerned mainly with mopping-up operations, filling in factual gaps, modifying oversimplified hypotheses, and generally tidying up the field. The one new impetus is coming out of the American Middle West, the so-called "new economic history," heavily reliant upon the formal econometric models and the advanced mathematical sophistication of pure economics.[19]

The extent to which this "new economic history" is likely to transform and revivify the subject is still very much an open question. There are grave doubts whether counterfactual history—described by one critic as "if my grandmother had wheels she'd be a greyhound bus" history—is of much practical use to historians, who are concerned with what happened, not with what might have happened but didn't. It is, after all, a fact that America *did* build railroads instead of relying on water transport for bulk goods. Counterfactual history is a useful methodological aid to clear thinking about historical hypotheses, but nothing more.[20] There are even graver doubts whether the very shaky statistical data surviving even for periods as late as the nineteenth century are firm enough to form a solid foundation for the fragile and sophisticated superstructures which the "cliometricians"—as they like to call themselves—delight in building. Dizzily impressive to look at, these edifices do not seem very securely built when subjected to detailed critical examination. One of the difficulties with applying economic theory to history is that it works best on problems where the variables are small and therefore manageable; but these problems are often so narrow as to be trivial. Another is that it deals with a world where choice is always free and always rational and is never distorted by personal prejudice, class bias, or monopoly power; but no such world has ever existed.[21]

It is noticeable that except for voting behavior and roll-call analysis, all of these areas fall under the broad rubric of either ecological, social, or mental history; that except for the history of science and individual psychohistory, they are all concerned with masses rather than elites; that they are mostly looking at change over long rather than short periods of time; and that their frame of reference tends to be either larger or smaller than the nation-state.

To deal with the problems in these new areas, historians have adopted a variety of new techniques, all borrowed from the social sciences. One of them is prosopography, as the classical historians have called it for a long time, or career-line analysis, as the social scientists call it. This is a key tool for exploring any aspect of social history and involves an investigation of the common background characteristics of a sample group of actors in history by means of a collective study of a set of uniform variables about their lives—variables such as birth and death, marriage and family, social origins and inherited economic and status position, place of residence, education, amount and source of personal wealth and income, occupation, religion, experience of office, and so on. This tool is used mostly to tackle the two problems of the social roots of political action, and social structure and social mobility. The studies of elites, which were until recently the principal object of such inquiries, borrowed relatively little from the social sciences, and the work of scholars like Sir Ronald Syme and Sir Lewis Namier owed little or nothing to Vilfredo Pareto, Gaetano Mosca, and other theoreticians of elitism in politics. Students of the masses, on the other hand, have been forced—or have deliberately opted—to follow in the footsteps of the survey researchers, to ignore the rich evocativeness of individual case studies, and to limit themselves to statistical correlations of many variables for a sample of the population, in the hope of coming up with some significant findings. This technique has now spawned a number of new sub-branches, such as psephology, or the study of voting behavior based on a correlation of voting patterns of the electorate with census data, and roll-call analysis, a study of the voting behavior of legislators.[22]

The second significant method is local history, the in-depth study of a locality, either a village or a province, in an attempt to write "total history," within a manageable geographical framework, and in so doing to illuminate wider problems of change in history. The greatest of these works have undoubtedly been produced by the French, such as Pierre Goubert and Emmanuel Le Roy Ladurie for whole provinces, Pierre Deyon for an individual city, and Martine Segalen and Gerard Bouchard for a single village. But New England colonial history has been revolutionized by similar studies by Philip Greven, John Demos, Kenneth Lockridge, and others, while English history has been enormously enriched by the school of local studies centered at Leicester, in particular the work of William G. Hoskins and Joan Thirsk.[23]

The "new" historians have also borrowed from the social scientists a series of new techniques, most of which have already been mentioned: quantification, conscious theoretical models, explicit definition of terms, and a willingness to deal in abstract ideal types as well as in particular realities. The one new tool they have borrowed is the computer, which was first devised for the natural scientists, was then adapted for and adopted by the social scientists, and is now increasingly becoming a fairly common adjunct for the working research historian in these new fields. About 1960 historians suddenly gained free access to this immensely powerful but very obtuse machine, which can process enormous quantities of data at fabulous speed but only if they are presented to it in limited, often rather artificial, categories, and if the questions are extremely clearly, precisely, and logically framed. Fifteen years of varied experience with the machine has led to a greater appreciation among historians both of its potential uses and its real defects. When dealing with large quantities of data, it can answer more questions and test more multiple correlations than any human mind could handle in a lifetime. But it cannot abide ambiguity and therefore demands that the data be processed in precise packaged form arranged in clearly defined categories, which may well distort the complexity and uncertainty of the reality. Secondly, the preparation of the material for the machine is immensely time-consuming, so that on the whole, while its use enormously increases the size of the sample and the complexity of the correlations of variables, it may slow down research rather than speed it up. Thirdly, its use precludes that feedback process by which the historian normally thinks, thanks to which hunches are tested by data, and the data in turn generate new hunches. When the historian uses the computer, this two-way process is impossible until the very end of the research, since it is only when the print-out is finally available that any clues are provided to possible solutions to the problems and therefore make possible the generation of new ideas and new questions. Unfortunately, it sometimes turns out that omissions or short-cuts in recording or coding the data preclude the possibility of obtaining the answers to these new questions generated at a later stage. Worst of all is the kind of atrophy of the critical faculties that the mere use of punch cards and computers seems to produce. As Dr. Hudson remarks, "Most social scientists who rely on punch-cards and compu-ers seem in practice to abandon their powers of reasoning, and as a result, their data are almost invariably under-analyzed, or analyzed in a clumsy ham-fisted fashion. The research worker seems subtly to become the creature of the data-processing machinery, rather than vice-versa."[24] The historian, despite his largely humanistic training, is as liable to this insidiously corrupting mental deformation as are his colleagues in the social sciences.

The computer is a machine in the elementary use of which most professional research historians should henceforth be trained—a six-week course is ample for the purpose—but it is one which should only be employed as the choice of last resort. Wherever possible, quantitative historians are well advised to work with smaller samples and to use a hand calculator. Despite its undeniable and unique virtues, the computer is by no means the answer to the social historian's prayer that once it was hoped it might be.

IV. *The Future of History and the Social Sciences*

There can be little question that the "new history" of the last forty years, which has owed so much to borrowings from the social sciences, has rejuvenated historical scholarship and has caused that time span to be, together with the forty years before the First World War, the most fruitful and creative period in the whole history of the profession. Anyone who has had the good fortune to have lived and worked throughout that time can have nothing but pride in what has been achieved in furthering the understanding of man in past society.

Today, however, the future looks rather less promising, partly because the very success of the movement is generating some signs of hubris. In the arrogance of victory, some of the more ebullient and aggressively self-confident supporters of some aspects of the new history are not only making exaggerated claims for their own achievements but are also treating the subject matter and the methodology of the more traditional historians with an undeserved contempt. This attitude is inevitably causing a backlash, so that there are signs of a renewed conflict of Ancients and Moderns—something that can only do harm to both sides. The lack of moderation in the new victors is best epitomized in the title and contents of some new handbooks by some of the most distinguished practitioners of the historical craft in America and in France. In 1971 David S. Landes and Charles Tilly published a collection of essays, *History as Social Science* (Englewood Cliffs, N.J.: Prentice-Hall), in which some very bold claims were made for the "new history." In 1974 Pierre Chaunu published *Histoire, science sociale: La durée, l'espace et l'homme à l'époque moderne* (Paris: Société d'édition d'enseignement supérieur), in which he asserted that history was neither more nor less than a social science. The basic assumption behind this attitude toward history as a discipline has been described by a hostile critic in the following terms: "In some eyes the systematic indoctrination of historians in all the social sciences conjures up a scene of insemination, in which Clio lies inert and passionless (perhaps with rolling eyes) while anthropology or sociology thrust their seed into her womb." The critic (E. P. Thompson) rightly pleads for a more active and energetic response from the Muse of History to this vigorous assault upon her person (and one more appropriate to the sexual revolution of our time).[25] The principal objection to the total integration of history into the social sciences, as advocated by Chaunu and others, is that "the discipline of history is above all a discipline of context." It deals with a *particular* problem and a *particular* set of actors at a *particular* time in a *particular* place. The historical context is all-important, and cannot be ignored or brushed aside in order to fit the data into some overarching social science model. Witchcraft in sixteenth-century England, for example, may be *illuminated* by examples of witchcraft in twentieth-century Africa, but it cannot so easily be *explained* by them, since the social and cultural contexts are so very different.

Looked at from the other side of the fence, in the eyes of some social scientists history apparently is now regarded as little more than a useful data source for the pursuit of their own theoretical investigations. History exists, it has been argued, in part "for the explicit purpose of advancing social scientific inquiries," an extreme position admittedly but one which is based on a fundamental misconception of the integrity and importance of history as a study of man in society in the past.[26]

Moreover, this seems in some ways an odd moment at which to choose to hitch the Muse of History to the chariot of the social sciences, almost all of which are currently in a state of severe crisis and in the process of an internal reassessment of their scientific validity. The notion of value-free anthropology has been blown up by the publication of Malinowski's diaries; value-free sociology has come under severe attack—to say nothing of its usefulness or wisdom; value-free psychology is clearly nonsense in the light of B. F. Skinner's self-evident ideological blinkers and the antithetical romantic ideas of R. D. Laing; while the hardest social science of them all—economics —has failed in its job of prediction and cure of the new problems of stagflation, the giant international corporation, and the limits on natural resources. To change the metaphor, it might be time for the historical rats to leave rather than to scramble aboard the social scientific ship which seems to be leaking and undergoing major repair. History has always been social, and it was attracted by the siren songs of the social sciences because it thought—perhaps somewhat mistakenly, it now appears—that they were also scientific.

On the other hand, since every social science is in a process of upheaval and transition, no one can predict their future. At one time sociologists seemed most likely to be useful to historians, and indeed Max Weber and then R. K. Merton were, but they retreated into quantitative survey research or highly abstract functionalist theory, neither of which was of much service. Today the most powerful influence is coming from demography and from symbolic and social anthropology. Ten years from now some other discipline, perhaps social psychology, may have most to offer to the historian. In this perpetually moving frontier the most influential discipline changes from decade to decade, and the historian has to be perpetually watchful for new trends and new ideas. We may today be in no more than a temporary period of reappraisal before a new leap forward.

What can be said with some confidence, however, is that there are at least three ways in which the social science-oriented historians seem at the moment to be in particular danger of allowing their enthusiasm to outrun their judgment. The first is through an intemperate and injudicious use of quantification as a solution to all problems.[27] It is only too easy to exaggerate the potentialities of the method and to allow the tool to become the end in itself. A classic case of the misapplication of this method is the revisionist work on American slavery of Robert W. Fogel and Stanley L. Engerman, *Time on the Cross: The Economics of American Negro Slavery* (Boston: Little, Brown, 1974). It now appears that the historical source materials were seriously misunderstood and misused, and that in the lust to quantify the authors came up with both false and meaningless results. It also seems that the statistical manipulations were themselves seriously defective. As a result, all the main conclusions of the book, about the relative mildness of slavery as a form of industrial discipline, about the rarity of the forced breakup of slave families, about the adoption by the slave workforce of the white Puritan ethic of hard work, and about the basic profitability and economic viability of the slave system are all certainly still unproved and perhaps untrue.[28] The claim to have successfully demolished a century of historical scholarship by the use of the most modern quantitative methods turns out to be a hollow boast.

There are several morals to be drawn from this example. The first is that no amount of quantitative methodology, however sophisticated, will compensate for misinterpreted or defective data. The only result is what computer experts call the "GIGO effect": garbage in–garbage out. All statistical information before the mid-twentieth century is more or less inaccurate or incomplete or unhelpful (being normally intended for quite a different use than that to which the historian wishes to apply it), and as a result, it is not only futile but positively deceptive to deal in precise numbers and percentages down to one or two decimal points. A modest proposal for improving slightly the honesty of our profession would be to pass a self-denying ordinance against the publication of any book or article based on historical evidence before the twentieth century which prints percentages to even one decimal point, much less two.

Another serious defect of some of the more ambitious of the quantifiers is their failure to conform to those professional standards, designed to make possible a scientific evaluation of the evidence, which have been built up over a century of painstaking traditional scholarship. *Time on the Cross*, for example, was published in two volumes. The first, containing merely the conclusions, was made available in large numbers, and the second, dealing with sources and methods, in much smaller numbers and at a later date. Worse still, it is impossible to find the evidence in the second volume to support many of the conclusions in the first volume, nor is it possible even to find a list of the records which have been used. The reader is merely assured that unprecedented masses of data have been examined, the full publication of which is only now being prepared, long after the conclusions were published.

On the other hand, it is fair to explain that even when they are scrupulously anxious to describe their sources and methods, it is impossible for quantitative historians dealing with vast masses of information to print all the raw data upon which their study is based, and impossible for them to give more than the most summary account of how the raw material was manipulated. At most, they can do no more than give brief descriptions of sources and methods in a separate (very lengthy and boring) article or appendix, which still may conceal as much as it reveals in terms of how the nuances and ambiguities of the raw data were compressed into simplified machine-readable form, since the full code book is not available. Almost equally obscure is any subsequent statistical manipulation, so that, taking all three problems together, the reader is often obliged either to take on trust or to reject out of hand figures whose methods of verification are not fully revealed to him and would probably be beyond his comprehension if they were.

An excellent case in point is the stimulating new book by Charles, Louise, and Richard Tilly, *The Rebellious Century, 1830-1930* (Cambridge: Harvard University Press, 1975). In order to discover the sources and methods that lie behind graphs 5 to 8, on acts of collective violence in France over a century—the collection, coding and analysis of which took countless man-hours of many researchers over almost a decade—the reader is asked to track down descriptions of the methodology spread over no fewer than six different articles (p. 314). Few readers will have the tenacity or curiosity to pursue the subject that far. The great majority will inevitably take the graphs at their face value, without probing any deeper. The major findings of the work stand or fall on the reliability of these graphs, and yet within the book itself there is no provision made for discovering how they were compiled, while the multivariate analyses used for explaining the ups and downs of the graphs are likely to baffle all but the most sophisticated of cliometricians. This is a book which lacks most of the basic scholarly apparatus but which apparently conforms to the best standards of scholarship of which cliometric history is capable. It is the product of a decade of massive research, and yet the reader is left in a state of helpless uneasiness both about the reliability of the data and about the validity of the explanations put forward. It therefore poses in its starkest form the problem of verification in cliometric history. If the conscientious reader is baffled even by this work, it is certain that he will be baffled by all the other massive undertakings of a similar nature. The conclusion seems to be that for projects of this size there is no way of making all the raw data, the code books, and the statistical methodology readily available to the reader. As a result, the normal processes of verification by a checking of the footnote references is not possible. How historical revisionism can proceed under these circumstances is not at all clear. The only solution seems to be to deposit all the raw data—the code books, the programs, and the print-out—in statistical data banks to which serious investigators can go to check through the whole process once again from start to finish. Such data banks are now beginning to spring up, as has already been noted, at Ann Arbor and elsewhere,[29] and they may eventually provide a partial solution to this problem, provided that scholars make available not only the end product—the computer tapes—but also the data sheets, code books, and other working materials.

It is only fair to add that the cliometricians are not the first to be guilty of this breach of scholarly standards. One of the most distinguished of all American intellectual historians of the past generation, Perry Miller, also failed to publish his footnotes but merely deposited them in the Houghton Library at Harvard. When, thirty-five years later, a curious scholar took the trouble to examine them, the results were disquieting in the extreme. It became apparent that so far from relying on the widest possible range of sources, as he had claimed, Miller had drawn very heavily indeed on authors who were very limited in number and one-sided in viewpoint.[30] But an occasional lapse by one of the great traditionalist historians is no excuse for the wholesale adoption of such habits by the cliometricians.

It would be less than helpful to repeat the hackneyed reactionary cliché of the baffled humanist that "one can prove anything with figures," since it is very much easier to prove anything with words, which are always put together for rhetorical effect as a means of subjective persuasion as much as for logical argument. But it must be admitted that there is also a rhetoric of figures, and especially a rhetoric of graphs. The whole aspect of a graph can be radically altered by changing the vertical or the horizontal scales; by using semilogarithmic rather than arithmetical graph paper; by the judicious selection of a base index number designed to highlight or downplay a trend; by using moving averages rather than raw figures. This manipulation of appearances is quite independent of the question of the reliability of the data and whether they have been compiled by extrapolation, adjusted by the application of an appropriate index error, or properly modified to take account of the rising or falling value of money. Percentages are equally open to manipulation, depending on the item which is selected as the base number. One of the major problems of quantification in history is that while the average historian has been trained to scrutinize words with the greatest care and suspicion, he tends to take a graph or table on trust and not to know how to evaluate its reliability or to examine how it has been arrived at. He is not trained to be a professional critic of numerical data.

Perhaps the most serious defect of some, but by no means all, of this new school of dedicated cliometricians, as they call themselves, is their tendency to ignore or neglect all evidence which cannot be quantified, whereas it is precisely from the combination of statistical evidence with literary and other materials of every possible variety that truth is most likely to emerge. Proof of an important historical argument is most convincing when it can be demonstrated from the widest possible range of sources, including statistical data, contemporary comments, legal enactments and enforcement, institutional arrangements, private diaries and correspondence, public speeches, moral theology and didactic writings, creative literature, artistic products, and symbolic acts and rituals.

A further danger arises from problems of scale. A peculiar combination of circumstances came together in the 1960s which made it possible for the first time to assemble and manipulate enormous quantities of data. The circumstances were the advent of the computer, whose use was *de facto* free, a growing interest in social mobility in the nineteenth century, the discovery by scholars of nineteenth-century census data, and a cornucopia of research funds suddenly made available for hiring large teams of helots to work on vast collective projects. The result was the emergence of the huge quantitative research project. Most of these gigantic enterprises, the grandest of which, the tyrannosaurus of the age, has already cost well over three-quarters of a million dollars, grew up on the fertile American soil, but there are also examples in France and England. In a joint American and French project, David Herlihy and others have put on computer tape the Florentine *catasto* of 1427, which lists 60,000 families and 264,000 persons. In France a team working with Le Roy Ladurie has computerized 78 variables for 3,000 districts from the census of French conscripts between 1819 and 1930, while Louis Henry has for years been supervising a gigantic inquiry—much of it by hand-counting —into French historical demography, based both on aggregative data for hundreds of villages and towns and on family reconstitution of a small selection. In England an equally ambitious enterprise of the identical kind is under way under the direction of E. A. Wrigley at Cambridge, including aggregative data for over 400 villages and family reconstitution studies for up to a dozen. The French are also hard at work putting their own census data for the nineteenth century on computer tape, while the same thing is being done for selected sample areas of England by a team directed by D. V. Glass. In North America there are in progress the most gigantic enterprises of all, such as the academic factory directed by Theodore Hershberg which is analyzing by computer the 2½ million people covered by the Philadelphia censuses from 1850 to 1880, and another very similar factory, but operating on much more sophisticated lines, directed by Michael Katz, which is at work on the town of Hamilton, Ontario. These vast undertakings have more in common with the modern scientific laboratory, with its teams of researchers and its massive equipment operating under the direction of a single professor, than with the traditional lonely scholar sitting with his books in his study or turning over manuscripts in a record office.

There are many dangers inherent in such projects, the most serious of which is that to some extent the conclusions drawn from these highly costly and labor-intensive quantitative studies still depend on the utility and reliability of the variables selected for study by the director before the data collection begins. Thus if any variable is missed in setting up the code book—for example, the social distribution of literacy as evidenced by signatures in the 1427 Florentine *catasto*—it is too late to go back and do it again once the omission is discovered. Another drawback is that they depend entirely on the accuracy and completeness of the original records, and there are good reasons for thinking that some records, like parish registers, are seriously and inconsistently incomplete, sometimes for burials, sometimes for marriages, and usually for the births and deaths of infants who die in the first week of life; that tax records are hardly every reliable; and that censuses, even today, are seriously inaccurate, especially in occupational categories and through omissions of the poor, women, children, and other subordinate groups. Moreover, even if the data are accurate, one still cannot be sure that all the research assistants are coding them the same way. There is nearly always some measure of personal judgment involved in the coding process. Worst of all is the fact that if the individual mentioned in one document is to be matched with that in another, record linkage problems become almost insuperable in the majority of cases, quite apart from the fact that those who move out of the area are lost to the sample altogether.

In view of all these problems, and in the light of the results which have hitherto been published, the question arises whether the concentration of such vast quantities of scarce resources of money and manpower on a few gigantic projects was altogether wise, and whether the funds might more usefully have been spread out to aid the researches of a large number of individual scholars. One can reasonably ask whether $7,000 each given to one hundred historians would have produced larger returns in terms of the advancement of knowledge than $700,000 spent on a single project. The evidence upon which to judge this issue is not yet in and will not be available for several years. In any case, even if some of these mammoth projects produce some really important conclusions in the next five years or so, it seems likely that they may die out altogether in the financial ice age of the 1970s. If so, some of them may leave nothing behind them but miles of computer tape and mountains of print-out, to be wondered at in years to come not so much for their potential value to scholarship as for their sheer size. Some may turn out to be rather like the project to put a man on the moon, more remarkable for the evidence they provide of man's vaunting ambition, vast financial resources, and technical virtuosity in the 1960s than for their scientific results in the advancement of knowledge.

Some of them do no more than prove the obvious, such as that the nineteenth-century laborer lived near his place of work, since he had to walk to get to it. Others provide information which seems to have no useful meaning and would not have been measured except for the fact that it was measurable—for example, the geographical distribution of hernias in early nineteenth-century France, or the average size of an English household from the sixteenth to the nineteenth century (4.75 persons).[31] Some threaten to get so bogged down in methodological problems, particularly those of record linkage—the struggle to prove that the John Smith or the Patrick O'Reilly in one record is the same John Smith or Patrick O'Reilly in another—that nothing of significance emerges for years or even decades. Indeed, the record linkage problem in tying one document to another is so serious that for projects looking at change over time it drastically reduces the number of usable items in the sample, often to those who happen to possess unusual names. The one book which deals with this problem is far from reassuring about the reliability of the results of quantitative methodology dependent on record linkage.[32]

It is likely that many of these excesses contain within them the seeds of their own destruction, but more dangerous for the profession is the growing belief among many graduate students that only a subject which is somehow quantifiable is worthy of investigation—an attitude which drastically reduces the subject matter of history and often leads to the same kind of scholastic triviality from which the early pioneers of the "new history" were trying to liberate the profession. As a result, many students, lacking the resources needed for these giant projects, plunge single-handed into quantitative studies, many of which do no more than prove something which was already well known from literary sources, and many of which are hopelessly flawed by defects in the raw data. Many others are based on too small a sample to be meaningful—for example, a graph of medieval crime rates over centuries based on the records of a single manorial court of a village whose population was literally decimated by the Black Death. Indeed, the now popular study of crime through quantitative study of court records raises very serious methodological questions about the changing perception and meaning of crime among different classes in the same society—the lower-class criminals and the upper-class prose-cutors and judges—at different times. It also raises the insoluble problem whether what is being quantified is the changing reality of the defined criminal activity or the changing zeal of police and prosecutors.[33]

This same conceptual difficulty applies to the work by the Tillys and others on changing levels of violence. Different societies take very different attitudes toward physical violence and draw different lines between the violent and the nonviolent. For example, in early modern European regimes, the popular revolt was a semilegitimate means of protest by the inarticulate; it was the only means of protest they possessed, and in the means used there was a "moral economy of the crowd" which had its own legitimacy.[34] Moreover, despite the terri-ble consequences of physical injury to individuals in an age when medical technology was either helpless or positively harmful, many societies took very calmly levels of interpersonal violence that would horrify us today. Until these difficult problems of relative historical perceptions are cleared up, quantitative studies of crime or of violence remain interesting but dubious ventures whose statistical results are open to a variety of interpretations.

Most disturbing of all are plans, now apparently in the develop-mental stage at Chicago, Harvard, and Rochester, by which graduate students in history will in future be trained in two significantly different ways.[35] The first group will be taught in the traditional manner, acquiring a mastery of the bibliographical literature in sev-eral major fields, a familiarity with broad interpretive historical con-cepts, and some experience in the handling of primary source ma-terials. The second group will spend so much time acquiring highly sophisticated expertise in statistical methodology, model building, and knowledge of the social sciences as to make it impossible for them to obtain that broad historical knowledge and wisdom and that familiarity with the handling of sources which have hitherto been regarded as essential prerequisites for the professional historian. This is clearly the beginning of the development of two significantly different kinds of historians. The reason for such specialized training is clear enough, but on balance this is a methodological split which should be resisted if our discipline is to survive as a humane collective enterprise in which we can all participate.

The second area which now threatens to get out of hand is psychohistory. It is obvious that anyone making a serious study either of an individual or of a social group is obliged to make use of psychological explanations of human behavior. If the psychohistorians would stick to the simple proposition that the function of psychology is merely to improve the biography of the individual, all would be well. But nowadays many begin by postulating that there is a theory of human behavior which transcends history. This claim to possess a scientific system of explanation of human behavior based on proven clinical data, which is of universal validity irrespective of time and place, is wholly unacceptable to the historian since it ignores the critical importance of changing context—religious, moral, cultural, economic, social, and political. It is a claim, moreover, that has recently been rejected by many of the more perceptive members of the psychological profession itself. Thus Sigmund Koch has observed that "modern psychology has projected an image of man which is as demeaning as it is simplistic." Moreover, the whole notion of quantifying rationality, so dear to experimental psychology, is now looked on in some quarters as a "disease in consciousness."[36] Secondly, many of the psychohistorians show an attitude toward the normal rules of evidence so cavalier that it would cause a student adopting such methods to flunk the course. Even the most brilliant of all works in this genre—Erik Erikson's *Young Man Luther*—depends for its data on a set of events many of which the author freely admits are mere posthumous legend and may never in fact have happened. "We are obliged," he says, "to accept half legend as half history." Finally, the historian finds it hard to swallow the act of faith by which the argument leaps from the trivial and the individual to the cosmic and the general—for example, from Luther's alleged constipation and his troubles with his father to his break with the Papacy and the emergence of the Lutheran Reformation. Most biographical studies using psychohistory have hitherto proved disappointingly unrewarding or unscholarly, and a more promising area seems to be the psychological study of well-defined social groups undergoing similar high-stress experiences, such as Ariès' dazzling *Centuries of Childhood* mentioned earlier. But this particular line of investigation is now also threatened by psychological reductionism of the most extreme type, as in Lloyd De Mause's *History of Childhood* (New York: Psychohistory Press, 1974) and regularly displayed on some of the pages of the *History of Childhood Quarterly*. Perhaps the most promising line of inquiry of all is that which modifies the rigidity of Freudian psychological theory in the light of the influence of social and cultural history. The most successful example of this genre is Carl Schorske's exploration of changes in all aspects of bourgeois culture in late nineteenth-century Vienna.[37] But so far, he has few imitators.

The third dangerous development is the habit of crunching historical explanation into a single one-way hierarchy of causation, which is now becoming the hallmark of much modern French scholarship. According to this dogma, there are three levels of explanation, of descending independence. First comes the infrastructure, the economic and demographic parameters which set the stage and are the prime movers of the historical process; then the structure, of political organization and political power; and lastly the superstructure, the mental and cultural system of beliefs. Treated too rigidly, this systematization threatens to strangle imaginative historical inquiry. It blocks off any possibility that historical explanation may, in fact, be a much messier and more loose-ended process. To borrow the language of the engineers, it may be a nonlinear, multiple-loop feedback system, with many semi-independent variables, each responsively reacting to the influence of some, or all, of the others.

The basic objection to these threats to the historical profession is that they all tend to reduce the study of man, and the explanation of change, to a simplistic, mechanistic determinism based on some preconceived theoretical notion of universal applicability, regardless of time and space, and allegedly verified by scientific laws and scientific methods. Both historians and social scientists must recognize at least three universal constraints on human cognition which affect all disciplines that are concerned with the nature of man. The sociologist Robert Nisbet has defined them as "first, awareness of the element of *art* that lies in all efforts to grasp reality, no matter how undergirded by pretentious methodologies and computer systems these efforts may be; second, that however one proceeds, with whatever degree of objectivity and devotion to truth, he cannot escape the limitations imposed by the form of his inquiry; and third, that many words through which social scientists, humanists and others approach reality are unalterably metaphoric."[38] These are truths of which too many of the exponents of the "new history" have today lost sight. The fundamental mistake, as Liam Hudson points out, is to think that "people are reducible to the form of evidence about them that we find it easiest to collect. The first, statistical, tendency is a form of scholasticism to which we are all subject in greater or lesser degree. The second, reductive, is one of ideology, crude and brazen."[39]

It would be misleading to end this paper on an unrelievedly pessimistic note. But it certainly looks as if the triumph of the "new historians" has brought into being signs of a new illusion of value-free science, a new dogmatism, and a new scholasticism that threaten to become as stifling and sterile as those which first came under attack some forty years ago. It is impossible to pretend that the great journals of the 1930s, *Annales* and *The Economic History Review,* are still as exciting and stimulating today as they were in their heady youth. The latter is far more narrowly technical than it used to be, and the former, though still as adventurous and innovative as ever, is so large and diffuse as to be difficult to digest. Nor does their newer rival, *Past and Present*, now have quite the same path-breaking significance that it possessed only ten years ago. This decline in excitement is not because of any deterioration in the quality of the articles published, but because it is more stimulating and rewarding to be successfully converting the unbelievers than to be preaching to the already converted. On the other hand, the most recent addition to such journals, the American *Journal of Interdisciplinary History*, is still on a rising curve of intellectual success.

It may be that the time has come for the historian to reassert the importance of the concrete, the particular, and the circumstantial, as well as the general theoretical model and the procedural insight; to be more wary of quantification for the sake of quantification; to be suspicious of vast cooperative projects of staggering cost; to stress the critical importance of a strict scrutiny of the reliability of sources; to be passionately determined to combine both quantitative and qualitative data and methods as the only reliable way even to approach truth about so odd and unpredictable and irrational a creature as man; and to display a becoming modesty about the validity of our discoveries in this most difficult of disciplines.

If this can be done, it will arrest the possible threat of a split in the profession, especially in America. On the one hand, the "new historians" are riding high on the crest of a wave of successful grantsmanship, laudatory articles in the popular press, the admiration of flocks of graduate students, and the capture at last of some of the key positions of power in the profession. On the other hand, some of the older humanists, like Jacques Barzun and Gertrude Himmelfarb, are now in full cry not only against the indefensible excesses of some of the "new historians" but also against a latitudinarian toleration for a many-sided approach to history.[40]

There is a growing mood of skepticism abroad about the value to historians of much of the newest and most extreme social science methodology. This comes out well in the cautious tone of the series of articles on the "new history" in the *Times Literary Supplement* of March 7, 1975, as compared with the optimistic euphoria displayed in the three issues of the same journal nine years earlier, in 1966, whose publication is now cynically described as being the result of an editorial decision "presumably in order to discharge avant-garde duties." Warning signals are flying about threats of a new theoretical dogmatism and a new methodological scholasticism. No doubt the conservatives are unduly alarmist. But if the profession does indeed begin to narrow its viewpoint and closes off its intellectual options, as it certainly did in the early twentieth century, it runs the risk either of growing sterility or of factional fragmentation. Only if the two principles of methodological diversity and ideological pluralism are vigorously defended will the necessary intellectual interchange between the historian and the social scientist continue to be a fruitful one, and will the "new history" continue to replicate its astonishing successes over the past forty years by helping to solve the fresh problems that will arise to preoccupy the next generation of professional historians.

NOTES

1. In this essay footnote references have been limited to direct quotations or to further developments of the argument. The authors and their works mentioned in the text are too well known to need documentation. I am very grateful to the students and faculty members of my seminar at Princeton, in discussion with whom the arguments of the essay have been modified and refined over the years. I am also extremely grateful for some trenchant and pertinent comments on a penultimate draft by my colleague and friend, Professor Robert Darnton, who saved me from many excesses and errors. For those that remain I am solely responsible.

2. Edward G. W. Bill, *University Reform in Nineteenth-Century Oxford: A Study of Henry Halford Vaughan, 1811–1885* (Oxford: Clarendon Press, 1973), pp. 69–72.

3. Walter Bagehot, *The English Constitution* (London: Chapman and Hall, 1867).

4. Elias H. Tuma, "New Approaches in Economic History and Related Social Sciences," *Journal of European Economic History* 3, no. 1 (Spring 1974):175.

5. Liam Hudson, *The Cult of the Fact: A Psychologist's Autobiographical Critique of his Discipline* (New York: Harper & Row, 1972), p. 12.

6. Carl Bridenbaugh in *New York Times Book Review Section*, January 24, 1965.

7. For a brilliant analysis of the development of *Annales* and the historical school it

represents, see J. H. Hexter, "Fernand Braudel and the *Monde Braudelien* . . .," *Journal of Modern History* 44, no. 4 (December 1972): 480–541.

8. Lucien Febvre, *Combats pour l'histoire*, 2d ed. (Paris: A. Colin, 1965).

9. Gabriel A. Almond in *American Sociological Review* 29, no. 3 (June 1964):418–19.

10. For an insight into the current approaches of this school, see Jacques Le Goff and Pierre Nora, *Faire de l'histoire* (Paris: Gallimard, 1974).

11. (London) *Times Literary Supplement*, July 28, 1966, p. 647.

12. Hudson, *The Cult of the Fact*, p. 13.

13. James Boswell, *The Life of Samuel Johnson*, 2 vols., Everyman's Library (London: J. M. Dent, 1949), 2:451.

14. E. J. Hobsbawm, "From Social History to the History of Society," *Daedalus: Journal of the American Academy of Arts and Sciences* (Winter 1971), 20–45.

15. Edward A. Wrigley, *Population and History* (London: Weidenfeld & Nicolson, 1969); and David V. Glass and D. E. C. Eversley, eds., *Population in History: Essays in Historical Demography* (London: E. Arnold, 1965).

16. For some examples of this eclectic approach, see Stephan Thernstrom and R. Sennett, eds., *Nineteenth-Century Cities: Essays in the New Urban History* (New Haven: Yale University Press, 1969); Harold J. Dyos and Michael Wolff, eds., *The Victorian City: Images and Realities* (London: Routledge & Kegan Paul, 1973); and Leo F. Schnore, *The New Urban History: Quantitative Explorations by American Historians* (Princeton: Princeton University Press, 1974).

17. W. S. Robinson, "Ecological Correlations and the Behavior of Individuals," *American Sociological Review* 15, no. 3 (June 1950):351–57.

18. For some discussion of psychohistory, see Cushing Strout, "Ego Psychology and the Historian," *History and Theory: Studies in the Philosophy of History* 7, no. 3 (1968):281–97; Alain Besançon, "Vers une histoire psychoanalytique," *Annales, Économies, Sociétés, Civilisations* 24, no. 3 (May–June 1969):594–616, and 24, no. 4 (July–August 1969):1011–33; Bruce Mazlish, "What Is Psycho-history?" *Transactions of the Royal Historical Society* (London), 5th ser., 21 (1971); and Frank Manuel, "The Use and Abuse of Psychology in History," in *Historical Studies Today*, ed. Felix Gilbert and Stephen R. Graubard (New York: W. W. Norton, 1972). Examples of the genre are to be found in Bruce Mazlish, ed., *Psychoanalysis and History*, rev. ed. (New York: Universal Library, 1971); and Robert Jay Lifton, ed., *Explorations in Psychohistory: The Wellfleet Papers* (New York: Simon and Schuster, 1974).

19. For two collections of representative work by this new school, see Robert W. Fogel and Stanley L. Engerman, eds., *The Reinterpretation of American Economic History* (New York: Harper & Row, 1971); and Peter Temin, ed., *The New Economic History: Selected Readings* (Harmondsworth: Penguin, 1973).

20. E. J. Hobsbawm, "Labor History and Ideology," *Journal of Social History* 7 (1974):376.

21. For assessments of the virtue of the "new economic history," see Thomas C. Cochran, "Economic History, Old and New," *American Historical Review* 74, no. 5 (June 1969):1561-72; M. Levy-Leboyer, "La new economic history," *Annales, Économies, Sociétés, Civilisations* 24, no. 5 (September–October 1969):1035-69; H. J. Habakkuk, "Economic History and Economic Theory," in *Historical Studies Today*, ed. F. Gilbert and S. R. Graubard, pp. 27-44; and Albert Fishlow, "The New Economic History Revisited," *Journal of European Economic History* 3, no. 2 (Fall 1974):453-67.

22. Lawrence Stone, "Prosopography," *Daedalus*, Winter 1971, pp. 46–79.

23. Pierre Goubert, "Local History,"*Daedalus*, Winter 1971, pp. 113–27; and Lawrence Stone, "English and United States Local History," *Daedalus*, Winter 1971, pp. 128–32.

24. Hudson, *The Cult of the Fact*, p. 64, n. *.

25. Review of Keith V. Thomas, *Religion and the Decline of Magic*, by E. P. Thompson, in *Midland History* 1, no. 3 (Spring 1972):41-55.

26. Michael Drake, ed., *Applied Historical Studies: An Introductory Reader* (London: Methuen in association with Open University Press, 1973), p. 1. For a powerful, witty, and well-argued statement of the more traditional view of history as a profession, see J. H. Hexter, *The History Primer* (New York: Basic Books, 1971).

27. For a good, well-documented summary of the most recent work in and claims for this methodology, see Robert W. Fogel, "The Limits of Quantitative Methods in History," *American Historical Review* 80, no. 2 (April 1975):329-50. It is not easy from this article to see what the limits are.

28. For three of many devastating reviews of this work, see H. Gutman, "The World Two Cliometricians Made," *Journal of Negro History* 60, no. 1 (January 1975):53–227; P.A. David and P. Temin, "Slavery: The Progressive Institution," *The Journal of Economic History* 34 (Fall 1974); and T. L. Haskell, "The True and Tragical History of *Time on the Cross*," *New York Review of Books* 22, no. 15, October 2, 1975.

29. Historical Data Archives, collected by the Inter-University Consortium for Political Research at the University of Michigan.

30. George Selement, "Perry Miller: A Note on his Sources in *The New England Mind: The Seventeenth Century*," *William and Mary Quarterly*, 3d ser., 31 (July 1974):453–64.

31. J.-P. Aron, P. Dumont, and E. Le Roy Ladurie, *Anthropologie du conscrit français* (Paris, 1974); and Peter Laslett, ed., *Household and Family in Past Time: Comparative Studies in the Size and Structure of the Domestic Group over the Last Three Centuries in England, France, Serbia, Japan, and Colonial North America, with Further Materials from Western Europe* (Cambridge: at the University Press, 1972).

32. E. A. Wrigley, ed., *Identifying People in the Past* (London: Arnold, 1973).

33. François Billacois, "Pour une enquête sur la criminalité dans la France d'Ancien Régime," *Annales, Économies, Sociétés, Civilisations* 22, no. 2 (March–April 1967):340–47; and J. M. Beattie, "The Pattern of Crime in England, 1660–1800," *Past and Present*, no. 62 (February 1974), 47–95.

34. E. P. Thompson, "The Moral Economy of the English Crowd in the Eighteenth Century," *Past and Present*, no. 50 (February 1971), 76–136.

35. Robert W. Fogel, "The Limits of Quantitative Methods in History," *American Historical Review* 80, no. 2 (April 1975):346–48.

36. Hudson, *The Cult of the Fact*, pp. 74–76. Dr. Hudson's book is a brilliant but alarming critique of the state of modern psychology.

37. Carl E. Schorske, "Politics and the Psyche in *fin de siècle* Vienna: Schnitzler and Hofmannsthal," *American Historical Review* 66, no. 4 (July 1961):930–46; his "The Transformation of the Garden: Ideal and Society in Austrian Literature," ibid. 72, no. 4 (July 1967):1283–1320; his "Politics in a New Key: An Austrian Triptych," *Journal of Modern History* 39, no. 4 (December 1967):343-86; and his "Politics and Patricide in Freud's *Interpretation of Dreams*," *American Historical Review* 78, no. 2 (April 1973):328–47.

38. Quoted by Hudson, *The Cult of the Fact*, p. 155.

39. Ibid., p. 155.

40. Gertrude Himmelfarb, "The 'New History,' " *Commentary* 59, no. 1 (January 1975):72–78; Jacques Barzun, *Clio and the Doctors: Psycho-history, Quanto-history and History* (Chicago: University of Chicago Press, 1974). See also Jacques Barzun, "History: The Muse and Her Doctors," *American Historical Review* 77, no. 1 (February 1972):36–64 and rejoinders ibid. 77, no. 4 (October, 1972):1194–97; and Elie Kedourie, "New Histories for Old," (London) *Times Literary Supplement*, March 7, 1975, p. 238.

2

The New Urban History

Stephan Thernstrom

The new urban history is, if not quite an infant field, at best only prepubescent. The term, at least, is a mere seven years old. It was first employed in 1969, in the subtitle of a collection of papers prepared for the Yale Conference on the nineteenth-century city, *Nineteenth-Century Cities: Essays in the New Urban History*.[1] The years since then have brought a substantial and rapidly growing body of scholarly work that could be considered to lie within the domain of the new urban history, work displaying three common characteristics: an interest in linking social theory to historical data; an eagerness to use relevant quantitative evidence; and a desire to broaden the scope of study to embrace the experience of ordinary anonymous American city dwellers.

Last year saw the publication of a volume which might be considered to mark a second stage in the evolution of this field: Leo Schnore's *The New Urban History: Quantitative Explorations by American Historians*.[2] Enough has happened for it to make some sense to pause and take stock, and to speculate about what opportunities and dangers lie ahead.

I. *Defining the Terms*

I have to say at the outset, however, that my views about this subject are colored by a growing feeling, perhaps a result of creeping middle age, that neatly fencing off the scholarly turf and finding the proper labels for our own turf is not the most important of tasks. To some degree it can even be counterproductive. Some narrowing of vision is necessary to obtain focus—the researcher cannot profitably take as his subject all of history, or even all of American history—but the excessive proliferation of exclusive fields and subfields fragments the past and balkanizes the profession.

But if labels do matter, "the new urban history" may be the wrong one. Over the years I have grown steadily less comfortable with the term. I am now inclined to believe that, just as the Holy Roman Empire was neither holy, Roman, nor an empire, the new urban history is not so new, it should not be identified as urban, and there is some danger that it will cease to be history.

On the first point, the newness of the new urban history, those of us who have marched under that banner have been typically American, as quick to applaud new, improved urban history as we are new, improved Pepsodent. We would do well to recall that an exhortation to the profession to write "the New History," the "real history of men and women" was the substance of Edward Eggleston's presidential address at the meeting of the American Historical Association in 1900, and it has been echoed by generation after generation of historians in the succeeding three quarters of a century.

This is perhaps understandable; at one phase of our lives, we all feel the need to proclaim how very different we are from our fathers. And it has sometimes been inconvenient, in identifying intellectual tendencies that do represent a genuine shift, and in providing a label for groupings or schools of thought. But too often there has been an arrogance in the claim of newness, and a blindness to the roots from which the supposedly new sprang. There was something of that, I fear, in the spirit of the new urban historians. Although it is sometimes quite difficult to avoid such terms, I sometimes think our profession would benefit from a moratorium on the use of adjectives "new" and "traditional" as modifers of the noun "history."

Nor do I think any more that the adjective "urban" is very helpful in sorting out historians into clusters of people who have most to say to each other. At least I do not find that it serves to specify my own particular interests very well any more. "Urban" is at once too broad and too narrow for me.

Too broad, in that the city is such a complex, multifaceted, and, in societies like ours today, so nearly all-embracing a phenomenon that it admits of study from *many* vantage points. It is a place where too many things happen to be the province of one urban history—or even two, the new and the old. Perhaps one could specify a sufficiently delimited set of urban phenomena to define a coherent field of urban history—Roy Lubove's conception of "the city-building process" is an interesting candidate—but much of the work that has been done by new urban historians falls outside that.[3]

In another sense, the new urban history is too narrow. Not long ago Robert Swierenga called for "a new rural history," on the ground that the same demographic, economic, and social processes emphasized by the new urban historians shaped the lives of rural people as well.[4] I agree, and would go him one better by saying that urban and rural historians should be joining forces. It makes particular sense in the American context, for until very recently the majority of American city dwellers have been people who were born outside urban areas and later migrated into them. We cannot understand their experiences in the city without knowing a good deal about who they were and how and why they came there. Whether our subject is the Irish of mid-nineteenth-century Boston, the blacks of early twentieth-century Chicago, or the Appalachian whites of Detroit today, we are dealing with rural people confronting the challenges of urban existence. A proper study of groups like these could best be described not as urban history or rural history, but as a history of population and social structure.

There can even be some doubt as to whether the new urban history is history at all. I have in mind something other than the claim that all valid history must be written in narrative form. That view seems to me to be long outmoded. There is another, more serious question that I shall return to toward the close of this essay. History, I shall argue, is more than mere data processing; it is *thought*, and some of the recent literature in this field does not appear to be the product of much reflection.

With these matters of definition out of the way, let me offer some sketchy remarks on three subjects: the historiographical roots of the new urban history; needs and opportunities for future study in the field; and pitfalls and dangers to be avoided.

II. *Historiographical Roots*

Whether the field be termed the new urban history, or the history of population and social structure, its roots in American soil extend back into the 1930s. Three major contributions stand out. One is Oscar Handlin's *Boston's Immigrants*, which showed how a knowledge of the other social sciences could enrich social history.[5] *Boston's Immigrants* was noteworthy too in its pioneering use of a source that has been the backbone of many recent studies—the manuscript schedules of the United States Census. Historians had long made use of published census data, of course, but here was a treasure trove of social data about every American, data that could be reaggregated and analyzed by categories more fruitful than those employed in the published census volumes.

In these same years, the manuscript census schedules were also being exploited to interesting effect by Frank and Harriet Owsley and their students at Vanderbilt University. The work of the Owsley school, summed up most conveniently in *Plain Folk of the Old South*,[6] was unsophisticated and marred by racist assumptions. To write the social history of the antebellum South with hardly a reference to the four million slaves who accounted for a third of its population was a feat that boggles the mind. But Owsley and his followers posed crucial questions about the antebellum Southern social structure and gathered an extraordinary body of relevant quantitative evidence. They were, to my knowledge, the first American historians to transfer their data to punch cards and to use mechanical methods for processing them.

Boston's Immigrants and the various studies of the Owsley school employed quantitative evidence of a cross-sectional type. To the extent that they attempted to measure change over time, they relied upon comparisons of two or more cross sections, a procedure fraught with peril. It was James C. Malin who pointed the way toward a solution.[7] In his studies of the turnover of the farm population in Kansas, Malin demonstrated the utility of tracing individual life histories over time. While his interest was confined to establishing rates of persistence and migration, the method itself had broader implications, and later investigators would extend it to the study of movement through social space as well as physical space.

For reasons that are not altogether clear to me and that I cannot take the space to speculate about here, a good many years were to elapse before the analytical possibilities that had been opened up by Handlin, Owsley, and Malin were actually pursued. And when research in this tradition first reappeared in the late 1950s, few historians paid any attention. Two significant volumes were published within a year of each other: Merle Curti's Trempealeau County (Wisconsin) study, *The Making of an American Community*,[8] and sociologist Sidney Goldstein's volume on Norristown, Pennsylvania, *Patterns of Mobility, 1910–1950*.[9] Methodologically, both were model specimens of "grass-roots" social history, reconstructions of the social structure of past communities based upon an accounting of the experiences of the individual residents. Whether it was the lackluster prose in which these books were written, their failure to address the issue that seemed most important to scholars then—the question of consensus and conflict in national politics—or some other circumstance, they were little noticed and quickly forgotten.

That was not the case with *Poverty and Progress*, published only five years later.[10] It is true that one leading journal failed at first to review it and instead consigned it to the "books received" category on the ground that it appeared to be a work of sociology rather than history! (That it is hard to conceive of a similar study's meeting such a reception today is an index of how much has changed in the past decade.) But *Poverty and Progress* did soon have a certain impact. Coming at what proves to have been a strategic moment, it alerted younger investigators to accessible sources and readily comprehensible methods with which to write systematic social history.

III. *Future Study*

After this hasty backward look, let me turn to the future. In what directions should coming inquiries move? Five come to mind.

1. If we are to understand the American past more fully, it will be necessary to broaden the geographical scope of inquiry. After preparing a tentative reading list for a course in American urban history, someone remarked to me, he realized that it could better be described as a course in the history of Boston! More work on communities outside of New England, and the Northeast in general, is badly needed.

2. Likewise, it will be necessary to broaden the temporal scope of inquiry. The current literature focuses heavily on the 1850–1880 years because of the fortuitous availability of the manuscript census schedules. This was justifiable, I think, in the first phases of research. It is hardly the first time that the direction of historical inquiry has been shaped by the accident that pertinent evidence is readily available for one time and place and not for another. But now it is time to realize that the manuscript schedules of the U.S. Census are not the *sine qua non* for systematic social history. A wide variety of vital records, city directories, tax lists, manuscript state censuses, and the like have already been located, and more will surely be turned up if we only look hard enough.

3. We must go about delineating the stratification system with more delicate tools than the blue collar/white collar dichotomy and other similarly gross categories. A much closer and more refined scrutiny of the occupational universe will be rewarding, as Clyde and Sally Griffen demonstrate in their forthcoming Poughkeepsie study.[11] We need to know a great deal more about the world of work and the changes that took place within it in the course of American development. At the same time, it will be fruitful to probe more energetically for other forms of evidence concerning economic status—wealth, in-

come, and other dimensions of the command of resources over time. Recent work on the changing distribution of wealth in the American past, based upon tax lists, probate records, and the census manuscripts, suggests how much more is to be learned here. The current literature, however, attempts to deal with change over time by analyzing successive cross sections; as suggested earlier, the results of such studies will remain inconclusive without longitudinal studies that follow individuals through time.

4. The nature of the evidence available dictates that we study people in particular places—Boston, Newburyport, or wherever. And yet the cruel fact is that the people of a community at any given time are an unstable compound. Many of them had not been in that place long, and their newness to the community profoundly affected their place within it. And many would not stay in it very long. Full comprehension of the lives of the people of a community requires that we find out more about them both before they arrived and after they left for new destinations. Recent studies of European immigrants to the New World display increasing awareness of the need to scrutinize origins more closely; a similar awareness on the part of investigators treating internal, native-born migrants is needed.[12] Similarly, a more sustained effort to explore the future destinations and fates of out-migrants is necessary. The task is immensely difficult, but the recent discovery of the Soundex indexes to the 1880 and 1900 federal censuses, and of indexes to some state censuses may permit a major breakthrough here.[13]

5. The literature on American mobility has focused too narrowly upon male heads of households and has neglected the familial context, except for that part of it that can be glimpsed by comparing the occupational achievements of fathers and their sons. We have overlooked the fact that it was not only the fabled farm family of pre-industrial days that was an economic unit. The economic contributions of women and children, whether or not directly income generating, need to be examined much more closely.[14]

IV. *Pitfalls and Dangers*

Optimistic though I am about what has been done in this field in the past and what promises to be done in the future, I do see certain dangers that we must be on guard against.

1. In our desire to see that work in this field is cumulative, there is some danger that we shall err on the side of being merely imitative. It is indeed desirable that studies in quantitative social history present

information aggregated into categories sufficiently similar to those employed by other investigators to permit proper comparison with the results of previous studies. The contention that there was less upward mobility in city X than in city Y will be meaningless if the two inquiries do not employ a common definition of what occupational changes constitute upward, as opposed to lateral or downward mobility. Nevertheless, the mere documentation of an established pattern, cranking data from a previously unstudied community through a framework established by others, is not a very exciting contribution to knowledge. I shudder at the prospect that a few years hence the table of contents of a typical issue of the *Journal of American History* might read: "Social Mobility in Little Rock, 1850–1880," "Social Mobility in Albany, 1850–1880," etc. While continuing to pay proper heed to cumulativeness, we must insist that a good book or article be innovative and that it offer some distinctive interpretative insight, or develop some innovative method.

2. Some work in quantitative social history has been marred by the investigator's failure to scrutinize his sources with the necessary care. One of the great achievements of the historical profession has been the methods it has developed for the close inspection of texts and its concern for evaluating possible biases in the evidence. I see some prophets of the new history, however, who appear to have developed something of a "run it up the flagpole and see if they salute" mentality—a "run it through the computer and see what comes out" mentality. The most sophisticated statistical analysis of the characteristics of the rich of nineteenth-century New York, say, will be of little value if its foundation is a highly incomplete, inaccurate, and socially skewed listing of who the rich were.

3. I have some trepidations about team research with fat budgets and an elaborate bureaucratic structure. Some issues can be fully explored in no other way, as Michael Katz's splendid new book, *The People of Hamilton, Canada West*,[15] demonstrates so well. But there is little prospect that in the near future many of us will be able to find funding at the high five- or six-figure levels. Nor should it be necessary. I know that it is quite impossible to carry out serious research in astrophysics these days without massive support, but history remains and is likely long to remain a discipline in which the creative individual can get by very nicely with very little help from his friends.

4. Finally, I am distressed at the prospect that in importing social science techniques into their own discipline, historians will also import the barbaric and slovenly writing habits that are too readily tolerated in the sister social sciences. Not that I would ban all jargon

—if by jargon we mean technical terms that serve as convenient shorthand for ideas too complex to spell out each time we wish to refer to them. Some such technical terms are indispensable to the writer of history in the social science vein. He need only define them clearly at the outset and use them correctly thereafter. But much of the language I read in social science periodicals is jargon in another meaning specified in my dictionary:"unintelligible or meaningless talk or writing; gibberish." And even where the extremes of utter gibberish are avoided, I see too much prose that could only have been written by someone with a tin ear, writing that is relentlessly murky, leaden, and soporific. Some critics of social science history regard this as one of its inherent traits, but it seems to me that there are enough distinguished exceptions to the general rule to make that unlikely. I see no reason why a willingness to experiment with new methods requires that we abandon the sense of literary craftsmanship that has been so fundamental in our professional heritage. But I cannot deny that if I were to rank all the history books on my shelves on two scales, a social-scientific/humanistic scale and a well-written/poorly written scale, the two scales would be strongly correlated and the correlation would be negative. I can only hope that that relationship is contingent and susceptible to reversal in the near future.

V. *Summary*

I am not, in sum, a spokesman for a new breed of revolutionaries, dedicated to a complete transformation of the discipline, eager to substitute FORTRAN for Latin, determined to remake history into a coldly objective, rigorous, mechanical science of human behavior The shape of the discipline in general, and my own field in particular, has been changing and ought to continue to do so. New sources, concepts, and data-processing technologies have in some instances made it possible to write books of unusual social depth and richness, as well as of greater rigor and precision. But the most thorough mastery of the new is not sufficient to make a good historian, much less a great one. A good course in computer programming, for example, enables you to make the machine do your bidding. But *what* you have to do is not a merely technical problem. The real difficulties faced by all historians are these: how to choose an intellectually strategic issue to investigate; how to find a body of pertinent evidence; how to develop concepts to organize and give meaning to the evidence; and how to shape the material into an intellectually coherent, lucid statement or argument. These are at least as much aesthetic as they are technical problems, and scholars who lack humanistic sensibilities are not likely to overcome them successfully.

N O T E S

1. Edited by Stephan Thernstrom and Richard Sennett (New Haven: Yale University Press, 1969).

2. (Princeton: Princeton University Press, 1975).

3. Roy Lubove, "The Urbanization Process: An Approach to Historical Research," *Journal of the American Institute of Planners* 33 (January 1967):33–39.

4. Robert Swierenga, "Towards 'the New Rural History': A Review Essay," *Historical Methods Newsletter* 6 (June 1973):111–22.

5. (Cambridge: Harvard University Press, 1941).

6. (Baton Rouge: Louisiana State University Press, 1949). Fabian Linden's critique of the work of the Owsley school in the *Journal of Negro History* 31 (April 1946):140–89, exposed a number of serious flaws, but a critical essay, by its very nature, cannot convincingly establish an alternative view. It is puzzling and regrettable that the Linden-Owsley controversy did not stimulate continuing research on the subject.

7. James C. Malin, "The Turnover of Farm Population in Kansas," *Kansas Historical Quarterly* 4 (1935):339–72.

8. (Stanford: Stanford University Press, 1959).

9. (Philadelphia: The University of Pennsylvania Press, 1958).

10. Stephan Thernstrom (Cambridge: Harvard University Press, 1964).

11. *Natives and Newcomers: Social Mobility in Poughkeepsie, 1850–1880*, to be published by the Harvard University Press in 1977.

12. Josef Barton, *Peasants and Strangers* (Cambridge: Harvard University Press, 1975).

13. Charles Stephenson, "Tracing Those Who Left: The Soundex Index to the U.S. Census," *Journal of Urban History* 1 (1974):73–84.

14. Joan W. Scott and Louise A. Tilly, "Women's Work and the Family in Nineteenth-Century Europe," *Comparative Studies in Society and History* 17 (1975):36–64.

15. (Cambridge: Harvard University Press, 1976).

3

Historical Demography

Kenneth A. Lockridge

For me, it all started in a study room in the Princeton University Library. I was a graduate student. I planned to do a dissertation on a New England town, partly because my girl friend lived there and partly because no one knew much about how ordinary human beings had lived in this or in any part of colonial America. The trouble was, those town records were all about pigs breaking out of one set of fences and into another. Lord, I thought, how am I ever going to make a dissertation out of this? How am I going to find out what those people were doing?

I'm not sure I ever found out, but there in that study room, as I read for exams and despaired of my topic, someone said a very helpful thing: "Hey," he said, " have you seen Pierre Goubert's new book on Beauvais?" "No," I said, and so picked up that massive tome to add to the pile of reading. Only, when I opened it, there were these charts and graphs, which turned out to be of births, and deaths, and marriages. Now, charts and graphs are dull, but births, and deaths, and marriages are life. And they are more interesting than pigs and fences (though eventually I got something out of pigs and fences, too). And I realized that I had a set of birth, and death, and marriage records, for my town. I knew how it had been, how life had been, and death, and marriage for those Frenchmen around Beauvais in the seventeenth and eighteenth centuries, and I could find out how the basics of life had been for my townsmen and women of colonial Dedham.

That was something to think about. How long did they live, these Americans, how old did they marry, how many children did they have, how many children survived, and how long did they live in turn? And then we could go on to ask, of course, how they all lived. And how did all this compare with conditions in Europe?

So I sat there, the next summer, in Manhattan, and carefully read the French, and carefully counted births, and deaths, and marriages. I knew so little about real demography, or even about historical demography, which had just been invented in France, but I learned a little, and figured some things out for myself, and counted. The simplest thing was to see how many births, or deaths, or marriages there had been, per 1,000 population, and how this had changed over time. I learned later that this was called "aggregative analysis." If I'd known that at the time, it probably would have scared me off. Anyway, that took some tricky guessing, because I was not sure how many people there were in town and I was pretty sure not all births or marriages and near certain that all deaths were recorded. There were various ways around this, and I got some rough estimates of the overall birth, death, and marriage rates in this town.

One thing you had to do, to get these, was to reconstruct the population present, at various moments, using all available records to be sure you had your total straight. Now, while you were doing that, you could as well follow these people and families through time, recording all their births, and deaths, and marriages for several generations. In the end you would have maybe half the families in town where you were pretty sure you had found all their births, deaths, and marriages (which, I learned later, are called "vital events") for about three generations. You could use their birth, death, and marriage rates, which were pretty reliable, to see if your crude estimated rates for the whole population were more or less in the right ball park. I learned later that this was called "family reconstitution analysis." I also learned that you could find out a lot more about these well-recorded families. You could find out about their exact demographic behavior and about the adaptation of that behavior to changing conditions. All you had to do was record a few more details and look more closely.

So I did the analysis, in my primitive way, and what I found set me back. These people lived and married and died pretty much like European peasants—or like Goubert's Frenchmen around Beauvais, anyway, and like others who had been studied by then. They had about the same number of children as some pretty impoverished Frenchmen, they married at about the same age (in their mid-twenties), and while they lived longer, that difference alone was not revolutionary. And they actually moved around a lot less than many Frenchmen. I discovered later that they ran their town in a corporate mode long dreamed of by peasants throughout Europe.

What did this mean? There began at that time, in my mind, a

wrestling with some big ideas which has not stopped to this day. What did it mean that the American environment did not transform these Europeans immediately into "new men," either demographically or socially, not for 150 years anyway? Or what did it mean that, when signs said that some sort of demographic and social transformation had finally arrived, around 1750–1850, there was evidence that similar changes were taking place over much of the Western world? Not just in America. Or what did it mean that even after these later transformations, some of the seventeenth-century patterns of family and communal life which I had detected remained intact into the very twentieth century? How profound and meaningful was the transformation which Western society experienced?

Well, this is the story of all historical demographers, in microcosm. It all started with Louis Henry, in France, trying to explain why the French population, which like all European populations had grown rapidly from 1750 to 1800, had suddenly leveled off thereafter leaving France at the mercy of a still-increasing Germany. The rest of us have taken his tools and developed them and applied them to ever-wider demographic and social problems of our mutual history. And increasingly it is a mutual history we deal with.

We start, of course, from different points of view. Some of us are "pure" demographers, searching to understand why populations rise and fall. Some are social science modelers, seeking to know the rules and laws of adaptability within the human ecosystem. Some, like myself, are cranky historians in pursuit of the past and, through it, in pursuit of the present. We have taken these methods of "aggregative analysis," whether on a small or a large scale, and of "reconstitutive analysis," always on a small scale, and applied these widely in France, yes, but also in England, the Netherlands, Sweden, Spain, Latin America, Canada, and early America over a period ranging from 1200 to 1900. These methods shed light on every demographic and social and historical issue imaginable—including, as you know, the problem of slavery. And increasingly, several great events, or issues, have emerged as most important in the eyes of all historical demographers whatever their points of origin. What are these events, these issues? They are, by and large, the ones into which I was led by my own little study in Dedham.

First, we wish to understand that great system of life, of economy, and of culture under which the human population regulated itself in the centuries preceding the modern era. From the time Western man adopted settled agriculture until the eighteenth century, the population of the European world rose only very slowly if at all. It went through short, violent fluctuations and long, massive cycles, but in the end it increased only slowly and in 1700 was not overwhelmingly larger than it had been in 1200. What are the mysteries of this delicately balanced and ancient system—a system which endured in many respects even in the early American environment?

Then came a whole series of changes which present us with the rest of our issues. We have barely discovered that some of these changes existed, and we do not understand them all. Let me present them roughly in chronological and perhaps in causal order.

For example, the population in the West and perhaps all over the world began to rise steadily, some would say as early as 1550 or 1700, and certainly by 1750. Why? Was it the potato, or some other key to increased productivity? Present theory is that the crucial cause was an exogenous and so far inexplicable fall in mortality which, leaving fertility as high as ever, resulted in a sudden rise in population. Eventually better nutrition and sanitation sustained this fall in mortality and took it to still lower levels. The population continued to rise at an unheard-of rate to unheard-of levels, well into the nineteenth century.

A rising population had to be fed. Late in the eighteenth and early in the nineteenth century, agricultural and other productivity per capita began to rise slowly, making it easier for many nations more or less to support that unprecedented rise in population with which they were faced. We have no idea how mankind was able to bring this about, after previous centuries of evident failure even in the face of temporary rises in population. Now something happened and not only general but per capita productivity increased. In all areas this change was apparently associated with a mentality of individual planning and calculation, for the self, for the family, and increasingly excluding others. In some areas the growth of productivity was modest and hard won, but in England it blossomed into a technological then an industrial revolution, which soon spread elsewhere. By 1900 Western productivity had passed all imagined bounds.

Before the industrial revolution spread, though, another event occurred throughout the West, giving rise to perhaps the most fascinating of all the issues which we face. Fertility began to fall sharply, beginning early in the nineteenth century in France and in America, the fall spreading across Europe during the nineteenth century. By 1930 fertility levels were far below their former level. Why did this happen? Was that rational or calculating mentality of the late eighteenth century somehow persuading certain couples to limit their fertility in order to survive in a time of population pressure? Added encouragement would come from the reassurance that, with falling infant and child mortality, they could have fewer children, spend less, and still be sure some would live to care for them in their old age. Or were couples limiting fertility more in order to prosper, encouraged by signs of increasing human productivity and its hope of prosperity? In this case, they might even be able to take care of their own old age. Or was it a mixture of these considerations? One thing seems clear: it was not the diffusion of new means of birth control which led to the dramatic decline in human reproduction. It was a subtle, diffuse, economic yet also social and cultural event, which took place in the minds of young men and women. It might truly be said that if we understand the decline in fertility, we understand much of the mind of Western man in the age of his most profound transformation.

The result of the earlier and continuing fall in mortality, coupled with the subsequent decline in fertility, was a new demographic regime with consequences all its own. Always before, for example, mortality and fertility had been sky-high and in a neck-and-neck race. Babies were produced, died wholesale in infancy, and the survivors hoped to live as long as their parents. Most of the population was under the age of fifteen, and a good number of these would die. They were not productive, and the drain on emotional and substantive resources which their deaths represented was appalling. By 1900, after the transition to low mortality and low fertility, the scene was utterly changed. For one thing, of course, because it had taken the decline in fertility a century and a half to catch up with the fall in mortality, the total population had grown enormously. Yet, in the end, it was a population in which far more children survived not only birth, but into their teens and twenties and thirties and forties, and this most pro-ductive portion of the population loomed relatively larger than ever in history. We could speculate forever on the impact of this demographic transition, and that is why it is one of our issues.

Finally, together with the completion of this demographic transi-tion, came the mass industrialization and urbanization which we think of as characteristic of modern society. The significances of this are largely for other social scientists, and for historians, but there is some evidence that under these influences and in the twentieth cen-tury a new demographic and possibly social regime is emerging, which we might call postmodernity. This is in part an issue for historical demographers to consider.

So: the mysteries of the old, static, high-mortality, high-fertility, low or zero-growth regime.

The sudden fall in mortality and accompanying rise in population.

The early, marginal rise in productivity which occurred almost simultaneously.

The subsequent fall in fertility, with all that involved and implied.

The consequences of the resultant demographic transition to a low-mortality, low-fertility regime.

And the consequences of urbanization and industrialization for possible postmodern demographic and social patterns.

This is the sequence of events which aggregative and reconstitutive analysis have helped delineate and may help elucidate and understand. It is a mutual history which will be understood to our mutual benefit.

In passing, let me introduce some of the men who have rather recently defined these issues of human history and who are now working with increasing effect to understand the causal interrelations, the inner structures, and the consequences of these events.

The most fascinating work on the nature of premodern demography and society is being done by such scholars as Emmanuel Le Roy Ladurie in France and Ronald Lee in the United States, and also by Jacques Dupâquier in France, by E. A. Wrigley in England, and by Daniel Scott Smith in the United States. Le Roy Ladurie and Lee together depict a vast cycle of rising population, crowding, falling wages and nutrition, demographic disaster, population depletion, renewed opportunity, and again rising population, a cycle whose pulses, eight generations long, once echoed massively and rendingly through European history. Dupâquier, Wrigley, and Smith have begun to show that the ways in which premodern villagers adjusted to falling or rising resources, by reducing or raising population, were incredibly subtle, were often collective rather than individual, and were heavily expressed through and limited by the imperatives of local and of national culture. The simple mechanisms of clockwork social scientists will not describe the villagers' tactics or the interrelations within this self-regulating sociodemographic system.

The fall in mortality after 1700 or 1750 and the early marginal rise in productivity have their demographical and statistical poets, too, most notably Le Roy Ladurie and Wrigley. Yet these are the least understood of our changes, and I shall only urge you to read Le Roy Ladurie on Languedoc and Wrigley's various writings to get into these events and into our efforts to explain them.

The subsequent decline in fertility has had more attention. All of the French scholars and, here in the United States, Maris A. Vinovskis and Daniel Scott Smith are exploring this event. Vinovskis has found that some supposed predictors, such as urbanity, really correlate very little with lower fertility, since fertility fell in rural areas as well. Rather, some process which is related partly to shortage of land and to commercialization and perhaps to expected income, and is also related to subtle matters of context and ethnicity and culture, seems to have been involved in the decline in fertility in mid-nineteenth-century America. Daniel Scott Smith has made an attempt to investigate the specific background of this declining fertility in his long-term study of Hingham, Massachusetts. Smith implies that one crucial element was the declining importance of inheritance in determining children's social mobility and demographic decisions. By 1800—partly because of overcrowding, which had reduced the size of holdings and so reduced the size of inheritances, and partly because agrarian and commercial opportunities elsewhere had become more compelling than reduced inheritances—children had begun to marry and move and prosper regardless of their potential inheritance. This implied the end of whatever controls inheritance had once enabled parents to exercise over these children. One result, Smith suggests, was that fertility control over young people was no longer exercised by their parents, through delayed marriage and delayed inheritance, but was exercised rather by the young people themselves in rational view of their life chances in the larger society. Their fertility decisions were also influenced by the evolving imperatives of a culture which transcended the locality. The net result was a widespread, voluntary, and unprecedentedly effective use of birth control—probably coitus interruptus—by young marrieds. Smith must now spell out the exact reasons for the young people's decisions and clarify the larger implications of this transition to low fertility, the implications for the history of Western man and for the fate of an overpopulated world.

As for the consequences of the entire demographic transition, to a low-mortality, low-fertility regime, and indeed for the further demographic consequences of industrialization and urbanization in the twentieth century, here let me refer to modern demographers and to journalists as well as to historians. In some ways we historical types have just begun to consider these issues.

One thing which may help with the study of all the issues raised by this whole series of events is a thing called the Swedish *Databas* project. The Swedish demographic and social records are nearly complete for every individual in Sweden from 1700, and certainly from 1750, right up to the present day. There were, in effect, yearly local censuses which were cross-referenced to migration, birth, death, marriage, and other records. Since these were all kept by the church, you might say they were kept religiously. Now, what they are doing in

Sweden is putting sample parishes into machine-readable form, so that scholars anywhere can analyze one or several parishes in instant and exquisite detail right through the period of all these critical social and demographic events we've been discussing. This is a kind of Swedish WPA project, and a mighty creative one, too.

As you can see from this hasty review of the field, we have some big events, and some big issues, and some talented people—but far from a conclusive understanding of these events and of these issues. If I *had* to sum up the latest research in a few statements, I would say something like this: (1) The economic and demographic interactions of stable and of changing Western society are more complex and subtle than we had imagined. (2) Culture and cultural lag are very much involved in these stable and changing interactions. (3) Fertility probably dropped in response to economic conditions, but whether it represented an effort to maintain economic position in crowded times or a means to improved position in worsening or in improving times, or all of these, is still very much open. Here, too, matters of cultural conditioning must be considered as very important, and (4) the common thread running through all the demographic and social changes since 1700 or 1750 seems to be a shift in the locus of decision to the calculating if not always rational individual, first in the context of his family, and increasingly and ever more, alone. It would be folly to equate this man, or woman, for all his or her choices, with the trite old idea of progress.

So, you see, we already have the grain of a wider knowledge. Demographers now know that the rise and fall of human populations can be an almost profoundly subtle phenomenon. Social scientists know that the great changes in the human condition began well before massive industrialization and involve not so much gross changes in family size or context as much as subtle changes which focused pressures on the individual in his family to make decisions—for example, production or fertility decisions. Historians, in turn, may ponder these mysteries and truths. Our common history is a garden of wonder and, just perhaps, of knowledge.

We must remember, in all of this, too, that history seen upward from births, deaths, and marriages is itself a mode of thought whose implications need to be considered. It is possibly this which concerns me more than anything else. I would be willing to suggest, as indeed my language throughout this lecture has suggested, that this mode of thought has some benefits, but not entirely in the ways usually intended.

The usual dialogue about social scientific history runs something like this: Well, say the critics, it all tends to social scientism, and to a vast and Faustian pretense to total knowledge on the basis of numbers alone. Linguistically and conceptually this leads to disaster, as John Kenneth Galbraith's famous parody has shown:

This rather optimistic estimate was derived by plotting a three-dimensional distribution of three arbitrarily defined variables; the macro-structural, relating to the extension of knowledge beyond the capacity of conscious experience; the organic, dealing with the manifestations of terrestrial life as inherently comprehensible; and the infraparticular, covering the subconceptual requirements of natural phenomena.

Values were assigned to the known and unknown in each parameter, tested against data from earlier chronologies, and modified heuristically until predictable correlations reached a useful level of accuracy.[1]

In modern times, this mentality led to McNamara's disaster in Vietnam. In historical circles, it leads to an image of Robert Fogel, in his laboratory amid swarms of scurrying assistants, crying through the steamy air, "Numbers, numbers, give me more numbers!" It is Faust, all over again.

Historical demographers and historical social scientists, among them Professor Fogel, set against this the real claims of social science history: that numbers are the residue of real human beings and are the skeleton of the patterns of their lives and so of history, and that these patterns of basic behavior, once reconstructed and supplemented with other sources, qualitative sources, may help us to understand why populations change, and why and how societies and economies change, and to what degree the whole manner of human existence has changed into modern times. And if this can get Faustian, that is an excess we shall have to watch out for in our search for knowledge.

That is the usual dialogue, and I think you are all familiar with it. You can judge for yourselves the merits of the critics and defenders. Faustianism is, of course, no small danger. What I wish to consider instead, however, is a related accusation often leveled against social science history. It is said that social scientific historians are inhumane as well as Faustian. By inhumane I do not mean so much the way they treat each other, which certainly is inhumane, but I mean instead the fact that these numerologists need and instead bleach out the very soul of human existence. Where, the critics say, where in all of this is man? And where, to please the feminists, is woman? Quantitative theories alone are not only incomplete but inhumane. They do not have the great resonances of human life. We have lost a whole dimension of history, that dimension which makes history also one of the humanities.

Well, I'm not so sure about this one, for many reasons. For one thing, the scholars who level this accusation are usually those who have used one or two or, at most, three quotations to twist history into whatever artistic shapes their own minds happen to conceive. This is the opposite sin from numerical Faustianism, and if this kind of history is humane, God save us. History as a humanity is, after all, supposed to evoke the real human resonances of the men of the past, not the resonances contrived by men of the present.

Moreover, I'm prepared to argue that the way to a revival of history as a humanistic discipline lies precisely through the social scientific analysis of historical structures, shocking though this may seem. I would argue that it is through a knowledge of the demographic and social structures of the past that we gain the best and most accurate sense of what it meant to be a man, or a woman. Think of it. When Dan Smith reconstitutes the lives of thousands of families in Hingham and shows us, marriage by marriage, birth by birth, move by move, even name by name, how the younger generations of the early nineteenth century slowly declared their economic and demographic independence of their parents, *and* slowly exercised their determination to limit their children and to control every thread of the fabric of their lives, what have we here but a sense of the human condition? Not a story, not a novel, but a real sense of hundreds, and thousands, and hundreds of thousands of lives. And what poignancy in those lives, simultaneously steeped in the heady wine of independence and plunged into the gall of Victorian self-control. There is an ambiguity worthy of a novelist: and there is such a thing as we have never had, such a sense that this was life, not invention.

Or what of Robert Fogel's and Stanley Engerman's *Time on the Cross*, to pick another example? What is this book on slavery, however clumsily expressed, but another effort again to delineate that structure of demographic and numerical reality within which we may better understand, yes, and appreciate the interplay of human emotions? Out of these numbers we know as never before that American black slavery was not a scourge of the body so much as of the soul. The black man was told that he could live—he and his woman would be fed, clothed, and housed until their reproduction rate and often life expectancy itself approached those of their masters—and then they were subjected to an attempt to obliterate both soul and pride which was unmatched in the annals of slavery. If you want a sense of what slavery was, then think of this paradox, and of its agonies.

Finally, a failed example, a book called *Wisconsin Death Trip*, by Michael Lesy. Here we have part of the soul of rural Wisconsin in the nineteenth century, tacked up from a newspaper in the form of suicide notices, and staring out at us with blank eyes from apparently melancholy old photographs. We are told, in effect, that men lost their souls in this dungheap, or fled to the stimulation of the cities in order to survive. But we do not have the suicide rate here, or the incidence of madness, or the migration rate, compared with the same statistical rates for the cities. Perhaps life in the cities was worse still. In which case, we should be able to find more than a few smiling memoirs of the springs or summers in rural Wisconsin, and of satisfying harvests. The interpretation would be reversed. Because we lack the demographic structures of life, here, and elsewhere, in the cities, we do not know how to interpret these casual newspaper clippings and these cryptic, wide-eyed, staring photographs. We lack the structure of reality which would help us understand how these men and women felt.

The promise of historical demography, then, and of social science history, is not merely social scientific knowledge. It is also a better sense of what, amidst the structures and changes of life, human beings really were, and did, and felt. Out of births, and deaths, and marriages, we have a renewed sense of humankind, of our great unities, of our joys, our pains, and our travails, and of our ambiguous coming of age.

NOTES

1. John Kenneth Galbraith in *Report from Iron Mountain on the Possibility and Desirability of Peace* (New York, 1967), sec. 6, n. 13.

BIBLIOGRAPHY

Dupâquier, Jacques. "Review Essay" on E. A. Wrigley, *Population and History* (London: Weidenfeld & Nicolson, 1969). In *History and Theory* 12, no. 1 (1973):141–46.

Fogel, Robert, and Engerman, Stanley. *Time on the Cross: The Economics of American Negro Slavery*. Boston: Little, Brown, 1974.

Galbraith, J. Kenneth in *Report from Iron Mountain on the Possibility and Desirability of Peace*. New York: Dial Press, 1967.

Goubert, Pierre. *Beauvais et le Beauvaisis de 1600 à 1730: Contribution à l'histoire sociale de la France du XVIIe siècle*. 2 vols. Paris: S.E.V.P.E.N., 1960.

Hareven, Tamara K., and Vinovskis, Maris A. "Marital Fertility, Ethnicity, and Occupation in Urban Families: An Analysis of South Boston and the South End in 1880." *Journal of Social History* 7 (Spring 1975):69–93.

Henry, Louis, and Fleury, M. *Des registres paroisseaux à l'histoire de la population: Manuel de dépouillement et d'exploitation de l'état civil ancien.* Paris: Éditions de l'Institut national d'études démographiques, 1956; new ed., 1965.

Henry, Louis, and Gautier, Étienne. *La population de Crulai, paroisse normande: Étude historique.* Paris: Presses universitaires de France, 1958.

Lee, Ronald. "Population in Preindustrial England: An Econometric Analysis." *The Quarterly Journal of Economics* 87 (November 1973):581–607.

LeRoy Ladurie, Emmanuel. *Les paysans de Languedoc.* Paris: S.E.V.P.E.N., 1966; abridged trans., *The Peasants of Languedoc.* Urbana: University of Illinois Press, 1974.

Lesy, Michael, comp. *Wisconsin Death Trip.* New York: Pantheon, 1973.

Lockridge, Kenneth A. "The Population of Dedham, Massachusetts, 1636–1736." *Economic History Review*, 2d ser., 19 no. 2 (1966):318–44.

Smith, Daniel Scott. "Parental Power and Marriage Patterns." *Journal of Marriage and the Family* 35, no. 3 (1973):419–28.

Vinovskis, Maris A. "A Multivariate Analysis of Fertility Differentials among Massachusetts Towns in 1860." Paper delivered at the meeting of the American Historical Association, New York, 1973.

———. "Rural-Urban Differences in Fertility." Paper presented at the meeting of the American Historical Association, Chicago, 1974.

———. "Demographic Changes in America from the Revolution to the Civil War: An Analysis of the Socio-economic Determinants of Fertility Differentials and Trends in Massachusetts, 1765-1860." Ph.D. dissertation, Harvard University, 1974; available with the permission of the author, c/o Department of History, University of Michigan, Ann Arbor, MI 48104.

Wrigley, Edward A. "Mortality in Pre-Industrial England: The Example of Colyton, Devon, over Three Centuries." *Daedalus*, Spring 1968, pp. 546–80.

———. *Population and History.* London: Weidenfeld & Nicolson, 1969.

4

The Many Faces of the History of Science

A Font of Examples for Philosophers, a Scientific Type of History, an Archaeology of Discovery, a Branch of Sociology, a Variant of Intellectual or Social History—*Or What?*

I. Bernard Cohen

The history of science[1] is primarily based on the application of the methods and values of historical inquiry to the subject matter of science. This makes for an odd combination, in that the physical and natural sciences are the most significant branches of academic learning in which the history of the subject appears to be of no immediate value or direct relevance to its practitioners. Artists, architects, musicians, poets, dramatists, novelists, literary critics, historians, philosophers, economists, and political and social scientists all study the works of their predecessors with great profit. No training would be considered adequate in these areas of scholarship or the creative arts without a sound knowledge of the history of the subject. There is, furthermore, a real curiosity as to the work done by predecessors in such fields, even if—in some cases—that curiosity has as its goal only to become better acquainted with a mode or style that is to be rejected: romanticism in literature, classicism in music, Victorianism in architecture, laissez-faire doctrines in economics, an outmoded scale of moral values in historical judgment.

How different it is in the sciences! Of course, scientists pay a kind of homage to the great men and women of their past. They put portraits in textbooks and on the walls of their libraries and laboratories,[2] and they commemorate their predecessors in named laws and effects, like Newton's laws of motion, Brownian movement, or Chagas's disease.[3] Scientists, however, seldom read the writings of their predecessors in the course of scientific research[4] and they do not generally require that their students study such writings; nor are they particularly concerned with the actual stages of discovery or with the detailed history of their subject, except perhaps for the recent past.[5] There are, of course, exceptions: scientists for whom the history of science may be a subject of genuine concern, on a more serious level than as a hobby, or something of cultural value. But it is very rare indeed to find historical aspects of the sciences conceived to have primary scientific importance, that is, having a significant role in the "doing" of science or the training of students to become scientific practitioners.[6] Of course, many scientists recognize that the history of science may make their students better human beings, better equipped to deal with the problems of science and scientists in current society.[7] This purpose is quite distinct from the preparation to do actual scientific research.

Let it be understood that I am not here making a value judgment; I am merely stating an obvious fact. Indeed, most scientists are convinced that all parts of science that are correct or useful have actually been incorporated in the present living science, the current science found in textbooks and handbooks.[8] This aspect of science has been well expressed, although a little inverted, by Herbert Dingle, who asserts that

the history of science is essentially a part of its own subject,—science itself,—in a way which, I think, is true of no other discipline. An outstanding characteristic of the philosophy which is science is that it is progressive, each advance depending on, and being validated by what has gone before. In any modern scientific paper there are references to previous papers, they themselves contain certain similar references, and so on, until ultimately the justification of the newest work rests on that of the earliest in that particular science. Every paper is thus implicitly the whole history of its own particular subject. . . .

But, of course, as Dingle is quick to note, the writer of such a paper today is "probably ignorant of all the previous work except that on which his own immediately rests." And he warns that such ignorance is "undesirable, and can be a source of much error."[9]

There is, moreover, a very significant difference between the sciences and most other creative activities of man, at least with respect to the classics of the discipline. The painter, the sculptor, the architect, viewing a great work of the past—whether of antiquity or the recent past—can grasp much of the essential beauty and meaning without needing a detailed guide to help him. Of course, full comprehension requires a knowledge of the traditions from which the work has sprung, of the nature of the problems which the creator attempted to solve, and of some of the conceits and conventions of those past times. Nevertheless, the greatest works of art or artistry, those that are really successful, have been able to make direct contact with the beholder down through the ages, without the need of a scholarly interpreter. The same is true of the classics of philosophy, history, and literature.[10] Often we may require that such works be in part translated into a modern idiom—Homer into English, Chaucer into modern English—and again the fullest comprehension does require historical or scholarly help. Yet millions of ordinary intelligent people have read the plays of Shakespeare or have seen them in performance and have grasped their message and drama without needing the *chevaux-de-frise* of academic scholarship. The same is true of Plato's dialogues, Thucydides' history of the Peloponnesian war, Guicciardini's history of Florence, Machiavelli's book on the prince, or Adam Smith's treatise on the wealth of nations. How different it is when a scientist decides to read Newton's *Principia*! Faced with a far more difficult problem than orthography, grammar, or archaic words and phrases, the reader must in the first instance be equipped to comprehend advanced dynamics and celestial mechanics. But even today's mathematician or physicist will find that this most modern of older classical scientific works appears in an almost unreadable form. A knowledge of today's mathematical treatment of physical problems in dynamics proves to be of less help than one might expect. One reason is that Newton does not explicitly use the algorithm of the infinitesimal calculus, even though he was its inventor along with Leibniz.[11] Newton seems to use the purely geometric or synthetic method of the ancients rather than the analytic method of the moderns; for this reason many commentators have said that Newton's *Principia* is like a treatise in Greek geometry. In fact, it is not. A close inspection shows that Newton no sooner sets up a geometric relationship than he applies his method of limits: the result is that the discourse on dynamics is written on the infinitesimal level rather than the finite. Indeed, the *Principia* opens with a discussion of the abstract mathematical theory of limits, possibly the first published systematic attempt at a rigorous clarification of what we mean by limit in modern mathematics. In this way Newton says to all readers that a condition for understanding the physics of his *Principia* is to know Newtonian mathematics.

Here is only the first of many difficulties for today's would-be reader. There are many others. Newton demands a knowledge of geometry, notably of the conic sections, and of the Euclidean rules of proportionality. The language is unfamiliar, invoking such long-out-moded terms as subtense (or subtangent), subduplicate and sesquiplicate ratios, and the like.[12] There is even a source of bewilderment in the discovery that in the *Principia* the second law of motion is essentially different from what we know as Newton's second law,[13] because Newton uses a different concept of force from the one to which we have become accustomed. If the unaided reader may thus have difficulty in making sense of Newton's second law, which is one of the three fundamental axioms upon which the whole treatise is constructed, how much of the *Principia* may be said to be readily intelligible to a reader, however well trained in science, who has not undertaken special preparation for the task?

The *Principia* may be an extreme example, because—from the day it was published—it was always a difficult book to read, even with a commentary. But almost any technical scientific treatise must be read slowly and carefully, whether it is ancient, medieval, early modern, or modern. The conceptual obstacles (including the use of mathematics) may be somewhat more severe in the exact sciences than in the life sciences or the earth sciences, but let the reader not underestimate the task of comprehending an anatomical, embryological, or physio-logical treatise of the past! This obvious and undeniable distinction between the literature of the sciences and other literatures implies that even if a scientist should become convinced that he wants to learn about the science of the past, he generally will not get very far un-aided, and in this he is set apart from his colleagues in other disci-plines. That is, he will not get very far unless he undertakes some special historical studies as an ancillary assignment. Alternatively, he may restrict himself to selected topics that may prove more readily accessible or that may be available in editions in which a historian of science has produced an explanatory comment to make the text more easily comprehensible to an untrained reader.

Because the scientific documents of the past are written in an exotic scientific language that differs from that of the present, the scientist who turns to history tends to do so not as a working scientist but as a kind of historian: he becomes a scientist temporarily more interested in history than in science. Obviously, the history of science may have a greater interest and significance for him than the history of some subject wholly foreign to his professional area of expertise, but it should be clear by now that the scientist does not study scientific documents of the past in the same way that he studies those of the present or that an artist may study works of art of both the past and the present. This point has been beautifully expressed by Erwin Panofsky:

[The scientist] deals with human records, namely with the work of his predecessors. But he deals with them not as something to be investigated, but as something which helps him to investigate. In other words, he is interested in records not in so far as they emerge from the stream of time, but in so far as they are absorbed in it. If a modern scientist reads Newton or Leonardo da Vinci in the original, he does so not as a scientist, but as a man interested in the history of science and therefore of human civilization in general. In other words, he does it as a *humanist*, for whom the works of Newton and Leonardo da Vinci have an autonomous meaning and a lasting value. From the humanistic point of view, human records do not age.[14]

This special aspect of the history of science needs to be made clear at the outset, since otherwise we would find it hard to understand why this subject so often tends to be esteemed by general historians (who are apt to be barred from fully understanding it by their lack of scientific training) even more than by scientists (whose intellectual traditions provide the subject matter).

It should now be clear that I consider the central core of the history of science to be the study of the actual contents of the scientific record as revealed in publications, records of conversations, correspondence, laboratory or reading notebooks, journals, lecture notes (both of lectures given and lectures attended), annotated books, any manuscript materials (from scraps to early drafts of finished works or written statements of speculations or of trial and error), and finally —where available—the actual artifacts of scientific work (instruments or other equipment, scientific specimens, or preparations). Before discussing the needs in this area and some of the spectacular successes of the recent past, let me introduce some of the other forms that the history of science takes at present and that will surely also shape the future of the discipline.

Whoever examines the state of the history of science today becomes aware at once of a considerable pressure to produce social histories. In part this is merely a reflection of the general demand for relevance at the expense of intellect. But it is also, no doubt, a secondary effect of the changing point of view of society at large with respect to science itself. Recent years have seen a progressive disillusionment with an earlier optimistic view of science as a simple provider of benefits that would lead to a newer and better world. We have seen the use of scientific discoveries on a large scale for the creation of instrumentalities of destruction. Even the betterment of the general condition of man through a science-based technology has apparently had the socially undesirable side effect of altering the environment for the worse.

The consequence of the fact that science has become so identified with the military-industrial complex of the last decades, and with the pollution of the environment, would seem to be that a historian of science can no longer be content to study the growth of scientific ideas without considering the new force of science in relation to society. But as yet there have not been produced a series of analyses and case histories of the actual links between discoveries in science of the recent past and their ultimate social effects through their embodiment in technological devices or systems (in which I include a good part of medicine). Despite a continuing moral dialogue about science in relation to society, historians of science have still the unfulfilled assignment of carefully documenting the ways in which scientific research both affects and is affected by the applied science that has produced the practical effects on man, his society, and his environment. It may perhaps seem that the neglect of such topics arises from the fact that they do not depend on historical studies so much as on analyses of the sociological variety, requiring more of a background in the area of science and public policy than in the history of science as such. But a more likely reason is that in the ordering of their priorities, historians of science have concentrated on the science of the past (as it existed in Mesopotamia, Greece, the Middle East and Asia, medieval and renaissance Europe, and the seventeenth and eighteenth centuries), and only recently have been approaching the present (that is, the nineteenth and early twentieth centuries). The history of contemporary or present science has been neglected to a degree often unimagined by an outsider to the field. [15] I believe that the reason for this state of affairs lies in the simple fact that the history of science is so young a professional subject. [16] Naturally, attention has been paid first to the great founding periods of science: its emergence in antiquity, its development and transmission in the Islamic and medieval worlds, its full flowering during the Scientific Revolution, and its maturation during the Enlightenment and early nineteenth century. With a conspicuous lack of complete scholarly editions of such masters as Kepler, Newton, Lavoisier, and Darwin, historically minded scholars have not seen their most pressing assignment to be to document and to analyze fairly recent science. [17]

It is easy to see, however, that the understanding of the relations between current science and society requires a historical base, if only because these relations have been changing so rapidly during the past century. To see the magnitude of this change in recent times, one needs only to recall that in the years prior to World War II, 68 percent of the total budget for scientific research and development in the United States came from industry and less than 20 percent from the federal government, whereas today those figures are just about reversed. In gross terms, in 1938, the total expenditures for scientific research and development in the United States came to 264 million dollars, whereas in 1974 one relatively small agency of the federal government (the National Science Foundation) had an annual budget that included 400 million dollars for the support of basic research alone, and the total research and development expenditures by the federal government came to more than 17 billion dollars.[18] It is an obvious corollary that the number of scientists in the country must also have risen by a large factor, and that there must have been a concomitant increase in the role of scientists in government. Thus the historians discern not merely a change to what is known as "big science," but an alteration of the traditional links between pure science and society.[19] No longer is it adequate to limit one's inquiries to the ways in which pure science provides the ideas, while applied science reduces these abstractions to practical reality. One must ask whether pure science itself may follow directions of advance determined by (or even limited by) considerations of specific applicability to well-defined social goals or technological needs. Moreover, the functions of pure scientists in today's complex world have come to embrace many assignments far outside such a simple model. For example, since World War II, academic or pure scientists have played a major role as technological consultants to government. The President's Science Advisory Committee (PSAC) was largely composed of mathematicians and physical scientists, primarily of the academic variety, and yet their opinion was sought not on the future of academic physics, biology, and genetics, but rather on technological and engineering problems such as weapons systems and supersonic transport.[20] The massive support for science all over the world in recent decades has been closely associated with (and to a large degree motivated by) problems of national defense. The existence of this new environment for science calls for sound historical analyses of the ultimate effects of this form of patronage on the nature of science itself, both as an institution and as a system of ideas. Here are some obvious tasks for the future of the history of science. In particular, the question must be faced as to whether the new "big science," characterized by group research rather than individual efforts,[21] may be producing a science so different from anything that existed prior to the mid-twentieth century that all traditional history of science may have been reduced to a kind of intellectual archaeology.

The recognition that science itself may have been radically altered by recent massive government support has quite naturally caused some historians of science to wonder whether various social pressures may not to some degree have affected the course of scientific development in the past. Thus the editor of a recently established historical annual devoted to the physical sciences states that the purposes of his publication are "to stimulate the study of the social function of the physical sciences and the professional role of their practitioners," and to "be concerned with the context—cultural, political, moral, socio-economic, technological—of the physical sciences, a concern that is not yet strongly reflected in publications in the history of science."[22] It is to be observed, however, that none of the articles in the inaugural volume in which this statement occurs makes any fundamental contribution to our understanding of the ways in which the socioeconomic matrix may have influenced either the genesis or growth of scientific ideas or the actual paths of development of the physical sciences. Indeed, in the first four volumes there is only one article that even begins to come close to the editor's ideal, a study published in 1971 on "Weimar Culture: Causality and Quantum Theory, 1918–1927: Adaptations by German Physicists and Mathematicians to a Hostile Intellectual Environment." In this pioneering article, Paul Forman sets forth his view on how the actual methods and contents of science may have been a response to the environment,[23] but it should be noted that in this case it is the "intellectual environment" that is under consideration and not directly the socioeconomic matrix. As such, Forman's article is a major pioneering attempt to do for modern physical science what Alexandre Koyré did on a somewhat different scale for the science of the seventeenth century.[24]

The more classical approach to the history of science has been to trace out a fairly continual development of scientific ideas, theories, and techniques of investigation, from at least the time of Galileo, Kepler, and Harvey to the present. Of course, there are gaps and even occasional quantum jumps in knowledge and method, but historians have been able to trace a regular sequence in the growth of science, ever moving forward. For the social history of science during this same period of some four centuries, this approach has not been possible. There have been too many changes of a sort that cannot be fitted into a simple linear time chart. One occurred soon after the Industrial Revolution. It consisted of the first stages of the emergence of science as a profession, with paid jobs for scientists (in government service and in universities, and on occasion in industry), well-established scientific or professional organizations, recognized methods of becoming acknowledged as members of a "scientific community," and regular training channels such as the École Poly-technique and École Normale. The name of "scientist" was invented at that time to fit the new situation. The total effect of this change has only recently begun to be investigated. A major part of this kind of study should be an examination of the history of scientific instruments.[25] In this general area there are very few studies that fully meet the canons of present-day scholarship; among them is Roger Hahn's recent work on the French Academy of Sciences.[26] In this area a major block to the historical imagination may be an overinsistence on the necessity of applying retroactively some of the findings of today's sociologists about such matters as "roles" and "sociology of knowledge." These may be very useful concepts for the under-standing of the behavior of scientists and "men of knowledge" in our own time, but perhaps they are not easily applicable to past situations or to societies of academic and scientific men that may have been fundamentally different from our own.[27] In any event, the rise of professionalization of science is a historical question of major impor-tance, one in which there is still much research to be done, following on the pioneering efforts of Bernard Barber and Everett Mendelsohn.[28]

Still another profound change occurred in the nineteenth century which has set a real challenge to historical inquiry: the influence of science on technology and the beginning of a division between "pure" and "applied" science, the latter entailing the rise of special-purpose industrial laboratories. The history of technology has yet to be written, a situation which is perhaps related to the fact that this field is still an underdeveloped subject of scholarly inquiry and was—until quite recently—the captive of economic historians.[29]

A sign of the general ignorance concerning science and practice is that both general historians and historians of science often confuse programmatic and pragmatic ideals with facts and records. This prob-lem arises in part from the eloquence of Francis Bacon in preaching that a sound knowledge of nature, based on true science, would lead man to master his environment. For at least two centuries thereafter, spokesmen for the new scientific academies and societies continued to express the Baconian sentiment that advances in the sciences would produce changes in actual technology. Historians have often tended to conclude from such statements that during the seventeenth and eighteenth centuries there was a pursuit of all science for utilitarian ends. It is even at times assumed that major practical results had actually been obtained from the application of the fruits of pure or academic scientific research. Yet, in fact, there were none. Pure science, basic science, basic research, academic science, never once until the end of the eighteenth century produced any knowledge that in any serious manner influenced or really changed the ways in which men earned their living, guarded their health, cured diseases, fed and clothed themselves, improved the national economy, killed their enemies, defended their shores, communicated with one another, or transported themselves and their goods.[30] By the end of the eighteenth century, the pressure to show that science could change technology, which it had not done, became so great that it even led to a falsification of history in the story of James Watt and the steam engine.

In editing Joseph Black's lectures, John Robison dedicated the volumes to Watt, saying that he did so because Watt had put the discoveries of Joseph Black to practical use in his invention of the steam engine.[31] A careful analysis shows that Black's discoveries of specific heat and latent heat, though known to Watt, had no significant role whatever in Watt's invention, which was a fundamental improvement of the Newcomen or "atmospheric" engine. The major innovative feature of Watt's invention was the separate condenser. It did not require a Black to show a clever mechanic how wasteful it was to heat a cylinder by the admission of steam, then cool the cylinder by an injection of cold water, and then have to heat the cylinder once again by new steam; Watt saw the advantage of having the cylinder remain hot all the time, allowing the steam to be condensed either outside the cylinder or in a separate condenser. Black's theoretical discoveries did not have anything to do with Watt's brilliant idea that the return of the piston in the cylinder could be achieved more efficiently by reversing the direction of the steam than by having the return stroke depend on mere atmospheric pressure, thus leading to the invention of the double-acting engine. Furthermore, it was Watt's discovery, and not Black's, that for maximum efficiency the steam should cease to be admitted well before the piston had completed its stroke, so that the final work in the stroke could be produced by the steam already admitted into the cylinder.[32]

There was one invention, however, prior to 1800 that did derive from pure science or the advance in fundamental knowledge: the lightning rod. It was based on Franklin's investigations of the action of pointed conductors, induced charges, grounding, and insulation, plus his discovery that the lightning discharge is in fact an electrical phenomenon. But clearly this invention did not affect the way in which men killed one another, communicated with one another, or made their living. However, it does show us (as perhaps the only major Baconian example in two centuries) why in the Age of Reason, when it was hoped and believed that science might lead to a better world, Franklin's invention and the discoveries on which it was based were more than ordinarily esteemed.[33]

Here then is a major field for the historian of science of the future: how and when did science become the potent force for technological innovation which we know today? And in the earlier period, how *did* men actually reconcile the stated goal of useful science with the constant production of useless science—useless, at least, from the point of view of technology? At this point, let me add a corollary; for I do not think that in the social scale the discoveries in pure science were, in fact, all that useless. There had been produced concepts and ideas, theories and models, which had consequences for human thought and action.[34] The practical consequences of science are not merely new modes of industry, warfare, or the maintenance of health. They include the lessening of superstition, as, for example, when the fear of lightning was reduced by showing that it was a natural phenomenon which could be tamed, or when Halley and Newton discovered that comets are regular periodic phenomena and not therefore special actions by an angry god sending warnings of doom to sinful man. Surely there is a practical aspect to scientific discovery when men are shown the contrast between a rational order as disclosed in the world of nature and an irrational order in society, or when a new biological concept of man emerges as a higher form of sapient animal rather than a divinely created being possessed of an immortal soul.[35]

No one needs to be reminded today of the profound influence of science-based technologies on every conceivable aspect of our daily lives and our environment. The historian naturally asks when did science begin to produce such large-scale effects through applications of fundamental scientific knowledge that have so changed our world. In fact, there is an easily discernible moment in the nineteenth century when pure science showed its potency to influence the fate of nations as well as individuals, a second scientific and industrial revolution that clearly separates all recent science from the traditional search for knowledge. In 1856, William Henry Perkin, then a student at the Royal College of Science, produced the first synthetic dyestuff, mauve, during the Easter vacation. He had been attempting to synthesize quinine in his home laboratory and produced instead a dark precipitate, from which "he succeeded in isolating mauve, or aniline purple, the first dyestuff to be produced commercially from coal-tar."[36] Within six months this new "Tyrian purple" was being used commercially; and about a decade later, two German chemists succeeded in synthesizing alizarin, a natural colorant (often known as "Turkey red") produced from the madder plant, and in getting it into commercial manufacture by the Badische Anilin und Soda Fabrik. To appreciate the significance of these breakthroughs it must be kept in mind that at this time "Tyrian purple" was an excessively costly dye, obtained from a marine snail or shellfish (*Murex brandaris*) that lives on the eastern Mediterranean shores; only 23 grains of the dye were obtained from 12,000 of these snails, and the pre-World War I cost was about $300 an ounce. The madder plant, the source of the red dye, was then extensively cultivated throughout southern Europe and the Middle East; in France alone some 50,000 acres were given over to its culture. The synthetic dyes were made from coal tar, a cheap and readily available substance that was a residue from the manufacture of illuminating gas. Not only were the new synthetic dyes far cheaper than the natural products, they had an unrivaled "range of colour and delicacy of tone" that almost at once sounded the death knell of a traditional industry. In 1870, some 750 tons of alizarin were extracted from roots of the madder plant, but within forty years the annual production of alizarin in chemical plants had passed the 2,000-ton mark, about three quarters of it made in Germany.

The big goal of dye chemists was to replace natural indigo with a synthetic counterpart. In Europe indigo had traditionally been obtained from woad (*Isatis tinctoria*) until the latter had been replaced by a cheaper source, various species of *Indigofera* or indigo plant, grown primarily in India, which "controlled the markets of the world."[37] This dye was synthesized in a German laboratory in about 1890, but it took a decade more of scientific research and development and an expenditure of some five million dollars to transform the laboratory discovery into a commercially workable industrial process. Never before had there been so incredibly large an expenditure of money and so sustained an effort on the part of pure and applied scientists for a single practical goal. There was required for success a combination of the research and development forces of government, universities, and industry. High-level research became a feature of industry, and there also arose the novel practice of building operative research teams (in the universities as well as in industrial laboratories). This occurred in a Germany that had gained world supremacy in theoretical organic chemistry. In explaining how all these phenomena were active in gaining for Germany the mastery of the synthetic dye industry, we must remember that Germany was then a rising nation, seeking its "place in the sun," and that the indigo market, controlled by British India, was a prize worthy of the capture. In 1896–97, there were 1,583,808 acres under cultivation to indigo in India, yielding 8,433 tons of dye, at a value of £4,000,000. With the introduction of synthetic indigo, the acreage in India for 1909–10 had dropped to 282,000 with a yield of 2,002 tons.[38] Germany not only captured the major part of the world's dye industry, but at the same time—since unstable dyes are explosives—was building up the greatest potential explosive industry the world had ever known. Of most significance for the history of science, however, was the fact that in a matter of a decade the fruits of scientific research and development could all but destroy forever the traditional established agriculture of regions as widely separated as Provence and Bengal. Here, then, was a convincing demonstration of how the whole world could be radically altered by the applications of a powerful science.

How rapidly did the world learn from this lesson about the need for research and the support of science by the state and industry working hand-in-hand? Apparently not for many decades. L. F. Haber has documented for us the rise of the dye industry in the nineteenth century, but thus far we have no fundamental studies of the reaction (or lack of it) to this vivid demonstration of the real force of science.[39] This absence of historical analyses showing how the force of science became linked to government makes it even more difficult for us to understand the problems of science in relation to government that arose with such intensity in World War II and the postwar years.

The primacy of such relatively unexplored problems underlines the present dearth of sound historical studies of science and society, of the social history of science. Most of the historians who have written concerning this aspect of our subject have put forth programmatic declarations but have not yet succeeded in producing scholarly articles and monographs. A major reason for this gap between ideals and performance is clearly the intrinsic difficulty of this variety of history. It requires of its practitioners both an understanding of the major social and political (and even economic) forces and a knowledge of the science in question. Few among us have the ability to handle simultaneously the conceptual part of science (including mathematics) and the techniques of analysis of the several social sciences.

Two recent works, however, may give a hint of the potentialities in this new area. Arnold Thackray has begun to explore the matrix in which science flourished in early nineteenth-century Manchester; in particular, he has shown "the sterility of any simple thesis about the technological purposes of Manchester science in the Industrial Revolution." Thackray, however, sees "natural science" in a "cultural context" more than in a social matrix, although he does use systematically some of the technical modes of analysis of recent sociology. Another inquiry into the sociocultural groundwork of science has been made by Yehuda Elkana, who seeks to find in the nature of the society the reasons why the concept and law of conservation of energy was developed in mid-nineteenth-century Germany rather than in other countries.[40]

Yet it must be a source of wonder that there are no other full-length studies to match Robert K. Merton's pioneering quantitatively based analyses of science, technology, and society in seventeenth-century England. This groundbreaking investigation (a doctoral dissertation of the 1930s) will long remain a model for demonstrating quantitatively a shift in intellectual interests from decade to decade, one that eventually came to have a strong scientific component.[41] Merton, developing a mode of analysis used first in the nineteenth century by Alphonse de Candolle,[42] showed, moreover, that a relatively large proportion of the proponents of the new science, and the scientists themselves, were apt to be Dissenters in religion. Merton, perforce, neglected the actual content of scientific work, since his major assignment was quantitative, although he did examine such a question as whether a given bit of science had any practicality. But it is extremely difficult to determine whether or not a scientist's research or even a result of research may be practical—either in terms of the motivation of the scientist or (to use a Mertonian expression) the "unanticipated consequences" of the outcome of the research. Thus Merton would see Newton as being uninterested in any mathematics that did not have some use, say, in physics—which is not in keeping with what we know of Newton as mathematician.[43] The historian finds it grossly misleading to see Newton's *Principia* in the light of problems of navigation, which were never of any primary motivation in Newton's research and may in fact represent the area of his most conspicuous failure.[44] The conclusion that Newton invented the calculus of variations in response to problems of ship design turns out to be totally erroneous.[45] Despite such criticisms, however, time has not diminished the general admiration for Merton's pioneering inquiry: his bold willingness to use quantitative data, his insight into the delicate interrelations between science and religious inclination, and his demonstration of the real thrust of military needs on the problems studied by scientists. Historians will equally commend him for his admirable restraint in using sociological categories of analysis—a factor that may have lessened the impact of this work on general sociology and that still gives it the appearance of a primarily historical investigation.

The limitations of social (or sociological) analysis of historical questions without attention to content analysis is shown by a recent study of the development of science in America, based on a sociological rather than historical content analysis mode. In particular, the author uses the number of pages published, plus the number of European citations of American publications, to establish that the United States became a truly significant scientific country at a time when most historians conceive America to have been an "undeveloped" (but "developing") nation in science.[46] Content analysis would lead to a somewhat different judgment. Even the Nobel Prizes given to Americans prior to World War II tended to be for new instruments and particular experiments, or new techniques and effects, rather than for the giant steps of fundamental experiment and theory that affect all of science, such as the work of J. J. Thomson, Rutherford, Einstein, Bohr, Pauli, and Dirac. That the sociological judgment is wrong may be seen in the simple fact that there was hardly a major American scientist produced before World War II who did not have some period of training in Europe; yet there were very few Europeans who then felt it equally necessary to come to America for this kind of training. As late as 1963, at the one hundredth anniversary of the National Academy of Sciences, over 40 percent of the members proved to be foreign-born. This opinion is backed up by personal insights and individual experiences. I. I. Rabi, Columbia University physicist and Nobel laureate, went to study in Germany in the early 1930s. At Hamburg, in the physics library, he asked if there were a subscription to the American *Physical Review*. The reply was in the affirmative, but he was told that there were no current issues available; the journal was held in such low esteem that the library did not receive the issues month by month but waited till the end of the year, when a single bound volume could be put on the library shelf for archival purposes.[47] No better index could be found of the low opinion of American science held by Europeans.

At this point, I should introduce an important corollary to my general conclusions about the want of studies in the social history of science, since I have been exclusively concerned with work done in the West. In the "Democratic Socialist Republics" there are many historians who write about the development of science from a social point of view, although they do so from a specifically Marxist standpoint.[48] Unfortunately, not very many of these works have been made available in English; many of them are likely to be of a high order and might even contain useful correctives for some of the attitudes of Western historians. Recently a splendid history of probability written by a Russian was translated into English.[49] The author disposes of many of the myths in the West, including the one that probability arose in the seventeenth century simply because of the interest in gambling. In particular, he calls attention to the significance of the rise of the mathematics of shopkeeping, and he indicates some of the economic needs that may have had formative influences on the development of statistical thought and methods. In the West, the main authors of Marxist-oriented histories of science have been nonprofessionals, especially in England. They include J. D. Bernal (crystallographer), Lancelot Hogben (statistician), and J. G. Crowther (science writer, journalist).[50] For the most part, their writings weaken the impact of social considerations, either because of the erroneous or superficial character of their history or because of the excessive attempt to relate the growth of science to such factors as the forces of production, the class struggle, and the rise of the bourgeoisie.

Sometimes Joseph Needham is linked with the Marxists because there is a discernible influence of Marxist thought in some of his writings.[51] But while Needham is obviously an "externalist" and believes the "internalist" argument to be weak and inadequate,[52] his concern for the social history of science is far deeper than any commitment to a single political or social philosophy.[53] His multivolume study of the growth of science in China is not only one of the greatest works in the history of science to come from a single author's pen;[54] it is also one of the real masterpieces of historical scholarship of our time. His presentation of the social and institutional history of science in China is, above all, tempered constantly by the discipline of the scientific content and the linguistic controls. In fact, never before have the actual facts of science and technology in China been presented in such quantity and depth, and interpreted at each stage of exposition by the kind of insight that can come only from a thorough mastery of the technical content of the science being studied. Here, then, may be the ideal of the social history of science—dominated, controlled, and everywhere informed by content analysis. In fact, many scholars find this multivolume work richer in content analysis of science and its background philosophy (along with technology) than in its societal interpretations. Above all, Needham avoids the pitfall of confusing sociology with social history.

In sampling the writings on the societal aspects of history of science, a special place must be reserved for Pio Rattansi (of University College, London) and Charles Webster (of Oxford). Rattansi's studies of the clashes between physician and apothecary in Restoration England are a model of sober, penetrating analysis, and they reveal the professional jealousies of caste and class in the formative years of our modern science.[55] Webster's penetrating analysis of the English medical reformers of the Puritan Revolution combines a view of the actual medical and chemical practices (and their religious and hermetic backgrounds) with the general reformist tendencies of a group of physicians; he shows how a command of the actual science and medicine may illuminate (and be illuminated by) an understanding of the social and political forces of the times.[56] Not least, he reveals how "the medical reform movement of the Puritan Revolution was intimately concerned, not only with the dialectic between ancient and modern medicine, but also the conflict between rival traditions of experimental natural philosophy."[57]

One of Webster's findings reinforces the importance of Paracelsian medicine and iatrochemistry as it developed in the "intellectual climate" of the Puritan Revolution.[58] This theme, of the interactions between Paracelsian science and Protestantism (especially the more mystical parts of Protestantism), has been most notably developed by Walter Pagel, who has given the history of science a new direction by his insistence (in precept and in his many studies of the history of science and medicine) that the older and traditional distinctions made by historians between the "scientific" and the "non-scientific" components of sixteenth- and seventeenth-century thought were misleading and even downright wrong. This theme has been illustrated in a constant stream of articles, monographs, and books on such persons as Harvey, Paracelsus, and Van Helmont, and on such topics as the general religious background of biological thought, the role of Aristotelianism in Harveyan science, and so on.[59] Pagel has shown how great a distortion occurs when we apply the limiting and restrictive canons of post-Newtonian science to the thought of the men of science of the sixteenth century.

Rattansi has also been one of that company of scholars studying the fringes of modern science—the work of those who were held in bond by the fancies of alchemy and astrology. Such figures have elicited increasing interest in recent decades, and they have even been assigned a significant role in the emergence of modern science in the late sixteenth and seventeenth centuries. The great pioneer in this area of inquiry has been Frances Yates of the Warburg Institute. In her first major work in this area (a study of Bruno), she disclaimed any intention of contributing to the history of science proper. This book, she concluded, "has nothing whatever to do" with "the history of genuine science leading up to Galileo's mechanics." And then she declared explicitly, "The phenomenon of Galileo derives from the continuous development in the Middle Ages and Renaissance of the rational traditions of Greek science."[60] But she now asserts that we err in picking out rational science from that which in the sixteenth and seventeenth centuries was a mixture of what we may see today as true science and those far-out subjects that never made it. More recently she has written:

When I think of the fear and trembling with which, only nine years ago, I published a book with the title *Giordano Bruno and the Hermetic Tradition*, I am impressed by the rapid rate at which the history of thought has moved toward the acceptance of the idea that the scientific revolution arose in a Hermetic atmosphere. . . . Newton . . ., one of the greatest figures of the scientific revolution, was . . . deeply imbued with Hermetic disciplines.[61]

What are we to make of such a statement? Are we really to believe that modern rational science is a direct descendant of Hermetic thought, whether that be conceived as a form of rationalism or of irrationalism? Is Newtonian science only the final stage in the development of the Hermetic tradition? I think not. The more recent studies of Miss Yates, Rattansi, R. S. Westfall, and others, seem to have shown that Newton's creative scientific work can be understood only in the light of this Hermetic background and direct influence.[62] Perhaps. But there is a possible alternative interpretation.

There can no longer be doubt that there was a greater interest in Hermetic subjects among many upper- and middle-class intellectuals of the seventeenth century than heretofore had been suspected. Whoever wishes to gain an insight into this topic has only to look at Christopher Hill's recent works on the English Revolution.[63] Thus, it is not at all surprising that a Newton should have been interested in prophecy and in alchemy (I except astrology, which was already a false science). But that hardly means—as I read the record—that Newton's science was born of (or was even influenced in a major way by) irrational nonscience of the Hermetic variety. Just the contrary! A cognizance of this general background should rather aggrandize the stature of Newton, who was able to produce so great a rational science and thus put aside whatever Hermetic taint might otherwise have deflected him.[64] The suggestion has been made that the Hermetic or alchemical *spiritus* became Newton's aether. Perhaps; we must reserve the Scottish verdict here. But even if this should be so, we would be little further in our understanding than before, since we do not know exactly what creative role the aether played in the development of Newton's science.[65]

I believe this example shows how content analysis controls and disciplines every aspect of the history of science. It is not enough to observe that Newton was interested in alchemy and prophecy, and even Hermetic and mystic philosophy; we must carefully analyze his scientific thought in detail to see whether in fact it makes sense to suppose that these extra-scientific concerns were in any way related to particular scientific concepts and methods of procedure, or could have been their source. Of course, especially since the work of Koyré and Pagel, it is no longer possible to ignore the philosophical (i.e., metaphysical) and religious aspects of the basic scientific thought of Newton or of any seventeenth-century scientist.

The debate on the role of Hermeticism, alchemy, and magic in the Scientific Revolution is apt to continue for some time. The arguments are persuasive but not conclusive—in some measure, no doubt, because (as Paolo Rossi argues[66]) those ideas that do not fit the magical tradition are ignored. A significant step has been made by Rossi (and by D. P. Walker) in clarifying the varieties of "magic" and their possible role in the background of the Scientific Revolution.

Thus far I have dealt primarily with the social and institutional history of science. Let me now turn to some of the more traditional aspects of the subject, which nevertheless have had their revolutions too! The very name and concept of history of science would seem to suggest that there is a science whose history is worth writing. Accordingly, whether the science in question is early or late one would look for a historian of science only at times when science has reached a recognizable maturity. One such early time would have been in Greece in the fourth century B.C. And, indeed, we find that the first historian of science of record was a pupil of Aristotle, Eudemus of Rhodes. Not much is known about his life or career. His "main importance . . . in the history of thought" has been said to be his part in "making the works of Aristotle available to the world." But, for us, Eudemus is notable for having been the first known historian of science. Eudemus wrote histories of arithmetic, geometry, and astronomy, all three of which appear to be lost. But "it is mainly through the use made of them by later writers that we possess any knowledge of the rise of Greek geometry and astronomy."[67] Eudemus seems to have been well grounded in the technical aspects of the scientific subjects whose history he wrote, thus setting up an ideal standard for those of us who follow him almost two and a half millennia later.

After Eudemus, there were many writers who mentioned their predecessors, describing or summarizing their writings and doctrines. These texts may be exceptionally precious in the absence of other source materials, but this fact alone hardly qualifies their authors as historians. During the succeeding Islamic and Latin medieval periods, chronologies of the sciences and biographical registers of scientists (among others) were produced, but these too are not histories in the senses in which we usually employ this term.[68] Some historians of science see the beginnings of their subject in the Battle of the Books,[69] or the *Querelle des Anciens et des Modernes*,[70] in which historical information concerning ancient and modern scientists was assembled to answer the question whether or not there had been real progress. Two major English works that recorded the advances of science were William Wotton's *Reflections upon Ancient and Modern Learning* (1694), which came out for the moderns, and Joseph Glanvill's *Plus Ultra: or the Progress and Advancement of Knowledge since the Days of Aristotle* (1668), which is more nearly a true history of science (and also invention).[71]

The major pioneering historian of science of those days is Bernard le Bouvier de Fontenelle, who—as *secrétaire perpétuel* of the French Royal Academy of Sciences (Paris)—wrote the official biographical *éloges* of deceased academicians, made annual surveys of the scientific work done in the Academy (or reported through the Academy's publications), and composed an admirable summary of the inaugural decades of the scientific activities of the Academy (from the founding in 1666 to 1698).[72]

Of these seventeenth-century authors, only Fontenelle attempted to sketch out a historical panorama, in the sense that we would fully credit today. Wotton, for example, was not basically interested in the historical record of his own days; rather he had as his primary aim to attack Sir William Temple, whose *Ancient and Modern Learning* (1690) had come out for the ancients at the expense of the moderns. Wotton was able to make a good case for the moderns in science and in medicine, areas in which he had a better argument than in art, literature, or philosophy. Today, he is more apt to be praised for his moderation than for his historical accuracy or insight. Curiously enough, he was a better expositor of the modern developments in the life sciences (notably anatomy and the circulation of the blood) than in the exact or physical sciences (being especially weak with respect to the significance of the work of Galileo, to say nothing of Newton).[73] The seventeenth-century histories of the separate sciences are not much better. John Wallis's historical exposition of algebra, for example, is noted primarily for its anti-French (primarily anti-Cartesian) bias.[74] Fontenelle, however, did more than make a genuine contribution to historical scholarly learning and insight. In his writings there emerged—perhaps for the first time—a clear concept that science progresses in a series of revolutions that are analogous to political and social revolutions.[75]

The eighteenth and early nineteenth centuries witnessed the production of histories of science by men of science who wrote primarily for other scientists or for those intending to become scientists. This company includes Jean Étienne Montucla (history of mathematics, but including the exact physical sciences), Joseph Jérome de La Lande and Jean Sylvain Bailly (history of astronomy), Abraham Gotthelf Kästner (history of mathematics), Johann Beckmann (history of technology or inventions), J. F. Gmelin (history of chemistry), Joseph Priestley (history of optics and history of electricity), Jean Baptiste Joseph Delambre (history of astronomy), and Thomas Thomson (history of chemistry).[76] It is fair to say that their works put to shame many a present-day counterpart, and not merely in relative terms of comparison but as actual sources of information and insight into the concepts and methods of the science of the past. Such writings show that the highest levels of comprehension of the history of science are possible only to those who are fully masters of the technical subject content. Priestley's histories are especially interesting to today's reader, since he had a dual aim: to record the past developments of optics and electricity, and to delineate the "present state" of these subjects. In this way these presentations aimed at introducing a scientific beginner to a branch of science along with its historical background. At least half of each of these works is devoted to the "present state," constituting a most valuable key to the problems and theories of the eighteenth century seen through the eyes of a perceptive scientific observer. Priestley also developed a philosophy of scientific discovery in which he analyzed the role of chance.[77]

In the nineteenth century there were many special and general works on almost all aspects of the subject. But there can be little doubt that the two most influential writers were William Whewell and Ernst Mach, the former a major philosopher of science associated with inductivism, the latter an equally important philosopher of science associated with positivism. Whewell is apt to be a little prolix for today's tastes, but he is continually rewarding to read even though the reader may recoil from his artificial language (including such bizarre names for branches of science as "atmology" and "thermiotics"). Although Whewell tended to rely on secondary sources, his *History of the Inductive Sciences* is more perceptive than at first sight may appear. It should, however, be read in conjunction with two other works, *Philosophy of the Inductive Sciences* and *Philosophy of Discovery*, since they elaborate the primary ideas and principles that are chronologically displayed in his general history.[78] For anyone interested in physics, Mach is a stimulating author. His well-known book on mechanics influenced the thought of young Albert Einstein. Mach's books continue to be primary sources for anyone interested in philosophy. For it is within a framework of history that Mach developed such famous notions as the principle of economy of thought.[79]

Many books were produced at the end of the nineteenth and in the early years of the twentieth century that exhibit scholarly expertise of a high professional level, shown in the extensive use of primary sources (including manuscripts), proper documentation and bibliography, and care and discrimination on the factual level. An international company of such scholars includes J. H. Heiberg (Danish) and Sir Thomas Little Heath (British) on ancient mathematics and astronomy; H. J. Zeuthen (Danish) and Moritz Cantor (German) on mathematics; Hermann Kopp (German), Marcellin Berthelot (French), and E. O. von Lippmann (German) on chemistry and alchemy; Agnes Clerk (British), John Louis Emil Dreyer (British), and Rudolf Wolf (German) on astronomy; Karl Friedrich Wilhelm Jessen (German) and Julius von Sachs (German) on zoology; Edmond Hoppe (German), Émile Jouguet (French), Isaac Todhunter (British), Ferdinand Rosenberger (German), and Ernst Gerland (German) on physics; Julius Leopold Pagel (German) and Karl Sudhoff (German) on medicine. The writings of such scholars, and others of that half century or so that spans the dividing year of 1900, still stand on our shelves as major working tools, though subject to revision by yet another half century of scholarly learning. It may be observed, however, that this group of writers often tended to be unilluminating as to the changing nature of science, and that they also wrote within the narrow confines of speciality. For these reasons, the scholar of today is more apt to turn to them as a first source of specific information than for an understanding of the historical processes of development within the sciences.[80]

The case is somewhat different for two members of that chrono-logical group: Paul Tannery and Pierre Duhem. Tannery was a graduate of the École Polytechnique who never achieved academic recognition in a teaching post but spent his life as an official in the French national tobacco manufacturing administration. His astonish-ingly many contributions to scholarship are the more impressive when it is seen that they were produced at night and on weekends.[81] His special interests were in early Greek science and in Greek as-tronomy and mathematics, and in French science of the seventeenth century. His most enduring monuments are the now-classic editions of the writings and correspondence of Fermat and (in collaboration with Charles Adam) of Descartes. His own correspondence, articles, and shorter monographs have been published in eighteen volumes: *Mémoires scientifiques*. In 1900, at the first international gathering of historians of science (in a section of Histoire des Sciences of the Paris Congrès International d'Histoire Comparée), Tannery was designated Président of the newly established Commission Permanente. In those years there had been some question as to whether the history of science would be organized on an international level with the philosophers or with the historians. It was Tannery who helped ce-ment the permanent bond which still exists with the historical community. Although Tannery was at his best in specialized mono-graphic studies, he had a broad vision of an "histoire générale des sciences."

Whereas Tannery's scholarly career was entirely bounded by his-tory of science, Pierre Duhem's reputation was made in the first instance as a physical chemist and thermodynamicist. He was responsible for the introduction of J. Willard Gibbs's work on thermodynamics into France. A second career opened up in philoso-phy of science, where his most important contribution was *La théorie physique, son objet et sa structure* (1906).[82] This had been preceded, however, by two historical studies, one on mixtures and chemical compounds, the other a bird's-eye view of the evolution of mechanics.[83]

Curiously, it was as a medievalist and not as a historian of modern science that Duhem made his mark. In his *Études sur Léonard de Vinci* (1906–1913),[84] he introduced an antitraditional viewpoint with re-spect to the thinkers of the late Middle Ages. No longer would they be characterized in Descartes's coarse terms of "the abuse of intellect by reason," but would be seen through Duhem's eyes as precursors of Copernican cosmology, Galilean dynamics, Cartesian coordinate geometry, modern statics, and the Scientific Revolution. The new heroes were to be Albert of Saxony, Jordanus of Nemore, Jean Buridan, Nicole Oresme, who not only were forerunners of Leonardo but of Galileo himself, whose position as the architect of modern science Duhem was pleased to minimize if not to destroy altogether. Duhem's work has been continued in our own day by E. J. Dijksterhuis, Anneliese Maier, A. C. Crombie, Marshall Clagett, Edward Grant, and others. Although we have rejected Duhem's more extreme points of view, there are few today who doubt that the late Middle Ages produced scientific learning of a considerable magnitude that conditioned the "new" exact sciences of the sixteenth and seventeenth centuries.[85]

This new approach to medieval science and thought has tended to shrink the traditional time gap between ancient and modern science. Above all, it showed that the medieval schoolmen were far from being universally slavish followers of Aristotle but had been developing new concepts and scientific laws by criticizing and extending Aristotelian principles. The gap has, furthermore, been all but eliminated by studies of Arabic or Islamic science, and of Indian science. Here we may not only document the transmission and survival of Greek and Hellenistic science and philosophy but see significant innovations resulting from the enrichment of that ancient science by contact with active currents of Islamic thought, and of technical science, plus those originating in Mesopotamia, Persia, and India. The development of science has thus been conceived on a more global scale, with its domain extended to include the Middle East, Asia, and North Africa. We have only recently learned that certain innovations in the West, notably in the sixteenth century, had been so closely anticipated in Islamic lands as to leave little doubt that, among others, Copernicus and Servetus were influenced by concepts and innovations of their Muslim predecessors.

The history of the sciences has not only been pushed back from the Renaissance to the end of antiquity; the exact sciences, at least, have had their beginnings pushed back into Mesopotamia. In our own times, this has largely been due to Otto Neugebauer and his school, who have revealed to us by text and interpretation the mathematical prowess and astronomical methods of that early day. Surviving texts show the equivalent of algebraic procedures using positive and negative numbers, and the computation of compound interest. Those of my generation can still recall the almost overwhelming intellectual excitement of the 1930s, when it was revealed that the recorded history of the exact sciences went back twice as far as we had been taught to expect and that this ancient mathematics and exact science was on so astonishingly high a level.[86]

In the years between the two world wars, the outstanding figure in the history of science was George Sarton, trained in Belgium as a chemist and a self-taught historian of science.[87] Sarton's career was dedicated to the thesis that if the history of science were to become a respected part of the academic world, there was need of the same kind of accurate and readily available knowledge that a chemist has at his fingertips in various handbooks. His aim was to produce a general *Introduction to the History of Science*,[88] which would trace the history of all the sciences in all regions of the world, half century by half century. In the published volumes (from Homer to the end of the fourteenth century), each half-centurial survey is followed by a set of biographies of the men and women concerned in any way with science, broadly conceived. For all such figures, Sarton listed the main writings together with all editions of their works and the principal commentaries, plus biographies and scholarly monographs. Sarton also founded a journal, *Isis*, of which a main feature was a critical bibliography of every aspect of the history of science but also containing supplements and corrections to those volumes of the *Introduction* already published. *Isis* also included original articles and book reviews. It rapidly grew to be the leading journal in the field, and became the official organ of the History of Science Society.[89]

Soon after the first issue of *Isis* appeared in 1913, Sarton's career as a private scholar in Belgium was interrupted by the German invasion. He fled first to England and then to America, where he lived for the rest of his life. In editorials in *Isis*, lectures, and a vast network of correspondence,[90] Sarton constantly pleaded for the establishment of the history of science as a recognized academic discipline. He wanted to see the foundation of at least one institute for the history of science, perhaps comparable to the Institute for the History of Medicine at Johns Hopkins, and he wanted also to have the subject taught in colleges and in universities (where there would be graduate programs leading to a master's and a doctor's degree). Eventually he succeeded in establishing the history of science as a graduate subject at Harvard University; and I myself am the first American to have gained a Ph.D. in history of science as such in the United States. Until that time (1947), other Americans who became historians of science would take their doctorates in history, or in literature or languages, or in philosophy, or in one of the sciences. One of the major centers was at Columbia University, where the history of science was cultivated by

Frederick Barry and Lynn Thorndike. The historians of science who received their doctorates from Columbia did so in the Department of History, in the Faculty of Political Science.

Sarton wrote and spoke about the history of science with an intensity of conviction and passion not usually found in academic presentations. Like Auguste Comte, who had been a strong influence in his intellectual development,[91] Sarton conceived of a pyramid of knowledge but with history of science as the main subject rather than Comte's *sociologie*. For Sarton, the history of science was not only the supreme subject, uniting the humanities and the sciences (or serving as a "bridge" between these two areas); the history of science embodied what he called a "new humanism." In discussing this theme, Sarton would use such expressions as "the gradual redemption of man." Today, this tone seems out of keeping with a world that has lost its simple faith in progress and in science as the "only progressive human activity of man" as Sarton phrased it, in an expression of his positivistic faith.[92]

Sarton's *Introduction* stops at the end of the fourteenth century. He never got as far as what he once called "the promised land" of the seventeenth century. But in the *Introduction* (as in articles, lectures, and two general books), he made a convincing case for the significance of Islamic science and culture and its supreme importance in what we call "Western Civilization." He later published a set of two volumes on Greek science based on the first of a four-course cycle of lectures on the history of science for Harvard and Radcliffe undergraduates. It is a pity that there are no tangible remains of his lectures on modern science from the seventeenth to the twentieth century.

Sarton had a special gift for evoking great personalities of the past: Stevin, Rumphius, Linnaeus, Lagrange, Faraday, Darwin. His voice and his pen not only brought them to life in unforgettable images and encapsulated anecdotal life histories but indelibly impressed on his hearers and readers the tribulations and failures of these scientists as well as their achievements. But Sarton was not of a cast of mind to be interested in deep conceptual analysis or to work at the origins, filiation, and development of ideas, even in science. This latter area has grown up in the last decades under the stimulus and influence of a series of philosopher-historians, notably A. N. Whitehead, A. O. Lovejoy, Ernst Cassirer, and a group of French scholars, including Léon Brunschvicg, Gaston Milhaud, Émile Meyerson (a Pole living and working in France), André Lalande, Gaston Bachelard, Paul Hannequin, Georges Canguilhelm, and—above all—Alexandre Koyré.

Born in Russia, Koyré was educated at Tiflis and Rostov-on-Don, and then (in 1908) moved on to Göttingen, primarily to work in philosophy with Edmund Husserl (but where he also studied advanced physics and mathematics, the latter under David Hilbert).[93] In 1911 he transferred to Paris and followed lectures by Henri Bergson, Victor Delbos, André Lalande, and Léon Brunschvicg. His studies were interrupted by the war and the Russian Revolution, but he eventually returned to Paris to complete a thesis for the university doctorate (begun under François Picaret) on *L'idée de Dieu dans la philosophie de St. Anselme* (1923), followed by a study of *La philosophie de Jacob Boehme* (1929) which won him the *doctorat d'état*. Almost all of Koyré's professional career was spent as a staff member of the École Pratique des Hautes Études, interrupted by periods as visiting lecturer at the University of Cairo. During the war years in exile, he was a staff member of the École Libre des Hautes Études and a lecturer at the New School for Social Research. After the war he again took up his post in Paris but returned to America to lecture at various universities and eventually (1956–62) became a permanent member of the Institute for Advanced Study at Princeton, where he spent six months of each year, returning to Paris in time to give a spring course at the École Pratique.

Koyré's oeuvre covers a wide range, embracing studies of Hegel, Spinoza, and the German mystics of the sixteenth century, plus studies of Russian thought and philosophy and also medieval religious philosophy. These topics, to which his contributions were more than ordinarily significant, are not of concern here, save that they help to explain the base of philosophical idealism and downright Platonism that is the underpinning of much of his work in the history of science.[94]

Koyré was primarily interested in ideas and in the ways in which ideas tend to arise in science and are conditioned by their intellectual environment, especially by the philosophical and even theological presuppositions of their progenitors. His findings were always based on an extensive and intensive study of primary texts. He quoted at length from each of his sources, in the manner of the great French tradition of literary history, the *explication de texte*. Basically, he sought to understand each scientific or philosophico-scientific work in its own terms, not merely to find out whether this or that part might be "correct" according to some later canon of scientific knowledge and understanding. What, he wanted to know, were the problems a scientist posed for solution? What intellectual tools (concepts, laws, theories, methods, and presuppositions) were available to him? How did he use them? alter or adapt them? or discard them, substituting new ones in their place? In thus elucidating or reconstructing thought processes of science of the past, Koyré saw himself exploring the structure and function of intellect. And for him, it was just as important to understand the lesser figures as to know the real giants: Copernicus, Galileo, Descartes, Kepler, Hooke, and Newton. Collectively, both groups of men created the Scientific Revolution, and Koyré sought the essence of their new view of the physical world, which he found in their approach to motion and their concept of space. Early in his career, he expressed in a footnote the anticipation of a lifetime of research:

All the disagreement between ancient and modern physics may be reduced to this: whereas for Aristotle, motion is necessarily an action, or more precisely an actualization (*actus entis in potentia in quantum est in potentia*), it became for Galileo as for Descartes a state.[95]

A major thesis centered on the new "geometrization" of space, eventually associated with a shift "from the closed world to the infinite universe." Galileo emerged from Koyré's pages, not as a founder of experimental science, but as a thinker, a man who helped transform the "physics of quality" into a "physics of quantity," in essence substituting "Archimedan for Aristotelian methods."[96] Galileo, Descartes, Kepler, Newton, were all subject to his analysis. He showed in each case the stages of development in science caused by minds wrestling with old problems and new concepts and eventually producing a true "mutation" in scientific thought (the phrase is Koyré's, adapted from Bachelard). This new science was fundamentally different from all that went before it in its higher degree of congruity to the physical facts revealed by daily experience as well as by experiment and controlled observation. The mutation, according to Koyré, consisted in a new way of man's thinking about himself and nature, revealed to us in retrospect by an understanding of the role of mathematics (not mere quantification) in scientific thought and the ontological bases, and theological implications of the new natural knowledge.[97] Koyré thus reminded us that even though metaphysics had been temporarily cast out of philosophy by the positivists, it must be part of the armory of the historian who wishes to understand the scientific thinking of the past. Koyré not only revealed the thought of the Scientific Revolution in new dimensions; he also produced new evaluations of traditional figures. An example is his attribution of the law of inertia to Descartes rather than to Galileo.

Koyré's influence on the history of science has been profound, notably in America. The list of those who have been his students or who have been influenced by him includes such scholars as Marshall Clagett, I. B. Cohen, Pierre Costabel, A. C. Crombie, Dominique Dubarle, Charles C. Gillispie, Edward Grant, George Goldat, Henry Guerlac, A. R. Hall, Marie Boas Hall, Erwin N. Hiebert, T. S. Kuhn, John Murdoch, François Russo, Wilson Scott, René Taton, and R. S. Westfall. But inevitably there has also been a reaction against Koyré's position, both in general and in particulars. As to the latter, there is general agreement that Koyré tended to overstress somewhat the Platonic elements of the Scientific Revolution; he was extreme in supposing that actual experiments were of little importance, and that many experiments reported by Galileo and others had never been performed (and would have failed if they had been performed).[98] Of even more significance has been a growing conviction that the history of science is more than a history of scientific ideas (concepts, methods, theories, presuppositions) and must embrace the social background, the matrix of *external* (i.e., social, economic, political) forces that condition the growth of science. The "externalists" thus oppose the work of Koyré and his followers as "internalist" and incomplete. As I have mentioned earlier in this essay, there is a strong movement at present to relate the development of science to these external factors and to seek to link the history of science to the history of technology.

Despite a general interest in the growth of scientific ideas or the possible effects of the socioeconomic matrix on science, it remains true that the outstanding need in history of science today is for accurate well-edited texts of scientific works and of the manuscripts and correspondence of the men and women who have made science. Such editions are wanting for most of the major figures of the last three centuries. And so we are more than ordinarily grateful to O. Neugebauer and Marshall Clagett, and their disciples and associates, who have given us original texts together with commentaries and translations.[99] The work of Neugebauer may especially elicit our admiration, as he had to do more than transcribe and translate; he had also to restore missing fragments of Mesopotamian clay tablets and to decode mathematical tables that were sometimes incomplete in order to disclose the processes and operations that had produced them.[100] No doubt, the greatest edition ever produced of the correspondence, manuscripts and published writings of a scientist is the twenty-two volume monument to Christiaan Huygens, sponsored by the Dutch

Academy of Sciences from 1888 to 1950. One of the most important editions currently in progress is D. T. Whiteside's *The Mathematical Papers of Isaac Newton*,[101] which not only presents all the manuscripts and printed materials of mathematical interest but provides a running commentary that is at once a major contribution to the general history of mathematics (and the allied astronomy and physics) in the seventeenth century and an original and profound interpretation and evaluation of every aspect of Newton's work in the exact sciences. It goes without saying that the historical message of this edition is not readily available to those who are unable to comprehend mathematics. Two other editorial projects are charting new ways in the history of science. Up to now, the history of science has been studied by countries and regions, by chronological periods, and by subjects. But there have not been similar studies of the development of science by "schools" or groups. A. Rupert Hall and Marie Boas Hall have laid the grounds for this new approach in their edition of the correspondence of Henry Oldenburg, the first Secretary of the Royal Society of London.[102] A somewhat similar undertaking by René Taton (Paris) and A. Youschkevich (Moscow) will present some aspects of the scientific exchanges between the French and Russian academies of science in the eighteenth century, as seen through the correspondence of Leonhard Euler with several mathematicians and physical scientists in Paris.[103]

A few further aspects of current work need to be commented on. No single publication in the history of science in recent years has aroused quite so much general interest or has touched off so much debate as T. S. Kuhn's essay, *The Structure of Scientific Revolutions*.[104] This work presents a challenging model for understanding scientific change, one that is based on a close study of the historical development of the sciences but informed by sociological considerations and philosophical insights. I shall not add yet another note to the discussions of the validity or applicability of Kuhn's analysis, but in the present context it should be observed that Kuhn is more concerned with the internal social structure of science than with the effects or influences of the social environment. Many historians believe that the concept of scientific revolution is of recent origin, foisted on historical events in an anachronistic and possibly unwarranted manner. But I have found that the image of a revolution in science, and the actual use of the term "revolution" in the context of scientific change, may be traced back to the days of Newton, in the first full flowering of the Scientific Revolution.[105]

A second new direction given to studies of the history of science is best seen in the pioneering work of Derek Price, who has also been a leader in the area of studying the actual construction and use of physical instruments in the advancement of science.[106] Price undertook a series of quantitative studies of the changes in the scientific community, including the size of its membership, the number of publications of different sorts, and the changes and varieties of modes of communication among scientists. A number of "laws" have been found, among them a rule for the time of doubling of the number of publications in any field and certain rules about the emergence of specialties.[107] In particular, Price has called our attention to the great crisis of about 1830, when it "became evident . . . that . . . no scientist could read all the journals or keep sufficiently conversant with all published work that might be relevant to his interest."

Price's work has led him into an area now called the "science of science," or science in relation to policy. Other historians have also become concerned with this challenging area of activity.[108] Here is an exciting new field for research into current and recent history of science and a possibility of applying the history of science to problems of national priorities and planning and of international organization. No doubt the coming years will be witness to yet other modes of application of history of science, such as in the teaching of science (especially to undergraduate nonscientists) and in presenting problems and examples for philosophers of science.[109]

In the United States at the present time there are a number of universities offering doctoral programs in the history of science, whereas in the late 1940s there were only three: Cornell, Harvard, and Wisconsin.[110] Many historians of science are at present associated with academic history departments and consider themselves as historians, though of a special sort. These historians consider that a special part of their assignment is to provide an additional dimension to general history, one that is necessary if a complete view of man, events, civilization, and society is to result. But historians of science also have the continued hope that their work may inform the scientific community and become a necessary part of the education and background of all scientists.[111] In their present state of newfound maturity, however, the primary responsibility of historians of science is to their own community and their own standards, without forgetting that their work has relevance of the highest order to historians and scientists, to philosophers and social scientists, to historians of literature and art: in short, to the whole academic and intellectual community.[112]

NOTES

1. The following presentation is not intended to be a survey of every aspect of recent and current research in the history of science. Rather, it is a presentation of selected topics, each of which should be of interest to the general historian. I have, in the main, limited my discussions to topics with which I have had some firsthand contact, but I believe that some reference has been made to the major fields of activity. I am fully aware, however, that there are certain aspects of scholarship in the history of science which have been barely mentioned or have been omitted altogether, notably the tremendous international "industries" that are concerned with Galileo, Kepler, Copernicus, Newton, Lavoisier, and Darwin. Nor have I said very much about the growing concern among historians of science for the scientific developments of the last thirty or forty years, including the preservation of source materials and the making of oral interviews (in which I have participated myself). Furthermore, the limitations of space have made it impossible for me to mention the names of many colleagues and scholars whose work I admire enormously; the inclusion or noninclusion of the name of any scholar should not be taken as a value judgment concerning his or her work but is rather related the degree to which a particular book or article may have served to illustrate a point made in the following pages. Finally, I have consciously chosen to refer—to the extent that it has been possible—to scholarly work in English (or in English translation), so that there may be no language block to prevent the student of general history from pursuing the leads he may find here. There is no "manual" for this subject, but a useful guide is available in David Knight, *Sources of the History of Science 1660–1914* (Ithaca, N.Y.: Cornell University Press, 1975).

2. A thoughtless disregard for history is manifested even in such use of portraits, as may be readily seen by the fact that so many scientists are portrayed at rather advanced ages, even though everyone is aware that the most significant and original work in science is done by men and women in their younger and more creative periods. Additionally, portraits of scientists that are reproduced in textbooks and scientific treatises or monographs are often nonauthentic. See, on this score, George Sarton, "Iconographic Honesty (followed by a bibliography of iconographic studies and a note on altered portraits)," *Isis* 30 (1939):222–35, and "Portraits of Ancient Men of Science," *Lychnos* (1944–45), pp. 249–56.

3. My own favorites are Lyman's ghosts (named after Theodore Lyman) and Andrade's creep (named after E. N. daC. Andrade). On the complexities and significance of the naming of scientific effects and laws, see I. B. Cohen, "Newton, Hooke, and 'Boyle's Law' (discovered by Power and Towneley)," *Nature* 204 (1964): 618–21; and the discussion of eponymy in science in Robert K. Merton, *The Sociology of Science: Theoretical and Empirical Investigations* (Chicago: University of Chicago Press, 1973), pp. 298–302. The names assigned to laws and effects may actually vary from country to country, as may be seen in the Continental names for what the English-speaking world knows as "Boyle's law": "la loi de Mariotte," or "das Gesetz von Boyle und Mariotte."

4. An exception is the occasional search of the earlier literature when writing up the results of research.

5. This was notably true in the teaching of quantum theory during the 1930s and 1940s, when almost every older teacher found it necessary to retrace for his students the steps that made the adoption of quantum theory inescapable.

6. Some notable exceptions (among many) include René J. Dubos, *Louis Pasteur: Free Lance of Science* (Boston: Little, Brown, 1950); Joseph Fruton, *Molecules and Life: Historical Essays on the Interplay of Chemistry and Biology* (New York and London: Wiley-Inter-

science, 1972); Carl Ramsauer, *Grundversuche der Physik in historischer Darstellung* (Berlin, Göttingen, and Heidelberg: Springer-Verlag, 1953); Edmund T. Whittaker, *A History of the Theories of Aether and Electricity from the Age of Descartes to the Nineteenth Century* (Dublin: Dublin University Press, 1910), rev. and expanded into *A History of the Theories of Aether and Electricity*, 2 vols. (Edinburgh and London: Thomas Nelson and Sons, 1951, 1953); Joseph Needham, *A History of Embryology* (Cambridge: At the University Press, 1934, 2d ed., 1959); Julius von Sachs, *History of Botany (1530–1860)*, trans. Henry E. F. Garnsey, rev. Isaac Bayley Balfour (Oxford: Clarendon Press, 1906); Erwin Stresemann, *Die Entwicklung der Ornithologie von Aristoteles bis zur Gegenwart* (Berlin: F. W. Peters, 1951), English trans. by Hans J. and Cathleen Epstein: *Ornithology from Aristotle to the Present*, ed. G. William Cottrell, with a foreword and an epilogue on American ornithology by Ernst Mayr (Cambridge: Harvard University Press, 1975). Needham's great work on science in China (see n. 54 *infra*) shows him to be an outstanding professional historian of science, yet in 1934 he was by profession a biochemist, specializing in chemical embryology, although genuinely interested in history. His *History of Embryology* was, in fact, expanded from the historical chapters of his three-volume *Chemical Embryology* (Cambridge: At the University Press, 1931). A large number of professional doctors have made major contributions to medical history. And there is many a scientist who, at the conclusion of a successful professional career in science, has devoted himself with great profit to the history of his subject.

7. Training to become a practicing research scientist today does not require the study of Newton's *Principia*, Lavoisier's treatise on chemistry, or Harvey's studies on the motion of the heart, in the same sense that any poet would find it necessary—or at least valuable—to study Homer, Dante, Shakespeare, Villon, Baudelaire, or Yeats. But not too long ago, the German chemist Wilhelm Ostwald argued that studying the classics of science would actually help young scientists to gain vicarious experience of research and would thus actually serve as part of their training. It was to this end that Ostwald established his famous series of pocket-sized editions, known as "Ostwald's Klassiker der exakten Wissenschaften" (published in Leipzig by Wilhelm Engelmann).

8. Accordingly, they often consider the historian of science to be engaged in the detailed study of error.

9. Herbert Dingle, "Comments [at a conference on the history, philosophy, and sociology of science]," *Proceedings of the American Philosophical Society* 99 (1955):348–49. The progressive quality of science was a main point in George Sarton's approach to the history of science. Thus he stated as a "theorem" that the "acquisition and systematization of positive knowledge are the only human activities which are truly cumulative and progressive"; this "theorem" led him to the "corollary" that the "history of science is the only history which can illustrate the progress of mankind." Quoted from Sarton's *The Study of the History of Science* (Cambridge: Harvard University Press, 1936), p. 5; see Arnold Thackray and Robert K. Merton, "On Discipline Building: The Paradoxes of George Sarton," *Isis* 63 (1972):473–95, esp. p. 479.

10. This is not to deny that we understand such works better by means of scholarly commentaries, both historical and critical, and by being guided by the fruits of scholarly research. But even an untrained eye and ear can easily recognize the genius of Michelangelo or Shakespeare or Beethoven, although there might be some difficulty with Le Corbusier or James Joyce or Stravinsky.

11. Not only are there no solutions of problems of dynamics by means of today's familiar differential equations, there are not even any occurrences of the dotted fluxions (the mature Newtonian form of the calculus). As to the latter, this notation was not conceived by Newton until the 1690s, some years after the publication of the *Principia*

(*editio princeps*, 1687); in any event, he evidently did not wish to make the acquisition of the newly invented calculus a necessary precondition for reading the *Principia*.

12. This difficulty can be overcome by means of definitions in convenient footnotes, plus a general glossary. This problem is akin to that faced by one attempting to read Chaucer without knowing medieval English.

13. There is an additional source of bewilderment in the discovery that in the *Principia*, primary concept of force is also different from the way in which we define force today. As a result, the *Principia*'s second law is not only dimensionally different from our second law, but it seems to us to be dimensionally unsound and even false; the two versions of this law, however, are seen to be true in both forms and to be derivable from one another once the reader becomes cognizant of Newton's concept of time and his use of the infinitesimal in the limiting process. On this point, see I. B. Cohen, "Newton's Second Law and the Concept of Force in the *Principia*," in *The Annus Mirabilis of Sir Isaac Newton, 1666–1966*, ed. Robert Palter (Cambridge and London: M.I.T. Press, 1970), pp. 143–85, esp. app. 1.

14. Quoted from Erwin Panofsky, *Meaning in the Visual Arts: Papers in and on Art History* (Garden City, N.Y.: Doubleday Anchor Books, 1955), p. 5.

15. Arnold Thackray has written: "The history of science emerged as a professional discipline in the Western World in the 1950s, primarily in the United States. . . . The fifties was thus the crucial decade for defining standards, agreeing on methods, enrolling students, and creating a discipline. It was also the decade of the H bomb, the Cold War, Senator Joseph McCarthy, loyalty oaths, militant anticommunism, and the 'silent generation' of students. There were therefore unusually complex political, ideological, social, and professional factors at work in the shaping of this new discipline." This statement occurs in Thackray's bold plea for a new history of science, in which social considerations will become a prominent factor, "Science: Has Its Present Past a Future?" in Roger Stuewer, ed., *Historical and Philosophical Perspectives of Science*, vol. 5 of *Minnesota Studies in the Philosophy of Science*, ed. Herbert Feigl and Grover Maxwell (Minneapolis: University of Minnesota Press, 1970), pp. 112–27.

16. On the rise of the history of science as a professional subject in the United States, see the special issue of *Isis* 64, no. 4 (1975), commemorating the fiftieth anniversary of the founding of the History of Science Society. The first doctoral program in the history of science in an American university was established at Harvard University in 1936. Prior to that time, historians of science took their degree in departments of history, philosophy, literature, or the sciences. A notable group of historians of science—including Carl B. Boyer, Marshall Clagett, C. Doris Hellman, Pearl Kibre, and Edward Rosen—took their doctorates at Columbia in history in the Faculty of Political Science. Right after World War II additional doctoral programs in the history of science were established at Cornell and Wisconsin. (I do not take account here of specialized programs, such as the ancient exact sciences at Brown or the history of medicine at Johns Hopkins.)

17. Additionally, it may well be the case that the study of recent science absolutely requires such advanced training in science that very few otherwise qualified historians of science would have the necessary competence for research in the history of science in the last half century or more.

18. For quantitative data on the pre-World War II expenditures for scientific research and development in America, see I. B. Cohen, *Science, Servant of Man* (Boston: Little, Brown, 1948), p. 58; Vannevar Bush, *Science the Endless Frontier: A Report to the President on a Program for Postwar Scientific Research, July 1945* (Washington, D.C.: National Science Foundation, 1960, a reprint of the 1945 ed.), pp. 85-89. On current expenditures,

see the *Databook* published in January of each year by the National Science Foundation (NSF). It must be remembered that the mission of the NSF has been primarily the advancement of pure science or basic research, and that its annual budget is but a trifle when compared to the similar budgets of the Department of Defense, the Atomic Energy Commission, or the National Aeronautics and Space Administration (NASA). On the other hand, whereas in fiscal 1974 the scientific research and development budget of the Department of Defense came to some 9 billion dollars, as compared to NSF's total for 1974 of some 525 millions, the NSF was responsible for $400,101,000 for basic research and the Department of Defense for only $274,200,000.

19. For two views on the rise of "big science" and its consequences, see Derek J. de Solla Price, *Little Science, Big Science* (New York and London: Columbia University Press, 1963); and Alvin M. Weinberg, *Reflections on Big Science* (Cambridge and London: M.I.T. Press, 1967).

20. On the rise and fall of PSAC, see David Z. Beckler, "The Precarious Life of Science in the White House," *Daedalus* 103 (Summer, 1974): 115–34.

21. On this subject see Gerald Holton, *Thematic Origins of Scientific Thought, Kepler to Einstein* (Cambridge: Harvard University Press, 1973), chap. 12, "Models for Understanding the Growth of Research," a condensed and revised version of an article, "Scientific Research and Scholarship: Notes toward the Design of Proper Scales," *Daedalus* 91 (Spring, 1962): 362–99; also Derek J. de Solla Price, "Diseases of Science," in *Science since Babylon* (New Haven: Yale University Press, 1961), chap. 5. The report of the Naval Research Advisory Committee (U.S. Navy Department), *Basic Research in the Navy*, 2 vols. (Washington, D.C.: Department of the Navy, 1959), is far broader in scope than its title suggests, and actually proposes an important model for scientific development.

22. Russell McCormmach, ed., *Historical Studies in the Physical Sciences* 1 (1969): vii–viii. McCormmach makes it quite explicit that he does "not intend to publish articles that fall into categories that are no longer viable, e.g., heroic biography, the history of chains of discovery, the identification of precursors." And he adds, "It should be unnecessary to declare policy on such long-dead issues, but there is a staggering number of methodologically bad articles still making the rounds."

23. Ibid., 3 (1971): 1–115. The failure to print such papers is not a fault of the editor; the desired socioeconomic historical point of view is still largely in the realm of desiderata and not of actuality.

24. Koyré's work is discussed toward the end of this paper. I should perhaps add that, as is the case with all pioneering studies, not all of Forman's colleagues have thus far found his argument to be wholly convincing, and they are apt to refer to it in those academic terms of "stimulating" and "suggestive."

25. There exist a number of valuable catalogues of collections of scientific instruments and inventories of special types of instruments, but there are all too few investigations of the actual use of instruments in scientific work or of their design, construction, and dissemination (including the economics of manufacturing and trade). Some examples of work in this area are Derek J. de Solla Price, *Gears from the Greeks: The Antikythera Mechanism, a Calendar Computer from ca. 80 B.C.* (New York: Science History Publications, 1975), originally printed in *Transactions of the American Philosophical Society* 64 (1974), pt. 7; Maurice Daumas, *Les instruments scientifiques au XVIIe et XVIIIe siècles* (Paris: Presses Universitaires de France, 1953); G. Boffito, *Gli strumenti della scienza e la scienza degli strumenti* (Florence: Libreria Internazionale Seeber, 1929); E. G. R. Taylor, *The Mathematical Practitioners of Tudor and Stuart England* and *The Mathematical Practitioners of Hanoverian England 1714–1840* (Cambridge: At the University Press [for the

Institute of Navigation], 1967, 1966); Silvio A. Bedini, "The Instruments of Galileo," in *Galileo, Man of Science*, ed. Ernan McMullin (New York and London: Basic Books, 1967), pp. 256–92; and Henri Michel, *Traité de l'astrolabe* (Paris: Gauthier-Villars, 1947).

Not unexpectedly, there are numerous writings on the telescope and the microscope.

26. Roger Hahn, *The Anatomy of a Scientific Institution: The Paris Academy of Sciences, 1666–1803* (Berkeley and Los Angeles: University of California Press, 1971). Another major history that relates the growth of science to its institutional setting is Alexander Vucinich, *Science in Russian Culture*, vol. 1, *A History to 1860*, vol. 2, *1861–1917* (Stanford: Stanford University Press, 1963, 1970). The want of studies in this general area may be seen in the fact that the most recent attempt to produce a full-scale history of the Royal Society is Charles Richard Weld, *A History of the Royal Society, with Memoirs of the Presidents. Compiled from Authentic Documents*, 2 vols. (London: John W. Parker, 1848).

27. An exception is to be made for the incisive studies by Robert K. Merton, notably those in which his sociological conclusions are based upon a study of primary historical sources. A number of historically based studies appear in R. K. Merton, *The Sociology of Science, Theoretical and Empirical Investigations*, edited with an introduction by Norman W. Stover (Chicago and London: University of Chicago Press, 1973), esp. nos. 11, 14, 15, 16, 17, 20. This collection omits at least two historical essays ("Puritanism, Pietism, and Science" and—notably— "Science and Economy of 17th Century England") to be found in R. K. Merton, *Social Theory and Social Structure*, rev. and enl. ed. (Glencoe, Ill.: Free Press, 1957).

28. Everett Mendelsohn, "The Emergence of Science as a Profession in Nineteenth-Century Europe," in *The Management of Scientists*, ed. Karl Hill (Boston: Beacon Press, 1964), pp. 3-48; Bernard Barber, *Science and the Social Order* (Glencoe, Ill.: Free Press, 1952), esp. chap. 2, "The Historical Development of Science: Social Influences on the Evolution of Science," and chap. 4, "The Social Organization of Science: Some General Considerations." Of notable interest is Joseph Ben-David, *The Scientist's Role in Society: A Comparative Study* (Englewood Cliffs, N.J.: Prentice-Hall, 1971), esp. chap. 7, "German Scientific Hegemony and the Emergence of Organized Science."

29. Economic historians no longer have a primary interest in the history of technology as such, and this subject has no other obvious academic locus. In at least two major universities in the United States (Pennsylvania and Minnesota), a historian of technology is associated with a group of historians of science. There have been founded a number of institutes for the history of special technologies, such as the Eleutherian Mills-Hagley Foundation in Wilmington, Delaware, for the study of the technologies and industries established on the Brandywine. At M.I.T. a new program combines the history of technology and the history of science under the general rubric, "Technology Studies Program." Information concerning the history of technology at large is available through the Society for the History of Technology and its journal, *Technology and Culture*.

30. On Bacon's role in the propaganda for the practicality of pure science, see Benjamin Farrington, *Francis Bacon: Philosopher of Industrial Science* (New York: Henry Schuman, 1949).

Of course, there were some pure scientists in the eighteenth century, as in the seventeenth, who were interested in practical applications; and most scientists did not consciously make a division between "pure" and "applied" science. In those days the antithesis of "pure" science was "mixed" and not "applied." Furthermore, practical considerations arising from medicine and public health, agriculture and industry, mining and metallurgy, transportation and communication, and warfare did have a significant effect on science, even setting problems for many a scientist whose primary goal was to do basic research, as may be seen most notably in the field of chemistry. On this complex issue, see Henry Guerlac, "Some French Antecedents of the Chemical Revolution," *Chymia* 5 (1959): 73–112; Charles C. Gillispie, "The Natural History of Industry," *Isis* 48 (1957): 398–407; Robert E. Schofield, "The Industrial Orientation of Science in the Lunar Society of Birmingham," ibid., 408–15, and "Josiah Wedgwood and a Proposed Eighteenth-Century Industrial Research Organization," *Isis* 47 (1956): 16–19. A major contribution that has never been fully appreciated and used by other scholars is Archibald Clow and N. L. Clow, *The Chemical Revolution. A Contribution to Social Technology* (London: Batchworth Press, 1952).

31. Watt himself denied that there was any close association of Black's specific discoveries and his own invention, granting only that "the correct modes of reasoning and of making experiments of which he set me the example, certainly conduced very much to facilitate the progress of my inventions"; quoted in Robert E. Schofield, *The Lunar Society of Birmingham: A Social History of Provincial Society and Industry in Eighteenth-Century England* (Oxford: Clarendon Press, 1963), p. 64. Cf. pp. 63–66 for a discussion of the scientific component of Watt's mechanical invention.

32. See Donald H. Fleming, "Latent Heat and the Invention of the Watt Engine," *Isis* 43 (1952): 3–5.

33. See I. B. Cohen, "How Practical Was Benjamin Franklin's Science?" *Pennsylvania Magazine of History and Biography* 69 (1945): 284–93, and "The Two Hundredth Anniversary of Benjamin Franklin's Two Lightning Experiments and the Introduction of the Lightning Rod," *Proceedings of the American Philosophical Society* 96 (1952): 331–66.

34. The various ways in which developments in the exact sciences and the life sciences specifically affected social and political thought and action have barely been explored. The writer is currently engaged in studying these topics.

35. Science provided a new way of knowing and led to the expectation that all knowledge could (and hence would) be based on a rational analysis of experience according to method. Linnaeus, who designated man as "homo sapiens" in his system of classification, set forth the motto, "Method, the soul of science."

36. Sidney Edelstein, "Perkin, William Henry," in *Dictionary of Scientific Biography*, ed. Charles C. Gillispie, vol. 10 (New York: Charles Scribner's Sons, 1974), p. 516. A complete list of Perkin's works is given in S. Edelstein, "Sir William Henry Perkin," *American Dyestuff Reporter* 45 (1956): 598–608. Cf. Raphael Meldola, Arthur G. Green, and John Cannell Cain, eds., *Jubilee of the Discovery of Mauve and of the Foundation of the Coal-tar Industry by Sir W. H. Perkin* (London: Perkin Memorial Committee, 1906), and also Meldola's obituary notice of Perkin, *Journal of the Chemical Society* 93 (1908): 2214–57. On the possibility that picric acid may more truly be called "the first synthetic dye," see Aaron J. Ihde, *The Development of Modern Chemistry* (New York, Evanston, London: Harper & Row, 1964), p. 455n.

37. See Alexander Findlay, *Chemistry in the Service of Man* (London: Longmans, Green, 1916), p. 236.

38. Cf. Sir William A. Tilden, *Chemical Discovery and Invention in the Twentieth Century*, 5th ed. (London: George Routledge and Sons, 1926), p. 322. In 1954, there were 11,500 acres under cultivation to indigo in India, according to the eighth edition (1957) of Findlay's book (cited in n. 37 *supra*), p. 221n. Haber (see n. 39 *infra*), p. 85, notes that by 1900 the production of synthetic indigo (actually indigotin, one of the components of natural indigo) had reached an equivalent of a yield of 250,000 acres. Cf. H. Brunck, *The History of the Development of the Manufacture of Indigo* (New York: Kultroft, Pickhardt & Co. [for the Badische Analin und Soda Fabrik], 1901).

I. Bernard Cohen

39. L. F. Haber, *The Chemical Industry during the Nineteenth Century: A Study of the Economic Aspect of Applied Chemistry in Europe and North America* (Oxford: Clarendon Press, 1958). Haber (p. 171) quotes a report made soon after World War I, that: "In Germany the whole community takes interest in the chemical industry and this is perhaps one of the predominating factors in promoting the welfare of that industry." He notes, however, that "it cannot be [any longer] determined whether it was the climate of opinion that stimulated the development of chemistry or, conversely, whether this development conditioned public opinion." While Britain was losing (primarily to Germany) the synthetic-dye industry which she had begun with Perkin's discovery in 1856, there were innumerable conferences and discussions in print as to why Britain was losing this prize. A general agreement emerged as to two causes: "first the neglect of organic chemistry in the universities and colleges . . ., and then the disregard by manufacturers of scientific methods and assistance and total indifference to the practice of research in connection with their processes and products"; cf. Tilden, *Chemical Discovery and Invention* (n. 38 supra), p. 318.

40. Arnold Thackray, "Natural Knowledge in Cultural Context: The Manchester Model," *The American Historical Review* 79 (1974): 672–709; Yehuda Elkana, *The Discovery of the Conservation of Energy* (London: Hutchinson Educational; Cambridge: Harvard University Press, 1974), esp. pp. 6–8. Cf. also Steven Shapin and Arnold Thackray, "Prosopography as a Research Tool in History of Science: The British Scientific Community 1700–1900," *History of Science* 12 (1974):1–28.

41. Robert K. Merton, *Science, Technology & Society in Seventeenth-century England* (New York: Howard Fertig, 1970), a photoreprint made from vol. 4, pt. 2 (1938) of *Osiris: Studies on the History and Philosophy of Science, and on the History of Learning and Culture*, with a new preface by the author.

42. Alphonse de Candolle, *Histoire des sciences et des savants depuis deux siècles* . . . (Geneva-Basel: H. George, Libraire-Éditeur, 1885).

43. "Even that 'purest' of disciplines, mathematics, held little interest for Newton save as it was designed for application to physical problems"; quoted from the work cited in n. 41 supra, end of chap. 8 (pp. 181–82 of 1970 ed.).

44. See I. B. Cohen, *Isaac Newton's "Theory of the Moon's Motion" (1702), with a Bibliographical and Historical Introduction* (London: Dawson; and New York: Science History Publications, 1975).

45. See I. B. Cohen, "Isaac Newton, the Calculus of Variations, and the Design of Ships: An Example of Pure Mathematics in Newton's *Principia*, Allegedly Developed for the Sake of Practical Applications," in *For Dirk Struik: Scientific, Historical and Political Essays in Honor of Dirk Struik*, ed. R. S. Cohen, J. J. Stachel, and M. W. Wartofsky, vol. 15 of *Boston Studies in the Philosophy of Science* (Dordrecht and Boston: D. Reidel Publishing Co., 1974), pp. 170–87, esp. p. 184, n. 5. See also A. Rupert Hall, "[R. K.] Merton Revisited, or Science and Society in the Seventeenth Century," *History of Science* 2 (1963): 1–16, esp. p. 8. See also n. 27 supra.

46. Joseph Ben-David, *Fundamental Research and the Universities: Some Comments on International Differences* (Paris: Organisation for Economic Co-operation and Development, 1968), pp. 22 ff.

47. This event occurred in 1927; see the "profile" of Rabi by Jeremy Bernstein, pt. 1, *The New Yorker*, October 13, 1975, p. 86.

48. For a critical review of an aspect of this literature, published two decades ago, see David Joravsky, "Soviet Views on the History of Science," *Isis* 46 (1955):3–13.

49. L. E. Maistrov, *Probability Theory, a Historical Sketch* (New York and London: Academic Press, 1974). Of course, in any such overall survey there are inadequacies and errors; see the review by Persi Diaconis in *Science* 187 (1975): 1190–91. But what is

exciting about this book is its freshness and new points of view, so often different from what we have traditionally encountered.

50. Of this trio, the most significant (in terms of actual contributions to history of science) was Bernal. See his *Science in History*, 3d ed., 4 vols. (Harmondsworth: Penguin Books; London: C. A. Watts & Co., 1969) and *Science and Industry in the Nineteenth Century* (London: Routledge & Kegan Paul, 1953).

The influence of Marxist history of science goes back to Boris Hessen's paper on "The Social and Economic Roots of Newton's 'Principia'," read at the London Congress of the History of Science in 1931. Hessen's communication was published in N. I. Bukharin et al., *Science at the Crossroads: Papers Presented to the International Congress of the History of Science and Technology, Held in London from June 29th to July 3rd, 1931, by the Delegates of the U.S.S.R.* (London: Frank Cass & Co., 1971 [a photoreprint of the original edition of 1931]), with a new foreword by Joseph Needham and a new introduction by P. G. Werskey. See another reprint, B. Hessen, *The Social and Economic Roots of Newton's "Principia"* (New York: Howard Fertig, 1971), with an introduction by Robert S. Cohen. It may be observed that Hessen's admirers are universally in agreement in excusing his many errors of fact and of interpretation, and his gross oversimplifications, in order to be able to hail him as a pioneer—which admittedly he was. For a rebuttal to Hessen, see George N. Clark, *Science and Social Welfare in the Age of Newton*, 2d ed. (Oxford: Clarendon Press, 1949).

51. Even more significant in Needham's thought as historian is his passionate belief in human social evolution and his warm sense of humanity, informed by an active Christianity. For Needham's own views on the forces influencing his intellectual development, see his article (under the pen name Henry Holorenshaw), "The Making of an Honorary Taoist," in *Changing Perspectives in the History of Science: Essays in Honour of Joseph Needham*, ed. Mikuláš Teich and Robert Young (London: Heinemann, 1973), esp. pp. 7, 9–10. On the issue of Marxism in relation to Needham's early career, see pp. xvii-xviii of P. G. Werskey's essay (cited in n. 50 *supra*).

52. Needham's views on the "internalist"-"externalist" debate are stated expressly and used as a guiding principle throughout his work on science in China (see n. 54 *infra*); see also his essay on Hessen (cited in n. 50 *supra*), pp. viii-ix. Some major documents on this question have been assembled and edited by George Basalla, *The Rise of Modern Science: External or Internal Factors?* (Lexington, Mass.: D. C. Heath and Company, 1968).

53. Needham's political, social, philosophic, and religious points of view may be found expressed in the following works: *The Skeptical Biologist* (London: Chatto & Windus, 1929; New York: W. W. Norton, 1930); *Order and Life* (New Haven: Yale University Press, 1935 [reprinted, 1968, by the M.I.T. Press, Cambridge]); (under the pseudonym Henry Holorenshaw) *The Levellers and the English Revolution* (London: Gollancz, 1939 [reprinted, 1971, by Howard Fertig, New York]); *Time, the Refreshing River* (London: Allen & Unwin, 1943); *History Is on Our Side* (London: Allen & Unwin; New York: Macmillan, 1945); also in the following works which he coedited, and in which he has a contribution: *Christianity and the Social Revolution*, ed. with J. Lewis (London: Gollancz, 1935); and *Science in Soviet Russia*, ed. with J. Sykes Davies (London: Watts, 1942).

54. Joseph Needham, *Science and Civilization in China*, vol. 1, *Introductory Orientations* (Cambridge: At the University Press, 1954). This monumental work is to be completed in seven volumes, of which vol. 4 has three parts, and vol. 5 has two parts (vol. 4, pt. 3, comes to more than 900 pages). As of 1974, only vol. 5, pt. 1, and vols. 6–7 remain to be completed and seen through the press.

Although Needham has, in the several volumes, made some use of one or more collaborators, this has been a one-man job in the sense that he has not used a large research team but has done most of the work himself and has carefully controlled every bit of research and writing.

55. See, especially, his article on "The Helmontian-Galenist Controversy in Restoration England," *Ambix* 12 (1964):1–23.

56. See C. Webster, "English Medical Reformers of the Puritan Revolution: A Background to the 'Society of Chymical Physitians,' " *Ambix* 14 (1967):16–41.

57. Ibid., p. 41. Charles Webster has edited a volume of essays from the journal *Past and Present*, under the title, *The Intellectual Revolution of the Seventeenth Century* (London and Boston: Routledge & Kegan Paul, 1974); of these, nos. 14–26 deal with various aspects of science and its political, social, philosophical, and religious milieu. See also Webster's masterly and encyclopaedic *The Great Instauration: Science, Medicine and Reform, 1626–1660* (London: Duckworth, 1975).

58. Webster, *Intellectual Revolution*, p. 26. See, further, P. M. Rattansi, "Paracelsus and the Puritan Revolution," *Ambix* 11 (1963):24–32.

59. See, especially, his "Religious Motives in the Medical Biology of the XVIIth Century," *Bulletin of the History of Medicine* 3 (1935): 97–128, 213–31, 265–312; "Religious and Philosophical Aspects of Van Helmont's Science and Medicine," *Bulletin of the History of Medicine* 12 (1944), supp. 2; *Paracelsus: An Introduction to Philosophical Medicine in the Era of the Renaissance* (Basel and New York: S. Karger, 1958); *William Harvey's Biological Ideas: Selected Aspects and Historical Background* (Basel and New York: S. Karger, 1967). A bibliography of Pagel's writings, and a short biographical sketch, may be found in Allen G. Debus, ed., *Science, Medicine, and Society in the Renaissance: Essays to Honor Walter Pagel*, 2 vols. (New York: Science History Publications, 1972). Debus himself has carried on the Pagel tradition in a continuing set of books and monographs on the Paracelsian and Hermetic component of science in England in the sixteenth and seventeenth centuries.

60. Frances A. Yates, *Giordano Bruno and the Hermetic Tradition* (London: Routledge and Kegan Paul, 1964 [reprinted 1971]), p. 447.

61. "Science in its Context," an essay-review of the *Festschrift* for Walter Pagel (cited in n. 59 *supra*), *History of Science* 11 (1973):286–91.

62. Notably Frances A. Yates, *The Rosicrucian Enlightenment* (London and Boston: Routledge & Kegan Paul, 1972), chap. 14, "Elias Ashmole and the Dee Tradition: Isaac Newton and Rosicrucian Alchemy"; P. M. Rattansi, "Newton's Alchemical Studies," pp. 167–82 of the *Festschrift* for Walter Pagel (cited in n. 59 *supra*); R. S. Westfall, "Newton and the Hermetic Tradition," ibid., pp. 183–98; P. M. Rattansi, "Some Evaluations of Reason in Sixteenth- and Seventeenth-Century Natural Philosophy," pp. 148–66 of the *Festschrift* for Joseph Needham (cited in n. 51 *supra*); R. S. Westfall "The Role of Alchemy in Newton's Career," in *Reason, Experiment, and Mysticism in the Scientific Revolution*, ed. M. L. Righini Bonelli and William R. Shea (New York: Science History Publications, 1975), pp. 189–282.

63. Christopher Hill, *The Intellectual Origins of the English Revolution* (New York: Viking Press, 1972, 1973), chaps. 2 and 4, esp. pp. 233 ff.; also *The World Turned Upside Down, Radical Ideas during the English Revolution* (New York: The Viking Press, 1972).

64. I am not here anachronistically superimposing on Newton's thought a dichotomy between positive or "hard" or rational science and Hermetic alchemy or speculative philosophy; it is Newton himself who made this separation, which has been a characteristic of science ever since. In the concluding *Scholium Generale*, written for the second edition of his *Principia* (1713), he said explicitly: "I feign no hypotheses. [*Hypotheses non fingo*.] For whatever is not deduced from phenomena is to be reckoned

an hypothesis; and hypotheses, whether metaphysical or physical, whether of occult qualities or mechanical, have no place in experimental philosophy." He had not been able "to discover the cause of the properties of gravity from phenomena," but no matter! "It is enough [*satis est*] that gravity does really exist and act according to the laws which we have explained, and abundantly serves to account for all the motions of the celestial bodies and of our sea."

65. It would seem as if the area in which to look for an influence of the aether concept on Newton's scientific thought might be in optics. But here the seminal concept was a system of corpuscles moving according to mechanical laws; cf. J. A. Lohne, "Isaac Newton: The Rise of a Scientist, 1661–1671," *Notes and Records of the Royal Society of London* 20 (1965):125–39. See also A. I. Sabra, *Theories of Light from Descartes to Newton* (London: Oldbourne, 1967), esp. chap. 12, "The Two Levels of Explanation: Newton's Theory of Refraction," and chap. 13, "The Two Levels of Explanation: Newton's Theory of the Colours of Thin Plates." On the optical aether, see R. S. Westfall, "Isaac Newton's Coloured Circles Twixt Two Contiguous Glasses," *Archive for History of Exact Sciences* 2 (1965):181–96, and "Uneasily Fitful Reflections on Fits of Easy Transmission [and of Easy Reflection]," in *The Annus Mirabilis*, ed. Robert Palter (cited in n. 13 *supra*), pp. 88–104; Henry Guerlac, "Newton's Optical Aether," *Notes and Records of the Royal Society of London* 22 (1967): 45–57; Joan L. Hawes, "Newton's Revival of the Aether Hypothesis and the Explanation of Gravitational Attraction," ibid., 23 (1968): 200–12. It should be noted that Newton at one time examined the hypothesis that the aether might have a role in the cause of gravitation, but we do not have any evidence concerning a similar possible role of the aether in the development of either Newton's gravitational celestial mechanics or his theory of attraction in general. Newton did, however, combine the concept of corpuscles of light with the aether hypothesis in his explanation of the "fits" of "easy reflection" and of "easy refraction" that he supposed to be the cause of such phenomena as what we call "Newton's rings."

66. Paolo Rossi, "Hermeticism, Rationality, and the Scientific Revolution," in *Reason, Experiment, and Mysticism* (cited in n. 62 *supra*), pp. 247–73; also Marie Boas Hall, "Newton's Voyage in the Strange Seas of Alchemy," ibid., pp. 239–46. Also, J. E. McGuire, "Newton and the Demonic Furies: Some Current Problems and Approaches in the History of Science," *History of Science* 11 (1973): 21–41. The reader interested in this topic should also consult Mary Hesse, "Hermeticism and Historiography: An Apology for the Internal History of Science," in *Historical and Philosophical Perspectives of Science* (cited in n. 15 *supra*), pp. 134–62. Miss Yates has conveniently summarized her views in "The Hermetic Tradition in Renaissance Science," in *Art, Science, and History in the Renaissance*, ed. Charles S. Singleton (Baltimore: Johns Hopkins Press, 1968), pp. 255–74.

Paolo Rossi has explored the significance of "magic" for the new science, primarily in his *Francis Bacon: From Magic to Science*, trans. Sacha Rabinovitch (London: Routledge & Kegan Paul; Chicago: University of Chicago Press, 1968). Cf. the very important work by D. P. Walker, *Spiritual and Demonic Magic from Ficino to Campanella*, vol. 22 of *Studies of the Warburg Institute* (London: Warburg Institute, 1958 [reprinted, 1969, by Kraus Reprint, New York, and again in 1975 by University of Notre Dame Press]), supplemented by *The Ancient Theology: Studies in Christian Platonism from the Fifteenth to the Eighteenth Century* (London: Duckworth, 1972), of which the final pages are devoted to Newton's renewal of interest in the aether.

Paolo Rossi's paper on "Hermeticism, Rationality, and the Scientific Revolution" is one of the most perceptive and incisive critical analyses of this complex subject. "What started off as a useful corrective to the conception of the history of science as a triumphant progress," he writes (p. 257), "is becoming a retrospective form of historiography, interested only in the elements of continuity and the influence of traditional ideas." In the attempt to consider Bacon and Copernicus, Descartes and Newton, "in their links with the past, and in their common 'descent' from earlier revolutions and cultural innovations," Rossi sees scholars today "in danger of ignoring, as totally irrelevant, the ideas, theories and doctrines that make these writers difficult to fit into the endless list of writers on Hermetic subjects or of exponents of rhetoric who published their works between the second half of the sixteenth century and the end of the seventeenth century." Without in any way discounting the existence of a Hermetic tradition that held attractions for many of the primary figures in the Scientific Revolution, Rossi points out that all too often nowadays, historians no longer ask "what new ideas have given these giants their place in history" and "consider exclusively what existed in the past or may be derived from the past without unwanted residues."

67. See Ivor Bulmer-Thomas, "Eudemus of Rhodes," in *Dictionary of Scientific Biography*, ed. Charles C. Gillispie (New York: Charles Scribner's Sons, 1971), 4: 460–65. This collective work provides an admirable first guide to the scientific thought, experiments, theories, and achievements of the men and women who have been in the mainstream of science from its earliest beginnings to the present.

68. It is probably a sign of the relative youth of the history of science as a professional discipline that we do not yet have a full history of the subject. Henry Guerlac, well known for his studies on Lavoisier and certain aspects of Newtonian natural philosophy, has written a number of articles on the development and current state of the history of science; his most recent one, "History of Science 3: The growth of the Literature," appeared in the *Times Literary Supplement* (London), April 26, 1974, pp. 449–90. A perceptive companion study by A. Rupert Hall (ibid., pp. 437–38) is entitled, "History of Science 2: Microscopic Analyses and the General Picture."

69. See Richard Foster Jones, *Ancients and Moderns: A Study of the Rise of the Scientific Movement in Seventeenth-century England*, 2d ed. (St. Louis: Washington University Press, 1961; Berkeley and Los Angeles, 1965); the first edition was more accurately subtitled, "A Study of the Background of the *Battle of the Books*," *Washington University Studies*, n. s., Language and Literature, no. 6, 1936.

70. Still valuable is Ferdinand Brunetière, "La formation de l'idée du progrès au XVIIIe siècle," in *Études critiques sur l'histoire de la littérature française*, cinquième série, 4th ed. (Paris: Librairie Hachette et Cie, 1907).

71. Some of the major publications in the Battle of the Books, or the Quarrel between the Ancients and the Moderns, are (in modern editions): Bernard le Bouyer (or Bovier) de Fontenelle's *Digression sur les anciens et les modernes*, edited, together with Fontenelle's *Entretiens sur la pluralité des mondes*, by Robert Shackleton (Oxford: Clarendon Press, 1955); Joseph Glanvill, *Plus Ultra: or, the Progress and Advancement of Knowledge since the Days of Aristotle, in an Account of Some of the Most Remarkable Late Improvements of Practical, Useful Learning* (London: printed for James Collins, 1668; facsimile reprint with an intro. by Jackson I. Cope, Gainesville, Florida: Scholars' Facsimiles & Reprints, 1958); Charles Perrault, *Paralelle des anciens et des modernes en ce qui regarde les arts et les sciences*, 4 vols. (Paris: chez Jean Baptiste Coignard, 1688–97; facsimile reprint "mit einer einleitenden Abhandlung von H. R. Jauss und kunstgeschichtlichen Exkursen von M. Imdahl," Munich: Eidos Verlag, 1964); Jonathan Swift, *A Full and True Account of the Battle Fought Last Friday between the Ancient and the Modern Books in Saint James's Library* (1697), available in Herbert David, ed., *The Prose Works of Jonathan Swift* (Oxford: Basil Blackwell, 1939) 1: 137–65; Sir William Temple, *Five Miscellaneous Essays*, ed. Samuel Holt Monk (Ann Arbor: University of Michigan Press,

1963); William Wotton, *Reflections upon Ancient and Modern Learning* (London: printed for Peter Buck, 1694; a "third edition, corrected" was printed for Tim. Goodwin, 1705), but no more recent edition exists.

72. See Leonard M. Marsak, *Bernard de Fontenelle: The Idea of Science in the French Enlightenment*, vol. 49, pt. 7, of *Transactions of the American Philosophical Society* (Philadelphia: American Philosophical Society, 1959).

73. See the account by Henry Guerlac, cited in n. 68 *supra*.

74. See J. F. Scott, *The Mathematical Work of John Wallis, D. D., F.R.S. (1616–1703)* (London: Taylor and Francis, 1938), pp. 133 ff.

75. This topic is explored in I. B. Cohen, "The Eighteenth-Century Origins of the Concept of Scientific Revolution," *Journal of the History of Ideas* 37 (1976):257–288.

76. For a convenient bibliographical introduction to the older literature on the history of science, see George Sarton, *Horus: A Guide to the History of Science. A First Guide for the Study of the History of Science* (Waltham, Mass.: Chronica Botanica Company, 1952).

77. See the introduction by Robert E. Schofield to the reprint edition of Joseph Priestley, *The History and Present State of Electricity, with Original Experiments*, 3d ed., cor. and enl., 2 vols. (London: printed for C. Bathurst and T. Lowndes . . ., 1775 [reprinted, New York and London: Johnson Reprint Corporation, 1966]).

78. There is no recent reprint of Whewell's *History of the Inductive Sciences*, or his *Philosophy of Discovery*, but his *Philosophy of the Inductive Sciences, Founded upon Their History*, 2d ed., 2 vols. (London: John W. Parker, 1847) has been reprinted in facsimile, with an intro. by John Herivel, by Johnson Reprint Corporation, New York and London, 1967. Cf. Walter F. Cannon, "William Whewell, F.R.S. II. Contributions to Science and Learning," *Notes and Records of the Royal Society of London* 19 (1964): 176–91.

79. Mach's most influential book is *The Science of Mechanics: A Critical and Historical Account of Its Development*, trans. Thomas J. McCormack, with an intro. by Karl Menger, 6th ed., with rev. through the 9th German ed. (LaSalle, Ill.: The Open Court Publishing Company, 1960); cf. J. Bradley, *Mach's Philosophy of Science* (London: Athlone Press, 1971). I believe it fair to say that Mach was the most influential philosopher who based his ideas on historical analyses. His originality, wit, and extensive use of primary sources make his works perennially attractive and stimulating.

80. See Sarton's *Horus* (cited in n. 76 *supra*).

81. Cf. George Sarton, "L'oeuvre de Paul Tannery," with a bibliography, *Osiris* 4 (1938): 690–705; "Paul, Jules, et Marie Tannery," *Isis* 38 (1947): 33–51; "La correspondance de Paul Tannery et l'histoire de nos études," *Revue d'histoire des sciences et de ces applications* 7 (1954) :321–25.

82. Pierre Duhem, *The Aim and Structure of Physical Theory*, trans. Philip P. Wiener (Princeton: Princeton University Press, 1954).

83. *Le mixte et la combinaison chimique: essai sur l'évolution d'une idée* (Paris: Gauthier-Villars, 1902); *L'évolution de la mécanique* (Paris: Librairie Scientifique A. Hermann, 1905).

84. *Études sur Léonard de Vinci, ceux qu'il a lus et ceux qui l'ont lu*, 3 vols. (Paris: Librairie Scientifique A. Hermann, 1906, 1909 1913). Another major work is *Les origines de la statique*, 2 vols. (Paris: Librairie Scientifique A. Hermann, 1905, 1906). His ten-volume *Système du monde* was left incomplete at the time of his death and was finally printed in full only a few years ago. See Hélène Pierre-Duhem, *Un savant français, Pierre Duhem* (Paris: Librairie Plon, 1936); Pierre Humbert, *Pierre Duhem* (Paris: Librairie Bloud et Gay, 1932).

85. There has been continuing debate as to the degree of influence of the medieval

thinkers on Galileo and other figures of the Scientific Revolution. See A. C. Crombie, *Augustine to Galileo: The History of Science A.D. 400–1650* (London: Falcon Press, 1952; Cambridge: Harvard University Press, 1953), rev. and repr. as *Medieval and Early Modern Science*, 2 vols. (Garden City, N.Y.: Doubleday & Company, 1959). Stillman Drake has argued against this influence on Galileo.

86. Cf. O. Neugebauer, *Mathematische Keilschrift-Texte*, vol. 2 of *Quellen und Studien zur Geschichte der Mathematik, Astronomie und Physik*, pt. A, *Quellen*, 3 vols. (Berlin: Springer Verlag, 1935–1937). Also his *Vorgriechische Mathematik* (Berlin: Springer Verlag, 1934). Convenient presentations in English are O. Neugebauer, *The Exact Sciences in Antiquity*, 2d ed. (Providence: Brown University Press, 1957); and B. L. Van Der Waerden, *Science Awakening*, trans. Arnold Dresden (New York: Oxford University Press, 1961). A measure of the astonishment is seen in the fact that the Pythagorean theorem was known in Mesopotamia as many centuries earlier than the time of Pythagoras as we find ourselves later than that time.

87. See the George Sarton memorial issue of *Isis* 48, pt. 3 (1957), containing a bibliography of all his publications. An intimate portrait was penned by his daughter, May Sarton, *I Knew a Phoenix* (New York, Toronto: Rinehart and Company, 1959).

88. This three-volume work, containing respectively 840 pp., 1252 pp., and 2155 pp., was published for the Carnegie Institution of Washington by Williams & Wilkins, Baltimore, 1927, 1931, 1948. Sarton was a staff member of the Carnegie Institution most of his scholarly life, though stationed in Cambridge, Mass., where he was a lecturer and then Professor of the History of Science.

89. See n. 112 *infra*.

90. Sarton's correspondence is now in the Houghton Library of Harvard University.

91. See G. Sarton, "Auguste Comte, Historian of Science," *Osiris* 10 (1952): 328–57.

92. On this aspect of his career, see the article by Thackray and Merton cited in n. 9 *supra*.

93. See Charles C. Gillispie's article on Koyré in *Dictionary of Scientific Biography* (New York: Charles Scribner's Sons, 1973), 7:482–90; Yvon Belaval, "Les recherches philosophiques d'Alexandre Koyré," *Critique* 5, nos. 207–8 (1964): 675–704.

94. A bibliography of Koyré's writings to 1967 may be found in I. B. Cohen and René Taton, eds., *Mélanges Alexandre Koyré*, vol. 1, *L'aventure de la science* (Paris: Hermann, 1964), pp. xiii-xvii. Major works or collections not included in that bibliography are: *Newtonian Studies* (Cambridge: Harvard University Press; London: Chapman & Hall, 1965), *Metaphysics and Measurement*, *Essays in Scientific Revolution* (London: Chapman & Hall; Cambridge: Harvard University Press, 1968), *Études d'histoire de la pensée scientifique* (Paris: Presses Universitaires de France, 1966), *Études d'histoire de la pensée philosophique* (Paris: Librairie Armand Colin, 1961). Koyré's masterpiece, the *Études galiléennes* (Paris: Hermann, 1939, reprinted 1966), is not available in an English translation.

95. This statement is translated by Gillispie (n. 93 *supra*), p. 485, from Koyré's statement published in German in 1922 and again in French in 1961; see *Études d'histoire de la pensée philosophique* (cited in n. 94 *supra*), p. 30, n.1.

96. Cf. Gillispie (n. 93 *supra*), p. 487.

97. *Études galiléennes* (cited in n. 94 *supra*), pp. 1–2.

98. Koyré doubted that Galileo's inclined-plane experiment would succeed as well as it does in the description given in the *Discorsi*, or *The Two New Sciences*, and dubbed this an "expériment imaginaire." But it was later shown that the experiment was easily reproducible, giving results equivalent to Galileo's. Cf. Thomas Settle, "An Experiment

in the History of Science," *Science* 133 (1961): 19–23. Koyré insisted on a Platonic influence on Galileo's thought, and supposed this to have led him to rely less on experiment than had been generally assumed by scholars. For a view contrary to Koyré's, see Maurice Clavelin, *The Natural Philosophy of Galileo: Essay on the Origins and Formation of Classical Mechanics*, trans. A. J. Pomerans (Cambridge and London: M.I.T. Press, 1974); and Stillman Drake, *Galileo Studies: Personality, Tradition and Revolution* (Ann Arbor: University of Michigan Press, 1970).

99. Neugebauer's editions are exemplary in that he gives us photographs of each clay tablet, then a drawing or transcription of it, followed by a transliteration and a translation. On this basis he then produces an interpretive commentary. Clagett also gives us a text, translation, and commentary for each major document.

100. It should be emphasized that the purpose of edited texts is to serve as a basis for interpretative commentaries. Often the latter follow the texts by many decades. An example is the *Commentariolus* of Copernicus, first published from a Vienna manuscript by Maximilian Curtze in 1878; republished, on the basis of a collation of this text with another manuscript, by Leopold Prowe in 1884. Translations appeared in German in 1899 and in English in 1937; and the latter was printed again (with annotations) by Edward Rosen in *Three Copernican Treatises* (New York: Columbia University Press, 1939). But it was not until 1973 that a full explanatory commentary was published by Noel Swerdlow—based upon a new translation of his own. Cf. N. Swerdlow, "The Derivation and First Draft of Copernicus's Planetary Theory: A Translation of the *Commentariolus* with Commentary," *Proceedings of the American Philosophical Society* 117 (1973):423–512.

101. The first volume was published by Cambridge University Press in 1967; the sixth in 1975. The edition will be completed in eight volumes.

102. The first nine volumes were published by the University of Wisconsin Press from 1965 to 1973; vol. 10 (1975) bears the imprint of Mansell (of London).

103. This work will appear in the Swiss edition of Euler's works. Euler's chief Paris correspondents included Clairaut and D'Alembert.

104. Thomas S. Kuhn, *The Structure of Scientific Revolutions* (Chicago: University of Chicago Press, 1962), issued also as vol. 2 of the *International Encyclopedia of Unified Science*, 2d ed., enl., 1970. For a response to Kuhn's analysis, see Imre Lakatos and Alan Musgrave, eds., *Criticism and the Growth of Knowledge* (Cambridge: At the University Press, 1970), comprising a primary paper by T. S. Kuhn, followed by critical discussions by J. W. M. Watkins, S. E. Toulmin, L. Pearce Williams, K. R. Popper, Margaret Masterman, I. Lakatos, P. K. Feyerabend, plus a final "Reflections on My Critics" by Kuhn. Among many reviews and review articles, particular attention may be called to those by Gerd Buchdahl, Dudley Shapere, and Israel Scheffler. The propriety of using the word and concept of "revolution" in relation to science is discussed by Stephen E. Toulmin, in the course of a lengthy historical narrative of, and critique upon, Kuhn's views, in his *Human Understanding*, vol. 1 (Princeton: Princeton University Press, 1972), pp. 100–117, and esp. pp. 117–18.

105. Cf. I. B. Cohen, *The History of the Concept of Scientific Revolution* (New York: Science History Publications, in press), and also the article cited in n. 75 *supra*.

106. Cf. the study of the Antikythera mechanism (cited in n. 25 *supra*); Price has also done considerable work on astrolabes.

107. *Science since Babylon* (cited in n. 21 *supra*), chap. 5. Among the important novelties reported by Price is that the number of journals has grown exponentially, rather than linearly. But, above all, the continuities he has found in growth since the seventeenth

century have emphasized the break in continuity or real mutation that occurred at the beginning of modern science, thus documenting in a wholly new way the existence and significance of the Scientific Revolution.

108. Two journals especially devoted to science and policy, *Minerva* and *Science Policy Studies*, contain historical articles. At the University of Montreal there is an active graduate program in which the history of science is combined with science policy studies.

109. One area that has been left out of consideration in this article is the relationship between the history of science and the philosophy of science. This omission is due to considerations of space and the necessary limitation to the central core of the history of science. On this topic in general, see I. B. Cohen, "History and the Philosopher of Science," in *The Structure of Scientific Theories*, ed. with a critical intro. by Frederick Suppe (Urbana, Chicago, and London: University of Illinois Press, 1974), pp. 308–73. See also the volume edited by Roger Stuewer cited in n. 15 *supra*, and Laurens Lauden, "Theories of Scientific Method from Plato to Mach, a Bibliographical Review," *History of Science* 7 (1968): 1–63. Of notable interest is John Lossee, *A Historical Introduction to the Philosophy of Science* (London and New York: Oxford University Press, 1972).

110. Cf. the earlier discussion of this topic on pp. 89–90.

111. An interesting format for the history of science has been developed at the University of Minnesota, where two professional historians of physics have been appointed to the physics department, a historian of biology to the biology department, and a historian of technology to the engineering school. There are also two full-time historians of medicine in the medical school.

112. I am all too aware of the fields of activity in the history of science that have not been mentioned in this report. They include Islamic and Indian science, science in Asia (notably Japan) other than the work of Needham, some aspects of ancient and medieval science, and the spate of scholarly activities on such figures as Copernicus, Galileo, Kepler, Newton, and Darwin. It should be clear that I have not attempted any overall survey of the many fields of the history of science, for which a ready introduction to the literature is available through the annual critical bibliographies published by the History of Science Society in *Isis*. These bibliographies, from 1913 to 1965, are currently being cumulated under the editorship of Magda Whitrow; the first two volumes have been published under the title, *Isis Cumulative Bibliography* (London: Mansell, 1971).

5

Intellectual History: Past, Present, and Future

Paul K. Conkin

I begin with a widespread response to the assigned topic: Intellectual history has had a brief but glorious past, suffers a beleaguered present, and has no future. But such a pessimistic judgment, expressed in a number of recent obituaries, is overly indulgent and thus irresponsible. It begs the crux of the issue—what does one mean by "intellectual history"? Quite apart from any definitional precision, intellectual history became a widely affirmed label of self-identity for American historians in the 1940s and 1950s. Its broad appeal undoubtedly lay, in part, in the very diversity of subjects that clustered under the ambiguous label. In the fifties, when I finished graduate school, it seemed the most fashionable label open to young historians, even as today other faddish and equally loose labels, such as social history, are ascendant. Intellectual history now seems as dated as narrow ties. It takes a peculiarly reckless graduate student to don the label and move with it into a perilous job market, where fads always reign supreme. But, as you suspect, I am not here to offer a postmortem on ephemeral fashions.

Definition leads us into the maze of historical subspecialities. Here any scheme is challengeable, for all such efforts are formal and to some extent arbitrary. We cut the human past up by chronological periods, by geographical area or political boundaries, by distinguishable areas of human interest, effort, or achievement (economic history), by reference frames (comparative history), by the breadth of people it encompasses (social history), or, quite misleadingly, by the extrinsic purposes of a historian (radical history) or even the research or analytical tools used (quantitative history). But in what I believe to be the most precise use of the term, intellectual history fits within none of these classifications. Its subject is too essential to the genus to be a mere species. It is not parallel to such subclasses as political and economic history, for its subject is as broad as the class—human history—and necessarily overlaps any subclass.

The use of a symbolic language, and thus talking out loud and talking to oneself, is a form of behavior distinctive to man. It interacts with other distinguishable modes of behavior. But these other modes are in all cases shared at least with the higher animals. Because of his linguistic ability, or in more expansive terms—his intellect, reason, mind, soul, or spirit—man has a cumulative verbal culture. Even his most unthought habits embody the conditioning effects of past thought. Differently expressed, almost everything man does reflects shared meanings and projective purposes.

By definition, any history is time-specific, for the order of events, when they take place and in what relationship to prior or subsequent events, is necessary to historical understanding. But this is true of natural history, of the history of an electron, a mountain, or a tribe of monkeys. What is most distinctive about human history is not time, but the essential role of a verbal culture. Loosely put, ideas are a part of any human history, and not only the most distinctive part but, by our usual interest, by far the most significant. We ask not only what people did, but in a special sense not applicable to mountains or dogs, why they did it. Our most crucial whys relate to purposes tied to language. When we have no access to a human language, we cannot understand what we as historians most want to know about a human society. We can record the wanderings of a past tribe, but until we have some clue to its meaning system, unless we can decipher its shared goals, we can only guess as to why each spring it moved up a mountain. We may assume its members sought greener pastures for their flocks, when in fact the summer solstice lured them to a closer communion with their sun god.

Man's enormous power over the rest of nature, his ability to unite in end-unified communities, the immense variety and richness of his conceptual creations all depend on language. Thus, any historian of the human past must attend to meanings and to the special teleology they make possible. To understand a battle, the military historian must grasp a general's strategic thought. The economic historian must unearth the economic concepts and normative beliefs that helped shape economic aspirations, work habits, or government policies. Since any historian has to understand the thought component of his subject, if he is to understand it at all, the intellectual historian cannot distinguish himself by his mere attention to concepts and beliefs.

This allows only a rather perverse definition. An intellectual historian is one who concentrates, if not exclusively, then predominantly upon past concepts and beliefs. He is thus distinctive, not by what he includes but only by what he leaves out. It is the unique character of language and thought that allows such an exclusive focus. The economic or political historian cannot ignore the concepts and beliefs that give sense to their specialized topics. But the intellectual historian can exclude or subordinate the nonideational events that always interact with man's conceptual activity. At least the more systematic products of human thought—a scientific theory, a philosophical movement—have a coherence and a thematic unity totally apart from all manner of conditioning circumstances. Even in isolation, they permit intelligible histories.

What about traditional distinctions between a broad, contextually rich and integrative intellectual history and a narrow, analytical history of ideas; or between an external and an internal approach to ideas? My definition is broad enough to encompass all such distinctions. One may use the label "history of ideas" to characterize specialized histories of a philosophy, a science, or a theological tradition, and reserve "intellectual history" for ambitious efforts to characterize the mentality of large groups, the intellectual characteristics of a whole country, or even the spirit of a whole age.[1] Thus, generality, breadth, synthesizing goals, and interpretive daring most distinguish the work of intellectual historians, who almost have to blend empirical data with speculative theory. This approach is most evident among European cultural historians, who often turn to Hegel, Marx, Freud, or Sartre for unifying but always controverted perspectives. But so long as a history, broad or narrow, focuses on concepts and beliefs, on the content of thought, it fits within the domain of intellectual history as I have defined it.

Language and the meanings it makes possible certainly alter the content of human consciousness, imagination, feeling, and perception, even as these influence the content of thought. But these mental attributes are all more primitive than thought. Neither is distinctive to man; neither requires language. A dog imagines, feels, perceives, and by almost any definition is conscious, at least when awake. Thus, by my definition, these aspects of mental life are not in themselves the subject of intellectual history. In Kantian language, intellectual historians do not deal with forms of perception but with conceptualization and categories of judgment. Likewise, expression and taste, however conditioned by thought, involve much more than thought. The history of an art, including literature, or of man's varied response to an art, is more than intellectual history, although all such subjects have their ideational components (a body of esthetic theory, or the beliefs that influenced artistic creativity or shaped an artistic movement). These alone exist exclusively within the domain of the intellectual historian.[2]

The distinction between external and internal usually encompasses, not the subject of intellectual history, but how the historian deals with a subject. The burden of any historian is to infer, from present artifacts, what happened in the human past and, within a very restricted range of causes, why it happened. This means he must fully understand a belief if it is the prime subject of his inquiry. Thus, external understanding must not mean some loose labels for an otherwise incomprehensible complexity. But we can validly distinguish between ideational causes and a broader, nonideational context that nonetheless has a great deal to do, if not with the exact content of thought, at least with its taking place. We can look only at the antecedent beliefs that made possible a new scientific theory. This ideational or internal explanation is most integral to my definition of intellectual history but, for complex reasons, often horrifies academic historians when it remains the only explanation. But once he has located such ideational causes, and I think this is his primary obligation, an intellectual historian can, often with great profit and without violating my definition, look to the external context—to a biography of the intellectual who produced the new theory, to the practical urgencies that motivated it or gained for it wide acceptance, to the public policies that supported research in the field, to the educational institutions that created a congenial work environment. But an intellectual historian does this only in order better to understand and explain the particular theory or the intellectual universe it occupies.[3]

Another inherited and confusing issue is ontological. The problem almost defies clear statement, although it involves the status or nature or role of something called ideas or thought or even reason. Do ideas precede or follow objective reality? How do they relate to action? Are they causal or caused? Here, in the very assumptions underlying such questions, we meet again the old ghost insecurely occupying a machine, or Platonic essences floating above a shadowlike material world. Such approaches to language and thought rest on psychological and philosophical assumptions at least a century out of date and lead to archaic conceptual ontologies, either idealistic or materialistic. They invite antinomic dualities. On one hand, ideas make up a higher reality, or even the only reality, and the dynamic and material world is a shadow of ideas or in some sense shaped and controlled by them. Intellectual history is thus the primary form of history, the essential key to all else. Nonsense, say critics. The material universe is alone real, and ideas are an ephemeral product of it, subsequent in time and in order of being, dependent, a reflective product rather than in any sense a determinant of what happens in the real world. The historian should seek concrete, material causes, and note ideas only as they reflect or provide clues to the underlying "forces" that control human destiny. Such reasoning accounts for some of the foolish and sophomoric dilemmas that, to my despair, I keep meeting in our profession.

By our most disciplined understanding of the world we keep bumping into, or at least that part that we have artfully reduced to manageable concepts, language and thus thinking is a natural tool despite all its wondrous gifts. It is a tool that we are now teaching chimpanzees. (We may soon be able to make sense of what other talking primates do, or write authentic histories of their colonies, for with language the apes will be able to live in true communities—that is, under modes of social organization and cooperation made possible by shared meanings.) The meaning of a word, the image or images it stimulates in the brain, rests on social convention. A child learns to form words, and learns their conventional meaning much as he learns to walk or to throw a ball. Insofar as there are any regularities, and there seem to be many, governing how higher animals learn, then man even in learning to talk and to think exemplifies these regularities, as behaviorists have always insisted. But how one learns is a distinct issue from what he learns. The meanings learned accumulate through time, change continuously and at varied rates, and are only roughly entombed in dictionaries. Meanings, as such, do not exist. For the word "exist," as we usually use it, properly denotes dynamic relationships and thus only physical objects. It is part of a "thing" language. What "exists" in a language, therefore, is only the physical entities that contain and convey meanings—memory cells, eardrums, explosions of air, or, as a secondary code, marks on paper. But meanings, though by definition nonexistent, are real enough and a vital, I am tempted to say the most vital, part of our experienced world.

A psychologist may rightfully focus on learning processes, on physiological or behavioral regularities. But the historian and the cultural anthropologist must focus also on the almost infinitely variable meanings used in human societies. But such a concern with meaning does not propel historians into an esoteric and separate realm of being. It simply changes the object of inquiry. The concepts I now employ in writing this essay, and which I hope I share with you, are fully correlate with many physical and behavioral processes, processes not distinguishably different if the meanings were the very opposite of those I now intend to convey. Given a physical perspective, talking is a physical process, involving atoms and molecules. Organically, it is physiological, involving cells and nerves and muscles. From a biological perspective, it is a highly adaptive mode of behavior. The sum of all this: talking and thinking are natural activities and not unreal or ethereal in any sense. But they do so separate man in function from other animals as to lend support to all his past pretensions of divine eminence. Finally, thinking is fully interactive with other modes of behavior, as much shaped as shaping, caused as causal. It invites only endless confusion to rend this interactivity, to search for some temporal or causal primacy either in ideas or in some material substance. Such a rending leads to the very ontological traps that have so long haunted that elusive word "idea." Many people habitually attach to it an ethereal connotation, either to demonstrate its sublimity or to damn its elusiveness and ineffectuality.[4]

As usual when I finish defining, I have a precise but very limited class. Few academic historians make concepts and beliefs the exclusive subject of their inquiry and teaching. I place no great value on such purity and deplore any overly myopic specialization. Yet, when I think of intellectual history today, I contemplate either a growing volume of narrowly specialized studies in such topical areas as the history of theology, philosophy, political theory, or scientific theory, or a few exceedingly versatile or at least very reckless college professors who either teach survey courses in one of these areas or, worse, try to blend the work of specialists into reasonably well integrated courses in American or European thought. Those who teach such broad surveys may bore deeply into only a few technical areas. Alternatively, they may skirt intricate theoretical subjects and instead trace the more generalized and derivative beliefs of a fashion-setting intelligentsia, with literature, criticism, and even types of journalism serving as sources along with popularized religious thought, philosophy, and science.

I am quite aware that my definition of intellectual history has only a tangential relationship to much that has passed as intellectual history in this country. But even from my narrowed perspective, the past is too complex for adequate summation here. Emphasis upon the role of language and thought in human history goes back to the Greeks. The place of ideas reached an exaggerated emphasis in the work of several nineteenth-century German historians and philosophers.[5] If we look at very basic and systematic beliefs, or to the self-contained disciplines in which they developed, we can find reasonably pure interludes of intellectual history in America as far back as the Puritan historians. In the nineteenth century, our theologians and our philosophers became increasingly self-conscious about their heritage. I still find Josiah Royce's *The Spirit of Modern Philosophy* (Boston and New York: Houghton, Mifflin, 1892) our most perceptive and useful history of German idealism. Religious historians still use Frank H. Foster's *A Genetic History of the New England Theology* (Chicago: University of Chicago Press, 1907). Since 1900 we have enjoyed or suffered a stream of books on church or denominational history, on European and even American philosophy, and on aspects of political and economic theory. Isaac Woodridge Riley's *American Thought from Puritanism to Pragmatism* (New York: H. Holt, 1915) and Randolph G. Adams' *Political Ideas of the American Revolution* (Durham, N.C.: Trinity College Press, 1922) fully conform to my definition of intellectual history and are clearer in concepts and more rigorous in use of evidence than their better-known successors. Extensive work in the history of the physical and biological sciences developed late in America, but today this field exemplifies, short of the multiplying studies of New England theology, our most fully developed and most sophisticated intellectual history.

The usually accepted American beginnings of a self-conscious speciality in intellectual history rests, not on such specialized scholarship, but on the sweeping generalities and sermonic purposes of Vernon Louis Parrington. Or, if one looks for his progenitors, in the literary history of Moses Coit Tyler, in the culturally sensitive work of Henry Adams, in Turner's efforts to account for distinctive American institutions, and in the broad social and cultural interests of such so-called new historians as James Harvey Robinson and Preserved Smith. These progenitors, and particularly Tyler, gave more overt attention to concepts and beliefs than most political and economic historians, although they rarely made ideas the primary object of their inquiry. In the twenties, both Carl Becker and Parrington did organize books around beliefs, however presentist they were in their understanding of such beliefs. Parrington first tried to characterize all of American thought, and thus set an enduring precedent, although few of his successors ever wrote as dramatically or distorted so consistently. Drawing on literary sources, broadly defined, he tried to find distinctive intellectual themes in America and, as Turner and Beard before him, gave particular honor to an elusive but much beloved "democracy."[6]

Parrington also attended to a beguiling but treacherous issue as old as Tocqueville, Emerson, and Whitman—the secrets of American exceptionalism. Concern with the distinctive attributes of an American civilization would long provide an almost irresistible motif for American historians. This was true in the more thematic and analytic approach of Ralph Gabriel [*The Course of American Democratic Thought* (New York: Ronald Press, 1940)], for the myth and image school begun in 1950 by Henry Nash Smith,[7] and in the endless search for an American character that so typified early programs in American Studies or American Civilization. This identity issue, born either out of national pride, a sense of cultural inferiority, or the concern over lost unities and purposes that so typified the cold war years, has usually led historians far beyond distinctive ideologies to broad social institutions and to artistic achievement. But even when broader in subject than intellectual history, such inquiry has usually been less than intellectual history in its propensity for loose labels and for its reliance on merely suggestive forms of evidence.

Academic historians, as they began to deal extensively with belief, usually remained loyal to their training and past interests. They eschewed narrow specialization and rarely had any competence in exceedingly technical areas such as science and philosophy. Thus, they tried to relate different modes of thought, find unifying and more general themes, and above all integrate "ideas" into a broader social context, often with a much greater concern for extrinsic causes and enduring influences than for the exact content of thought. Such goals precluded a myopic narrowness but discouraged loving attention to nuance. This contextual and integrative approach influenced Crane Brinton's pioneering text in European thought and spread even to specialized areas, as reflected in Herbert Schneider's contextual approach to American philosophy or in Joseph Dorfman's tedious efforts to fit economic thought into a broader background.[8]

Merle Curti, who began his honest and almost encyclopedic *The Growth of American Thought* (New York and London: Harper Bros., 1943) in the thirties, did more than anyone else to shape postwar research and teaching in an increasingly self-conscious but still ill-defined field. His book defies easy classification. He keyed it both to the life of the mind in America and to its varied products. He encompassed conventional and popular beliefs but also, within severe space limitations, offered revealing summaries even of highly specialized thought. Yet, Curti was not so concerned with the exact content of thought, or with ideational continuities, as with the social need that underlay the creation or wide acceptance of new ideas, with the fostering agencies of intellectual life, and with the role of various ideas in a society. Since he placed the greatest stress on the external context, he correctly identified his book, not as intellectual history, but as a social history of thought.

But the very technical limitations which Curti acknowledged begged for other integrative or synthetic strategies that could do fuller justice to the content of highly systematic thought. Two such strategies of the late thirties remain milestones in American historiography. In his 1936 book, *The Great Chain of Being* (Cambridge: Harvard University Press), and again in 1940 with the launching of the *Journal of the History of Ideas*, Arthur O. Lovejoy asked historians to locate and trace the rise and fall of very basic concepts, or what he called unit ideas. This was a program fully consistent with my definition of intellectual history and one that invited a less myopic concern with national characteristics. His very difficult analytic approach, borrowed in part from his earlier scientific training and related to his tasks as a professional philosopher, suggested great vertical depth, for key concepts lurked behind changing fashions of language and in the thought of people in many diverse nations, and helped shape many different intellectual disciplines.[9] Few historians had the interest or talent to buy his complete program. Instead they followed the alluring example of Perry Miller, who published the first volume of his *The New England Mind* in 1939.[10] In this book, Miller explored in loving detail every nuance of Puritan religious doctrine, which seemed to serve as a unifying ideology for a whole society. Miller displayed, not the analytical and philosophical rigor of Lovejoy, but an unprecedented sensitivity to language, to its rhetorical form as well as its overt content, its metaphors as well as its syllogisms. By limiting his study to a few small, homogeneous communities, he was able to display a horizontal breadth lacking in Lovejoy, yet without the vagueness or presentist distortions of a Parrington.

Miller was not always as circumspect as in his first masterpiece; few of his disciples were ever so circumspect. In such influential essays as those in *Errand into a Wilderness* or in his tortured biography of Jonathan Edwards, Miller indulged some very suggestive speculation.[11] In a limited text, a sermon, even in a key word or repeated image, he found profound psychological insight or apt symbols for gauging momentous shifts in beliefs and values. He also offered rather sweeping generalizations about something as elusive as an American mind. He thus left a double legacy. His more cautious and precise labors would continue in the detailed monographic exploration of New England thought, often in a narrow community context. This has led, appropriately, to major revisions of Miller's own work. But his example also influenced the growth of much more speculative and sweeping efforts to characterize all of American thought, efforts often tied closely to literary texts and to the less rigorously empirical standards of literary criticism. In some cases, these joined what I have called the myth and image school.

I know of no new approaches to intellectual history. One can still deal with the broad social context of thought, use rigorous analytical methods to explore key concepts or words, work within highly specialized subdisciplines such as the history of science, join Perry Miller in a holistic attempt to chart the most determinant world view of homogeneous societies, or make the treacherous effort to isolate some minimal ideological cement for whole nations or civilizations. Despite the challenging work of John Higham and others, I sense a steady erosion of interest in this last approach, at least for American history.[12] Such a synoptic or interpretative approach begs critical questions. Have all Americans or even most Americans shared any common beliefs or values? Even if we assume they have, can we move beyond presently typical mixtures of speculation and evidence to clear hypotheses and precise research goals? Finally, can we develop research strategies sufficient to give us unambiguous answers to broad questions about collective belief? My doubts multiply with each passing year.

In the last decade, a few intellectual historians have flirted with what might appear to be new approaches. Thomas Kuhn's definition of paradigm, which he used as a key to understanding basic shifts in scientific belief, has become an overly fashionable and near jargonistic term in several disciplines. I now meet it ad nauseam in history. Kuhn joined most pragmatists and positivists in affirming a non-ontological yet instrumental understanding of scientific concepts and laws. This means that scientific formulations are best understood as culturally variable, time-specific historical products, yet as reliable guides to action because of objective canons of verification. Among scientific communities, in a given period, specific theories cohere with a larger disciplinary matrix or, loosely put, with a common body of basic assumptions. When adherence to such a paradigm leads to practical failures or intellectual anomalies, the scientific community moves on to some new paradigm. This theory has led to extensive and very intricate controversies among both historians and philosophers of science. It easily devolves into truisms or, subtly distorted, supports a form of solipsistic relativism. Whatever its validity for understanding major breakthroughs in science, or possibly in other tight-knit intellectual disciplines, I doubt that the paradigm concept fits within broader and looser contexts, such as the thought of a whole society. When intellectual historians use paradigm, I already sense the verbal pretension that usually accompanies new labels for old bottles. I hear faint echoes of "spirit of an age," and "climate of opinion."[13]

Another beguiling temptation for intellectual historians, particularly when challenged by behavioral scientists, lurks in the structural anthropology most often identified with Claude Lévi-Strauss. More broadly, this reflects goals long present in several strands of continental European thought—to develop an autonomous science of mind or of culture, as rigorous, as predictive, as useful as the physical sciences. This entails either some underlying structure in all languages (a metagrammar), some universal cultural symbols, or some controlling mental substratum. In some very abstract theories in anthropology and linguistics, theories accepted by only a minority of experts, historians have found new support, if such was needed, for the interdependence of language and thought and for the essential role of both in human behavior. But the universalist motif of all such theory, the desire to develop generalizations and laws that either govern or set specific limits to cultural creativity, is as ahistorical as past attempts to reduce human thought to mere reflections of controlling material laws. Here is a path, not to improved history, but beyond history.[14]

If it is difficult to find the history of intellectual history as a field of inquiry in America, it is almost impossible to isolate the story of intellectual history as an academic subject. Here I know very little, and limit my guesses to courses in American intellectual history. As Henry Lee Swint found in a 1955 survey, the origins of courses in American intellectual history remain obscured by an early anarchy of course titles and content. Merle Curti began a course in American thought at Harvard in 1928 and believes that was the first such course in the country, although some medieval historians had already oriented their instruction toward ideas. Curti faced ridicule and had few early imitators. Swint was able to identify less than one hundred hybrid courses with compound labels (social, cultural, and intellectual) before 1945, but noted a rapid expansion after the war. Available texts by Gabriel and Curti surely guided much of the course development. Swint found too varied a content in 1955 for any clear characterization but no evidence of courses devoted exclusively to concepts and beliefs. Outside the special program in the history of ideas, which Lovejoy developed at Johns Hopkins, I doubt if any analytical and rigorous intellectual history courses existed until well into the fifties.

At least, anyone who tried such a course had no textbooks as a guide until Stow Persons published his *American Minds* (New York: Holt) in 1958. A brief, necessarily oversimplified survey, it did move the controlling emphasis away from social context to the actual content of thought.[15]

For those who, like myself, developed new courses in the late fifties, Persons offered a challenging guideline. We tried to do a Perry Miller on each epoch of our past, moving from the religious concerns of the seventeenth century to the scientific and political interests of the eighteenth. We indulged sweeping and loosely unifying labels, such as enlightenment, romanticism, naturalism, and irrationalism, or labels I now just as carefully repudiate. We also turned to such thematic books as Herbert W. Schneider's *The Puritan Mind* (Ann Arbor: University of Michigan, 1930); Daniel Boorstin's *Lost World of Thomas Jefferson* (New York: Holt, 1948); Richard Hofstadter's *Social Darwinism in American Thought, 1860-1915* (Philadelphia: University of Pennsylvania, 1944); and Morton G. White's *Social Thought in America: The Revolt Against Formalism* (New York: Viking, 1949). To note how superficial Hofstadter or White seem to me today is only to indicate how much detailed monographs have fleshed out and deepened our understanding of every epoch and almost every topic that then seemed almost manageable. With greater sophistication came unbearable complexity and also room for divergent tastes to lead instructors off in a hundred highly individualized directions. Persons' book is now out of print. No one has tried better to fulfill his purposes, publishers indicate no clear market, and I doubt if any scholar is now brave enough, or competent enough, to try to integrate even a few major topics, such as religion, philosophy, and science.

A brief, and surely very unrepresentative, sample of a few intellectual historians (29) at the 1974 American Historical Association meeting revealed almost as much anarchy as Swint found in 1955. The most popular course titles in American history, among twenty-three listed, included slight variations of "American social and intellectual history" (6), "American intellectual history" (5), and "American thought and culture" (4). Single titles included "Movements and ideas," "History of American thought," "Major themes in American thought," "American ideas," and "American thought and language." Only three courses reflected any narrower specialization, and these were all in religion. By the instructors' own judgments, very few courses (only 4 of 22) dealt exclusively with ideas. In all other cases either social or cultural themes shared the billing. Likewise, exactly half of the instructors described their approach as largely integrative, or an effort to fit concepts and beliefs to a broader social context. Five more included this as one of two approaches. Only three described their course as primarily analytical or as tied to specialized belief systems, although two more made this one of their concerns. Only two emphasized popular beliefs, and only two made national culture or character a primary concern. Almost all courses were junior-senior level. The size of the university did not correlate with any of the above patterns. If at all representative, this survey indicates that hybrid courses, with diverse subjects and a broad contextual approach still prevail, or roughly what Curti outlined in his 1943 text. Perhaps because of my own experience, I had expected more specialization, a clearer separation of social and cultural history into distinct courses, and a more analytical or technical approach to ideas.

What is the future for historical inquiry and instruction devoted almost exclusively to past concepts and beliefs? What seems to me most important for history is not how many people specialize in such a narrow field, but that all historians correctly understand the concepts and beliefs that are interactive with their research topics. This means that all historians need skills that are presently best understood, appreciated, and taught by intellectual historians. More important, I find valid educational goals, and thus a moral imperative, behind my own research and teaching in intellectual history. But such lofty vindication may have less to do with recruiting young intellectual historians than personal interest. Even here I am sanguine. The very difficulties of intellectual history—the specialized training and philosophical skills required to master highly original and systematic beliefs, and the difficult research skills demanded by the elusive, formless, and well-hidden beliefs of mass men—should continue to fascinate some of our most brilliant and versatile graduate students and overcome the negative pull of presently ascendent fashions.

Intellectual historians often feel defensive and beleaguered today, not so much because of valid criticisms of their past failures as because of certain superficially persuasive objections to their whole approach. They are, so critics argue, elitist in subject and archaic in methods. In a new age of scientific history, they remain captive to older, humanistic biases and resist both the new revelations of the social sciences and new research techniques that are now revolutionizing historical inquiry.

The elitist charge raises many issues, particularly since the word "elitist" is as vague as it is pejorative. But in one possible sense of the word, intellectual historians surely want to plead guilty. John Dewey, whom no one could accuse of elitism, tried for much of a lifetime to fathom the distinctive attributes of human communities and the sources of cultural change. The secret of such change, he found, is in man's luxuriant and almost infinitely variable conceptual creativity. In the midst of complex conditioning environments, and out of a qualitative rich experience, man continuously adds new images or meanings to an inherited language. The most intense or problematic experience is the most fruitful fount of meaning modification. And, despite a necessary social context and at times immense public implications, meanings always undergo change in the mind of an individual. Some new meanings remain private, or seem of no interest to anyone else. But some new concepts, and the new propositions and anticipations they allow, eventually become commonplace in a society. New concepts and beliefs are adaptive tools that literally transform the world, as have religious and scientific beliefs in the West. The point is clear. If the intellectual historian seeks out the origins of enduring belief he will always end up with creative individuals. They may not have been brilliant or powerful, but they had immense influence. For example, if I want my students to understand the beliefs of millions of Mormons today, I would begin by taking them back to the early doctrines of one man—Joseph Smith. If this is elitism, I enthusiastically endorse it.

It is true that most present intellectual historians, not only in seeking out the origins of belief but in selecting topics for research and teaching, choose to deal with exceptional men and women and with more coherent and systematic types of thought. In this, they join literary historians who focus on more gifted and influential writers. Their choice of subject reflects, not any necessity of definition, but their own selective criteria. As all historians, they have to select a few topics, for they have neither the time nor the tools to explore more than a few aspects of man's past thought. I hope they, as all historians, select those topics that seem most appropriate to their moral and educational goals. Surely we should try to discover the truth about those aspects of the past that seem most important or instructive. More often than not, as I struggle to inform students of a vast heritage of religious, philosophical, or scientific beliefs that live on either in their own unremarked beliefs or, more often, in their behavior, I find I must turn back to original or influential progenitors. Does this mean that I have contempt for the beliefs of the common people? I can only ask—which common people? From all that I can gather, the typical students who sat before me, however intelligent, are almost completely ignorant in these areas. Are they not part of the common people? I want to provide them with a better understanding of who they, or their immediate neighbors, really are. I want to show even casual Presbyterians why they still reflect certain attitudes or do certain things. To so inform them, I often lead them back to John Calvin or even Augustine and Paul. I see nothing elitist in my purpose, and I can think of no better way to fulfill it. But I do admit that such purposes are not all controlling. Intellectual historians become connoisseurs of belief systems, almost collectors, and most easily respond to elegant or systematic products of the human mind. Esthetic and logical criteria have a great deal to do with their selection of subjects.

But what about the beliefs of common people in the past? All people think, and all reflect the conditioning influence of past thinking in their habits. Also, the brilliant scientist may be depressingly conventional in religious beliefs, a novice in comparison to a zealous and uneducated Bible expert from the hills. Originality is cheap, easily attained by anyone and most easily of all by undisciplined minds. Subtlety marks thought at every social level, and if anything nuances multiply when we move away from the already structured and carefully restricted intellectual disciplines. Of course, the eccentric and original, the undisciplined or unprophetic beliefs of individuals rarely have enduring significance. They persuade few others and, being unwritten, become lost as soon as village memories fade. What most historians want to understand are widely shared beliefs, however stereotyped and conventional. These influence the rich and powerful as much as the poor or inarticulate; in fact, politicians usually are experts at voicing them. Commonplace beliefs, or even unarticulated assumptions, may not exert any considerable influence on the development of an intellectual tradition, but they surely help determine enduring patterns of behavior—how people organize their societies, how they worship, how they appease or control the physical world, how they vote. Such beliefs are the most critical but also the most elusive variables in group behavior. The data on such conventional belief are often thin, opaque to detail and nuance where these make all the difference. Here the historian often has to turn to a type of elite, past or present—back to the prophetic originators of now widely accepted beliefs or to literate and perhaps systematic advocates in the present. For example, one may have to turn to church confessions, to printed sermons, or to denominational periodicals even to risk any inferences as to what parisioners believed about God.

In the sixties, both fervent political commitments and a widespread fascination with new research tools underwrote an increasing historical interest in mass man and added to the growing status of social history, however defined. This pushed the issue of mass belief, or of popular mentalities, into the forefront. If intellectual historians would only explore the beliefs of the working classes, they could be on the right side politically and also make use of the newly fashionable research tools required for disciplined inferences from massive but usually thin data. But then the question: what educational objectives justify making popular belief the sole object of study? The pioneering thought of great scientists or philosophers often has immense influence on a society, although usually not for several generations. For a time it remains the property of narrow intellectual communities and often involves such intricate logic or such esoteric language as to be comprehensible only to a specialist. If specialized intellectual historians do not attend to such belief, its origin and development will remain a hidden and uncriticized aspect of our past. Other historians simply do not have the needed interest or skill to understand it. This helps justify the exclusive focus of specialized intellectual historians.

What about more conventional beliefs? I do not mean to imply that these are transparent to any historian. Far from it. Such beliefs may be very elusive and require great sensitivity in a historian. But my point is this—if we are to have truthful history in any field, then all historians have to deal successfully with conventional belief. In no sense can this be a separable task reserved for a few intellectual historians. Social historians have to fathom, in subtle detail, the shared beliefs of the population whose behavior they want to understand. Why not leave the task of understanding mass belief to them, with their broader research goals and, presumably, broader educational goals? Why not, indeed, if they do it well? By my observation, few historians acquire enough conceptual sensitivity to treat basic beliefs, particularly religious beliefs, other than loosely or superficially. Few appreciate fully the role of language, the importance of meaning, and the essential place of belief in the life of common people. At present, intellectual historians may need to bring their skills to bear on conventional beliefs in order to raise the quality of nonintellectual history. But I doubt that many intellectual historians will develop a sustained interest in the most conventional forms of belief or feel it educationally worthwhile to isolate them from the broader and often more fascinating social context in which they function. Esthetic and logical tastes, plus educational goals, work against such a choice. Thus, my guess is that intellectual historians who become absorbed with mass beliefs will soon move on to much broader nonideational aspects of the past. And I bless them in their new task. If they retain their sensitivity to meaning, and learn statistics, they should become our best social historians.

Now that I have conceded that most intellectual historians are elitists, I want to give my blessings to their humanistic purposes and their purportedly archaic methods. But first I must admit that much criticism of something called American intellectual history is well taken. For critics, the field often seems to consist largely of the earliest and crudest myth and image approach, the most hackneyed quest for an American character, the consensual and idealistic excesses of the 1950s, or the loose generalities and moralisms of a Parrington. It means vague generalizations about an American mind or an American civilization, based upon a highly speculative interpretation of a few literary artifacts with open-ended evidential value or upon very loose sociological or psychological theories. That is, it entails largely what I have excluded by definition. When I think of intellectual history, I think above all of conceptual precision, of endless definitions and distinctions. I also assume the highest possible canons of verification. In fact, the well-trained intellectual historian will never make confident inferences beyond his immediate subject, whether it is what one man believed or what certain doctrines or theories really entailed. Almost by definition, contemporary training in intellectual history involves the highest possible analytical and methodological standards. This alone may push intellectual historians even more toward highly specialized but very narrow subjects.

Because the intellectual historian concentrates so exclusively on meaning, and thus on the ever-variable and least general facet of human activity, he has come to epitomize a humanistic approach to history. The word "humanistic" is, of course, loaded and serves variously as both a compliment and an indictment. But it does, I believe, open to light some issues that vitally concern the future of history. If anything is clear to me, it is the bogus nature of any allegedly inherent conflict between history as a social science and as humanistic understanding. All historians, I presume, want to understand the distinctively human past. Since temporally and spatially variable meanings are the crux of such understanding, all human history is an inescapably humanistic form of knowledge (it encompasses variable cultural determinants and thus what is unique to man). If one wants to understand only the most general and time-neutral aspects of man's past—his environment, physiology, or patterned behavior—and to understand these in isolation from interactive cultural variables, then in purpose he is a generalizing scientist and not a historian, although he may turn to ancient artifacts to increase this understanding. If one concentrates on language and meaning, and thus entirely on the nongeneral aspects of past human behavior, he is by my earlier definition an intellectual historian. Most historians avoid these extremes. They look both to meanings and to a more general or lawful context in behalf of understanding the human past. Their attention to meanings makes them humanists; their attention to a uniform context or universal patterns often leads to a major and fruitful overlap with the work of social scientists.

The historian has a quite distinctive subject—the past career of acculturated, end-seeking mankind. This subject very much shapes the final product of historical inquiry, but in method the historian is at one with all other empirical truth seekers. He has to adhere to the same semantic rigor as any scientist in stating questions, problems, or hypotheses, has to utilize the same logical rules in drawing inferences, and must base his final truth claims on the same evidential tests. Any apology for alternative historical methods, for any form of special insight or vicarious identification, easily becomes an excuse for conceptual sloppiness or for loose modes of verification. Physical and behavioral scientists aspire to general knowledge, to propositions that apply to all members of broad classes—to all electrons, all organic cells, all animals, or all men. They also seek lawful or rigidly probabilistic knowledge, that is, relationships and transformations that hold for all like objects at all times. But for these aspects of behavior conditioned by meaning, we can never verify any such complete generality or lawfulness. Meanings change continuously. Culture seems unlimited in its variability. So far, we have been unable to chart any limits to conceptual invention or to find any clear pattern or stages that necessarily characterize it. To know why, in the sense of linguistically conditioned purpose, one tribe climbs a mountain is to have no sure clue as to why another tribe climbs even the same mountain. Some meanings and some beliefs have endured over long periods within particular societies. If we know these, we can isolate stable norms and customs and thus develop limited or closed generality in our historical accounts. I can affirm, with full confidence and excellent evidential support, that all nineteenth-century Hutterites believed in certain specific Anabaptist doctrines. I am not sure they still do and would not dare predict their beliefs or behavior very far into the future. But present beliefs do provide several limiting conditions for any early cultural change; I shudder at the problems that would face any policymaker who tried to rely only upon purportedly general theories in trying to work with the Hutterites.

These commonplace or even truistic observations illustrate, not a fatal weakness in history, but its inherent difficulty and challenge. The human past is the most difficult area of inquiry open to man. To the impediments posed by the passing of time and lack of direct accessibility to a subject, the historian further accepts the difficulty of decoding the elusive secrets of an always heavily nuanced language. For this most critical task, he can fall back on no shortcut, on no general theories that encompass all mankind, on no common human nature, on no preexistent or set body of concepts or any all-controlling grammatical structure, not even on any lawful pattern of cultural development. He has to dig into the particularities of each human community for his answers. This is not to deny generality and uniformity in many aspects of man's physical environment or in aspects of his animal behavior tied to organic structure. Here the historian can take his shortcuts, but these are at best peripheral to much that he wants to know—not why the tribe sought food, or how its members learned to eat or to talk, but what common purposes led them to climb a particular mountain at a certain time of the year. Of course, the more general aspects of life set outer limits, if not for playful conceptual invention, at least for meaning-conditioned behavior. If he wants to survive (even this is subject to a culturally induced veto), man must eat. But given physical options, the beliefs and values of a society determine how its members produce its food, how often they eat, what foodstuffs they consider legitimate, how they eat it, and what larger importance they give to certain forms of eating, up to the redemptive meaning of the Christian Eucharist.

Even if one grants the possibility of humanistic understanding, one can deny the value of such knowledge. And here I can plead but may not persuade, for what I value another may not. Among other uses, historical understanding helps shape our sense of identity, suggests new goals and aspirations, allows us a more creative and varied response to natural imperatives, and either informs our most sweeping criticism of existing institutions or reinforces our deepest loyalties and commitments. And intellectual history, because it focuses so exclusively upon language and thought, seems particularly well fitted for these goals, which are my goals in writing and teaching it. But because of the fragility of many concepts and beliefs, the endless shift in meaning even for the most familiar words, historical knowledge never gives us the universality and necessity that characterizes much scientific knowledge, and it does not lend itself to the same practical technology. If man, even cultural man, were everywhere the same, then the study of his history would be so simple. We could also finally eliminate the sources of human conflict. But because of the way he is, we can only understand cultural man in specific and limited contexts and epochs, as participants in an ever-changing cultural continuum. He remains an irreducible subject, the one nonobject in the world. He only has his past as a secure source of identity. If he comprehends this past, he knows who he is and is well-equipped to determine who he will become. If he knows it not, he is lost, futile, a creature of determining but unrecognized habits. If he thinks he understands his past, but does not, he falls into a very common and very comforting deceit, but sooner or later his unexamined and uncomprehended habits, the heritage of an unknown past, will catch him up in contradictions, ambivalences, and confusion.

My primary concern is with the survival of history, not intellectual history. Today even historians often seem overly fascinated with shortcuts. Maybe we are not up to all the effort. Young people respond to the heady delights of general theories or models of human behavior, which may correctly encompass the physical and behavioral regularities that men share with other animals. But these theories often seem, deceptively, to apply even to culturally conditioned aspects of behavior. If we so understand them, we move back to the parochial optimism of the eighteenth century, and so very quickly will reap the disillusionment that faces anyone who relies upon the early achievement of a complete science of man. I do not offer these precautionary warnings in order to interdict interdisciplinary cooperation or to deny the legitimate contribution of general theories or abstract models to hypothesis formation by historians. Above all, I do not want to deprecate research tools that historians, even intellectual historians, may first learn from researchers in other disciplines, although I must emphasize that formal tools belong to no empirical discipline (it is misleading to talk of social science methods) but to such formal or relational disciplines as logic and mathematics. I very much appreciate electronic tools for storing and sorting massed data and for making rapid computations, just as I esteem statistical tools that both expand and discipline the inferences we draw from that data. Techniques only become dangerous when adopted by the simple-minded, who are inclined to make them an end rather than a tool of inquiry, who easily confuse formal and empirical relationships (statistical determinants are not "causes"), or let familiar techniques rather than moral ends dictate the topics they select for investigation. Yet, one who deplores such tools, or refuses to use them when they could possibly benefit his investigation, is as much a fool as one who believes they constitute some new form of history.

The future of history entails the continued and arduous search for man's multidimensional past, including in every case his beliefs, if possible down to the exact nuance. Even if narrow-gauged intellectual historians should retire from the research frontiers, their concerns and their tools would still need to become the working equipment of all historians lest we continue to pass off distortions to our students. As I work in political history, as I agonize over the limitations of available texts, I most deplore a pervasive superficiality and a vicious presentism in the description of basic beliefs. The highly specialized works of intellectual historians have not had much influence on other historians; their methods remain unknown or unutilized. This is understandable. It is so difficult to know what people meant even by familiar words in the past, and so easy to read our meanings into them. Where present meanings or images are very different, where Dewey's meaning modification has gone on for centuries, we can scarcely avoid imposing some present nuances upon the thought of our progenitors. We all appreciate the past difficulties with words like individualism, democracy, capitalism. Religion now seems the hardest nut to crack, perhaps because of the highly suggestive and metaphorical language of religion or possibly because of more rapid shifts of meanings and interest in this area. Except for a few specialists, I find almost all historians culturally blind in their treatment of religion, a blindness many are at least beginning to recognize.

I am encouraged by three all too gradual developments in our profession—a much greater skepticism about explanatory theories developed in other disciplines or pseudodisciplines (surely we will never have another Langer urging the speculations of Freud upon a gullible profession), a much greater sophistication in research design and in the use of massed data, and at least an expressed concern for greater conceptual precision. The last most pleases the intellectual historian. Because of our interests and the tasks we set for ourselves, we are the technicians of the word. We have to work endlessly with meaning, moving interminably from half-clear concepts to a larger and fuzzy intellectual environment, hoping that the larger whole will inform the part, and then using every new nuance at the conceptual level to further expand our grasp of the whole. We have to build the larger picture, construct, in a particular empirical context, the picture of how a particular people conceived their world and how they acted within it, and only then allow such an empirical and nongeneral and always incomplete picture to provide us guidelines for understanding more and more of the details. To do this, we have to master the logical and analytical tools of the most careful philosophers and become working experts in semantics. We have our special tools, as demanding as any ancillary tools required by historians, from foreign languages to diplomatics to modern statistics. Whether we use these analytical tools in specialized intellectual history or not, we must needs share them with all graduate students, because, unlike diplomatics or statistics, they are needed in every historical field. If historical inquiry is not only to survive in America but continue to mature toward greater clarity and truthfulness, the universities have to maintain a few people with the skills that are the daily bread of intellectual historians. In fact, I fear for the broader dissemination of these tools, for the continually increased rigor they encourage in students, if our profession and our academies do not continue to honor even the most specialized and esoteric masters of pure abstraction.

NOTES

1. As an example of the confusion of labels, Hajo Holborn (in "The History of Ideas," *American Historical Review* 73, no. 3 [February 1968]: 683-95) uses the label "history of ideas" for such broad goals, while Hayden V. White, a historian equally influenced by classic European historians, prefers the term "intellectual history" (see his article, "The Tasks of Intellectual History," *The Monist* 53, no. 4 [October 1969]: 606-30). Maurice Mandelbaum (in "The History of Ideas, Intellectual History, and the History of Philosophy," *History and Theory* 4 [1965], Beiheft 5, "The Historiography of the History of Philosophy," pp. 33-66) carefully distinguishes the broader goals of intellectual history from the narrow and analytical purposes of the history of ideas. Thus, many historians use the two labels to designate the same product, and others to designate quite different products.

2. Despite its inherent ambiguity, I usually employ the term "cultural history" both for the history of the fine arts and for attempts to gauge the spirit of an age or to locate a complex group of mental traits in a population.

3. John Higham draws these same distinctions between internal and external explanation in "Intellectual History and Its Neighbors," *Journal of the History of Ideas* 15 (June 1954): 339-47, but he views them from a more dualistic perspective and sees in the difference a need for basic philosophical choices by historians. I disagree. Mary Hesse, in "Hermeticism and Historiography: An Apology for the Internal History of Science," in *Historical and Philosophical Perspectives of Science*, vol. 5 of *Minnesota Studies in the Philosophy of Science*, ed. Roger H. Stuewer (Minneapolis: University of Minnesota Press, 1970), pp. 134-60, makes the same distinctions but in order to reject an internalist approach.

4. I have borrowed much of this naturalistic, nonreductive, and nonontological understanding of language and thought from Chauncey Wright, Charles S. Peirce, and John Dewey. I sense that such an understanding, so congenial to one in the American philosophical tradition, has as yet had little influence upon European historians. Rush Welter (in "The History of Ideas in America: An Essay in Redefinition," *Journal of American History* 51, no. 4 [March 1965]: 599-614) has used the philosophy of Dewey to defuse some of the polarized conflicts about intellectual history, and comes close to my briefer attempt to do the same thing.

5. See Holborn, "History of Ideas," for an appreciation of Dilthey's contribution to the history of ideas.

6. Carl L. Becker, *The Declaration of Independence: A Study in the History of Political Ideas* (New York: Harcourt, Brace, 1932); Vernon L. Parrington, *Main Currents in American Thought*, 3 vols. (New York: Harcourt, Brace, 1927-30). For the origins and development of intellectual history in America, see Robert Allen Skotheim, *American Intellectual Histories and Historians* (Princeton: Princeton University Press, 1966); Arthur A. Ekirch, *American Intellectual History: The Development of the Discipline* (Washington: American Historical Association Pamphlets, No. 102, 1973); John Higham, "The Rise of American Intellectual History," *American Historical Review* 56, no. 3 (April 1951): 453-71, and "American Intellectual History, a Critical Appraisal," *American Quarterly* 13, no. 2, pt. 2 (Summer 1961): 219-33; and Arthur Bestor, "Intellectual History to 1900," in *Interpreting and Teaching American History*, 31st Yearbook of the National Council for the Social Studies, ed. William H. Cartwright and Richard L. Watson, Jr. (Washington, D.C.: 1961), pp. 133-55.

7. Henry Nash Smith, *Virgin Land: The American West as Symbol and Myth* (Cambridge: Harvard University Press, 1950).

8. [Clarence] Crane Brinton, *Ideas and Men: The Story of Western Thought* (New York: Prentice-Hall, 1950); Herbert W. Schneider, *A History of American Philosophy* (New York: Columbia University Press, 1946); Joseph Dorfman, *The Economic Mind in American Civilization*, 5 vols. (New York: Viking Press, 1946-59).

9. Arthur O. Lovejoy, "Reflections on the History of Ideas," *Journal of the History of Ideas* 1, no. 1 (January 1940): 3-23. See also his *Essays in the History of Ideas* (Baltimore: Johns Hopkins University Press, 1948). Both Mandelbaum, "Ideas, Intellectual History, and Philosophy," and Quentin Skinner ("Meaning and Understanding in the History of Ideas," *History and Theory* 8, no. 1 [1969]: 3-53) dissect what they perceive as severe limitations in Lovejoy's approach.

10. *The New England Mind: The Seventeenth Century* (New York: Macmillan, 1939). This followed his more limited *Orthodoxy in Massachusetts, 1630-1650: A Genetic Study* (Cambridge: Harvard University Press, 1933).

11. Perry Miller, *Errand into the Wilderness* (Cambridge: Belknap Press of Harvard University Press, 1956), and *Jonathan Edwards* (New York: W. Sloane Associates, 1949).

12. John Higham restates the problems, and poses tentative answers, in "Hanging Together: Divergent Unities in American History," *Journal of American History* 61, no. 1 (June 1974): 5-28.

13. The best discussion of "paradigm" as it relates to intellectual history is Robert Berkhofer, Jr., "Does History Have a Future? The Challenge of New Ways of Understanding Past Human Behavior for Traditional Historical Analysis," an as yet unpublished paper delivered at the Organization of American Historians' annual convention in April 1974. A loose defense of the paradigm concept appears in Skinner, "History of Ideas." For a detailed critique of this article and of other purported new strategies developed by John Dunn and J. G. A. Pocock, see Charles D. Tarlton, "Historicity, Meaning, and Revisionism in the Study of Political Thought," *History and Theory* 12, no. 3 (1973): 307-28.

14. See Berkhofer, "Does History Have a Future?" and Hayden V. White, "Tasks of Intellectual History."

15. Henry Lee Swint, "Trends in the Teaching of Social and Intellectual History," *Social Studies* 46 (November 1955): 243-51.

6

The Future of Southern History

C. Vann Woodward

The closest the historian can legitimately get to making pronounce-
ments about the future is the recent past, and the closer the recent past
gets to the present, the more insecure the historian feels in whatever
he has to say about it. His instinct is to withdraw from the present,
which is the brink of the future, and put distance between himself and
the brink to gain the security he likes to call "perspective." The trouble
with the future from the historian's point of view is that it has not
happened yet. Whatever glimpses beyond the brink I shall venture
here will be afforded from a point well back from the edge.

My first impression of the recent past of Southern history is that
there has been more of it. Here I speak in crudely quantitative terms of
sheer number and volume of publications during the last twenty years
or so. For that observation to have much meaning, it would have to be
endowed with that cherished quality of "perspective." It would have
to be placed in context of productivity in other fields of history, indeed
in other fields of learning. The 1960s were exceptionally prosperous
years for universities and for scholarship. Foundations and government agencies were generous with funds, graduate schools were
crowded, jobs were plentiful. It is likely that productivity increased
markedly in many disciplines, including other fields of history be-
sides Southern history. Whether Southern history was exceptional in
this respect, and if so to what degree, it would be premature to say. All
that seems possible at this time is a few tentative soundings and
estimates.

With apologies for citing a personal experience, I might offer the recent historiography of the brief period between Reconstruction and the First World War. In 1951 there appeared a volume treating that period entitled *Origins of the New South*. Twenty years later a second edition was published that included a supplementary bibliography prepared by Charles B. Dew, who compiled a critical list of works on this field that had appeared in the two decades since the original edition was published. A comparison of the bibliography of 1951 with that of 1971 is rather startling. A valid comparison requires elimination of the half of the list of 1951 that covered primary sources, government documents, newspapers, periodicals, and such materials. A comparison confined to secondary works of scholarship, however, discloses only 16 pages listing such works in the first edition and 112 pages in the second, and a count of individual titles comes to 311 in the one and 1,905 in the other.[1]

I hasten to say that this does not necessarily prove that more than six times the number of works were produced in the period between 1951 and 1971 than were published in the period of more than three times that length since 1913. For one thing the original bibliographer was probably more selective than the second, and for another the second bibliographer was probably more thorough and systematic than the first. I am at least sure that the second was more scrupulous in rounding up dissertation titles—granting there were more such titles to be rounded up in the latter period.

Allowing for these and other probable discrepancies in the comparison and for the delinquencies of the party of the first part, I am still persuaded that the contrast is significant. While I doubt that the ratio of productivity between the periods was quite six to one, I would feel confident in guessing that considerably more scholarly works on the New South era were produced in the two decades following 1951 than had been produced in all the years preceding, perhaps twice as much, perhaps more than that.

In all these estimates and those that follow it is well to keep in mind how brief has been the enterprise of scholarly investigation of Southern history. Putting aside the literature on the Southern Confederacy, especially its military aspects, and that on the local history of various Southern states, David Potter remarked in 1961 that "the history of the South as a region—of the whole vast area below the Potomac, viewed as a single entity for the whole time from the settlement of Jamestown to the present—is largely a product of the last five decades."[2] In that foreshortened perspective, it is less surprising that the products of two decades can account for such a large proportion of the whole. Especially so when it is recalled that those years came in the period after most of the learned journals of the field were launched, the great research collections were established, and courses and seminars in the subject had gained recognition in the leading universities of the country. Earlier historians of the South had labored without many of these advantages.

Whether activity on the post-Reconstruction period has been representative of productivity on other periods of Southern history it is difficult to say. No comparison of bibliographies such as those used for the New South period has been attempted for any other period. Were such comparisons available, they might well prove that other periods have outstripped the one observed. For what it is worth, my impression is that at least in the last fifteen years publications on the antebellum period, the Civil War, and Reconstruction have exceeded in number those on the period following. I have also been impressed with recent activity in colonial history, and the Revolution would seem to be undergoing a somewhat artificially stimulated boom that is, of course, national rather than regional.

So far we have spoken only in crudely quantitative terms—titles listed, books published, productivity in the market and manufacturing sense. These terms are not appropriate to the measurement of products of the mind. They do not even prove that the mind is involved. In too many instances it is not. The mindlessness of much academic productivity is all too apparent. If I have appeared to be rather casual in my quantification methods so far, it is attributable not merely to laziness but also to contempt for numbers as evidence of things of the mind. They may constitute mere evidence of misdirected energy or lax and low standards on the part of professors, editors, publishers, and critics. My guess is that these latter influences play a large part in accounting for bulging bibliographies and publishers' lists in recent years.

Any serious reckoning of the progress and future of a field of learning will shun numbers and turn from criteria of quantity to criteria of quality. These are, of course, even more difficult to apply and to agree upon. I can report, however, a considerable amount of agreement among knowledgeable critics with high standards that there has indeed been a gratifying improvement in quality. One evidence of improvement is found in the learned journals, and I quote the present managing editor of the *Journal of Southern History* as follows:

On the whole, I agree that there has been an improvement in the quality of the *Journal* articles over the years. There are fewer narrative and descriptive articles and more interpretative ones; there are more articles on blacks and slavery with a more balanced approach; there are more articles on urban history and more on the recent South; and there are more sophisticated quantitative articles. Much of the material is in a sense less southern than it is writing about topics relating to the South.[3]

I have undertaken no survey of professors offering graduate and undergraduate courses in Southern history, but I suspect that the experience of many in selecting essential secondary works for required reading would correspond with my own—viz., that a large percentage of such books in the required list have been published in the last twenty years. In my own list of required books for a yearlong graduate course, for example, 14 of a total of 29 fall in that category. I hope this does not merely betray a vulgar bias for the contemporary as against the old—a bias especially repugnant in historians—and I do not think it is that. At least a lot of old-timers, including U. B. Phillips and Charles Sydnor still retain honored places. It would be interesting and possibly revealing to see how many of what are now considered the most essential or important scholarly books on Southern history are missing from Rembert Patrick and Arthur Link, *Writing Southern History*[4]—not because that excellent study of historiography ignored or overlooked them, but simply because they were published later —that is, since 1965. My guess is that it might take more than the fingers of one hand to number them. And again I disavow the vulgar bias of contemporaneity.

Whether one finds this impressionistic evidence persuasive or not, it will be my assumption that something unusual has happened recently to a field of scholarship long considered parochial, out of the mainstream, marginal in importance, and comparatively dormant. What has happened, I believe, is that this field has suddenly emerged in a position of central importance in national history, disclosed more relevance to the history of foreign peoples than any other American field, and attracted more than its share of first-rate talent. In addition, or as a consequence, it explodes with innovations in interpretations, findings, revisions, and methodology, and discharges a flow of intellectual excitement that spills over into other fields.

My second assumption is that this is a phenomenon of American academic and intellectual life that calls for explanation of a kind to which the historian himself is peculiarly qualified to contribute. A start on this task is the main purpose of this essay. An incidental hope is that the effort might also lift a corner of the curtain that veils the future of the field of Southern history.

It will nessarily be an exercise in multiple causation, for the explanation is complex. The causes might be divided tentatively into two categories—the fortuitous and the inherent. By the fortuitous I mean the unforeseeable accidents of history, the shifting fortunes of chance and coincidence, the unearned increments. By the inherent I mean causes more directly attributable to the nature and riches of the subject—of Southern history itself. It will quickly become apparent that this dichotomy is of limited usefulness because the fortuitous and the inherent tend to overlap and intertwine. Since there is likely to be less controversy about the unearned than the earned, the rewards of chance than those of merit, it might be best to turn first to the fortuitous.

It was not chance that brought on the Civil Rights Movement, the drive for Negro rights, the demand for the study of black history and culture, or the great northward and cityward migration of millions of Southern black people. But it was chance or coincidence that all these events served to stimulate interest and work in Southern history. That certainly was not the intention of these upheavals. But anything touching Afro-American experience leads inevitably back to Southern history, and black history is inextricably interwoven with white.

Undoubtedly much of the historical writing inspired by those movements was superficial, propagandistic, or chauvinistic. On the other hand, without the direct or indirect stimulus of the social upheavals it is impossible to explain or even imagine the subsequent advances of serious scholarship in the history of slavery, abolitionism, emancipation, sectional conflict, reconstruction, segregation, and race relations—not to mention progress in the neglected field of black history more strictly defined. The main, if not exclusive, historical theater for all these subjects, of course, lay below the Mason and Dixon line.

For a century after the Civil War the South was an importer and consumer of cultural determinants and subjects for historical investigation—the North the exporter. The Southern historian was consequently concerned with the impact of such importations as big business, the corporation, Wall Street, urbanization, progressivism, and radicalism. A common response was that the South also had its urban problems, progressivism, and radicalism—even its frontier democracy: that the South was "American too." More recently the balance of trade in cultural determinants seems to be swinging the other way, with the South the growing exporter, the North the main importer. For one thing, the South has exported millions of its black people and along with them patterns of culture, housing, schooling, poverty, segregation, and politics—generally called "urban problems"—that had long been considered peculiarly Southern. By 1975 they were more commonly associated with Boston than with Little Rock. It has been seriously suggested that Northern politics is being "southernized." Increasingly, the North looks to the South for the historical roots of its problems, as the South had once looked to the North. To a degree Southern history has been nationalized as a subject of concern.

This is one, but by no means the only, reason for the rapid recent influx of non-Southern historians into the field of Southern history. In the old days there were always a few Northern historians who kept a hand in Southern history. Some of them, like Albert Hart, Frederick Bancroft, or Dwight L. Dumond, whose chief concern was to set Southerners right "on the goose," continued the old tradition of sectional debate and confrontation. Others like William A. Dunning and later Paul L. Buck carried on the nationalist tradition of sectional reconciliation. In the main, however, Southern history was written and taught by Southerners. When the editors of the multivolume *History of the South* planned their series in the 1930s, every one of the ten authors originally selected was a Southerner. It has not been so many years since Northern visitors to a meeting of the Southern Historical Association were relatively rare. One met Southerners and heard papers by Southerners. All that has changed. The attendance at a Southern Association meeting is now little more regional in character than one of the national association meetings, and the same applies to the authors of the papers. In the scholarship of certain fields, notably slavery, Reconstruction, and social history, non-Southerners have taken the lead and set the pace. Fortuitous or not, this has surely been a powerful cause of the renaissance in Southern history.

More clearly fortuitous and unearned as well as more subtle was the heritage of the Southern Literary Renaissance. Although its heyday was over before the boom in Southern history was well started, it served as an example and inspiration in several ways. For one thing the men of letters demonstrated beyond doubt that there was nothing in the subject matter of Southern history that prevented it from being treated with utmost seriousness by men of higher talent or from commanding the attention and capturing the imagination of the reading world at home and abroad. If historians had been inhibited by the feeling that their subject was somehow too discredited or parochial or backward or degraded to deserve the highest concern, they could banish their doubts. The novelists and dramatists taught historians other lessons, if any needed them: that to understand they need not justify, that to recount or recapture the past was not to celebrate it, and that defense had best be left to propagandists. The hallmark of the highest Southern fiction was history-mindedness. Historians could derive such pride as they might from evidence that their own muse won homage from craftsmen who served another muse with such fidelity and distinction.

There was yet another means at hand for overcoming the sense of parochialism and isolation under which Southern historians once labored. This was the rather recent discovery of the possibilities of comparative history with which the Southern experience was peculiarly endowed. And here we shift from the category of the fortuitous to that of inherent causes. For a long time the South suffered under the sense of the irrelevance of its past, a past that was out of step, a throwback to forgotten eras, a perverse survival of bygone styles and ways into modern times. In that way the modern South thought of its experience of aristocracy and hierarchy, of slavery and patriarchy, of paternalism and deference, of race and caste, of personalism and the familial ambiance, of colonial dependence and economic backwardness. Of course, the South's point of reference as the supposed norm in all those matters was the Northern or non-Southern part of the United States. What the South forgot was the North's boasted exceptionalism, its pride in escaping the ills that plagued the South's experience and that of other unfortunate peoples, together with its well-grounded myths of affluence, innocence, and invincibility—The American Way. What the South has recently discovered is that in the very peculiarities of its past that it had long considered eccentric, irrelevant, and out of step, the South's historic experience was more relevant and in step with many other peoples of the world and their heritage than was the history of the North. If any history was eccentric and out of step, in this respect, it was that of the rest of the country.

The South could claim shared experiences and institutions with many Old World peoples, but its closer claims lay to commonality and historic kinships with New World societies. The South was the major member of the great community of nations and colonies that made up Plantation America. That vast cultural community stretched eastward from Texas along the Gulf and through the Caribbean to remote Barbados, and southward from Virginia to far-off São Paulo. With dozens of societies once under the flags of several empires the Southern states shared the experience of slavery and plantation, the presence and influence of large numbers of people of African origins, styles of racial subordination and intermingling, and styles of aristocracy, patriarchy, paternalism, authority, caste, and deference, patterns of abolition, emancipation, and reconstruction, and post-manumission experiments with apprenticeship, sharecropping, and peonage. The antebellum South was the largest, wealthiest, and most powerful of the Plantation America societies. It clung to slavery longer than most, but not so long as Brazil and Cuba, and it was the only one of them that chose to fight an all-or-nothing war for survival.

The South, like most societies, sought to understand its past in part by comparison. It was only belatedly that it discovered that in picking the North it had chosen an incongruous partner for comparative purposes. Only lately and more logically has it turned for comparative illumination of its past to those countries of old Plantation America which had shared so many aspects of it. The result has been much more light upon the South's history than could be shed by comparisons with Massachusetts, Michigan, or Minnesota. Suggestive studies have been made comparing slavery in Virginia and Cuba, South Carolina with Barbados and Jamaica, and various aspects of the history of race relations by comparing the South with Brazil and with Caribbean societies.[5] So far, New England and the Middle West seem to have inspired no such comparative history, and short of the sociological abstractions of mobility, demography, and technology, it is difficult to know where such opportunities lie or where suitable comparative partners for such an enterprise might be found. The point is that Southern history has benefited singularly from this line of inquiry because of its special character and that this development has contributed significantly to its enlivenment as a field of study.

The next explanatory variable, to borrow a sociologism, might be said to combine the fortuitous and the inherent. At least elements of each category play a part in the explanation. Here the categories overlap and intertwine. On the fortuitous side is a secular slump in the national morale cycle. This happens whenever the national myths of affluence, innocence, and invincibility are seriously threatened, especially when all three are jeopardized simultaneously as they have been by the combination of depression, Watergate, and South Vietnam—to mention only a few of several such menaces to myths. A familiar side effect of such slumps in the morale cycle is a falling off in Yankeedom of the normal enthusiasm for such perennial historical themes as progress in urbanization and industrialization, technological advance, the westward movement, immigration, ethnic voting, social mobility, and the rise of the middle class.

As usual when that happens, historians turn away from familiar themes of the bland, the homogeneous, and the hopeful that sustain nation myths and seek contrasting themes. This may take any of several directions. The oldest alternative, the one William R. Taylor chronicles in *Cavalier and Yankee*,[6] is escapist and romantic, the quest for lost grandeur: silver on polished mahogany, white-columned porticoes, and, to quote a forgotten poet, "pistol-hearted horsemen who could ride like jolly centaurs under the hot stars." It still has lingering appeal for some, but other alternatives take priority. One is the search for what went wrong, the moral lesson, the serpent in the garden, the American genesis of wickedness and perversity. Broader still is the simple need for something different, some striking contrast to the bland, the hopeful, the homogeneous—even something wickedly un-American, darkly tragic, or catastrophic. All these "explanatory variables" fall in the category of the fortuitous.

The consequences, however, take us at once into the category of the inherent. Where else could the seekers more logically turn for that which they sought than to the history of the South and its notoriously inherent qualities? Where else, within national boundaries, could they have found so abundantly available all the varieties of contrast? Both the substance and the trappings of grandeur were there, and also the serpent, the perversity, the wickedness of aristocracy, the inequality, the towering pretensions and the precipitous fall, the catastrophe and the tragedy—all as un-American as one could well wish. As for the pall of blandness, homogeneity, and cheerful optimism, the rise and fall of the slave empire and the heritage of defeat that followed provide the perfect contrast. Between master and slave or white and black there were few ambiguities in the line of authority, little blurring of class lines, and no nonsense about homogeneity and equality on those fronts. The myths of affluence, innocence, and invincibility strike few roots in such soil.

The attractions of these riches have been irresistible to many seekers from above the Potomac and the Ohio—seekers of the exotic, seekers for new moral lessons to teach the South, seekers for startling new interpretations of its history. They have swelled the ranks of non-Southerners in the field and contributed substantially to the recent expansion of activity in Southern history. Their stay will probably be as temporary as the impulse and the needs that attracted them southward. Many of our scholar carpetbaggers will soon withdraw with what they came to get. They will leave behind many contributions, some of undoubted value, but in the process of evaluating the whole it might be well to count our spoons, so to speak, and take a close look at the fine print in the documents bequeathing the legacy they left.

Among the many types of newcomers attracted southward recently, none were so strongly attached to the field and none left a more ironic legacy than the newly spawned tribe variously named quantifiers, econometricians, or cliometricians. Whether the explanation is mainly of the fortuitous or the inherent type, the fact is there seems to be a fatal attraction and a durable relationship between the quantifiers and Southern history, particularly but not exclusively the history of slavery. From the very inception of the econometric movement with the famous essay by Conrad and Meyer on the profitability problem in 1957[7] down to the ambitious volumes of Fogel and Engerman in 1974[8] and the deluge of controversial criticism and comment, pro and con, precipitated by their work since then, the field of battle has lain below the Potomac. It has not been North versus South, but rather a battle waged on Southern soil between factions of an alien army. A few Southerners were recruited in their ranks, but mainly Southerners have remained noncombatant if fascinated spectators. No other theater of scholarly historical activity of all the varied Southern theaters has attracted so much attention or prompted so many bets on the outcome as this. Few of the spectators have mastered the weaponry or understood the tactics of the new warfare, but they had no trouble grasping the issues involved.

The stakes have not been so high since Grant and Lee squared off in the Wilderness. What was at issue was the outcome of a renewed debate over virtually all the ancient issues of the furious nineteenth-century sectional conflict that ended in the blanket moral indictment of Southern society. All the old issues were dragged forth: cruelty, slave breeding, brutal punishment, the whip and the branding bar, family separation, child sales, sexual exploitation, feeding, clothing, housing, medication, the horrors of the slave block and the slave trade, the whole abolitionist bill of indictment. Only this time the contestants were not fierce-eyed abolitionists and infuriated planters, but factions of fierce-eyed econometricians ranged in confrontation behind their batteries of computers.

The tide of battle swayed back and forth, and the outcome seemed doubtful. First Manassas raised false hopes and perhaps Vicksburg and Gettysburg were still to come. It would be a long war. But during the campaigns of '74 and '75 hopes soared along the Rappahannock and rebel yells echoed all the way to the Mississippi. It looked for a time as if Generals Fogel and Engerman and their disciplined regiments had turned the flank of opposing forces and were driving all before them. They had the advantage of numbers, and numbers counted—so to speak. Numbers were said to prove that slaves of the South were well fed, adequately clothed, comfortably housed, and reasonably well medicated. Materially they enjoyed many advantages over contemporary industrial free labor in the North and Europe, since they received larger real wages, had longer life expectancy, and a lower percentage of their output was withheld from them as profits. Brutality was rare, whippings were few, broken families were exceptional, child sales minimal, family integrity was carefully fostered, and slave breeding was virtually nonexistent. Under expert planter management and dedicated overseers, the majority of them black, slave labor far outstripped free agricultural workers of the North in efficiency and productivity and accounted for one of the wealthiest, most productive, and rapidly growing economies in the world. And furthermore, the 70 percent of whites who owned no slaves and the slaves themselves, to a degree, are said to have shared these blessings.

Many of these points were strongly contested, and pockets of resistance that were overrun in the general advance put up determined defense behind the lines. They were expecting reinforcements and their ammunition was not yet exhausted. On the other hand, the broad strategic advances seem rather more secure: that slavery was highly profitable, slave labor comparatively efficient and highly productive, and the Southern economy, at least in the closing decade of the old regime, extremely wealthy, sanguine about the future, and booming along at a great rate. Most of the shooting that continued among the hosts of quantification was not over these major points, but rather over the correct explanation: whether the stick or the carrot, the cowhide whip or the Protestant ethic. This is not the place to assess the merits or predict the outcome of this running war between cliometricians.

The only concern here is to estimate its impact upon the field of Southern history and particularly upon the Southerners who write and teach in this field. There can be little doubt that the work of the quantifiers has contributed substantially to the recent revival of interest and work in slavery and related subjects. Indeed it has altered the whole landscape of the old field. The question is how Southern historians will respond, particularly to the bold revisionism that professes to lift the whole subject out of the plane of moral recrimination in which it has so long languished.

Before making this timid foray into the future, however, the historian would characteristically halt for "perspective." First we should recall that when the cliometricians unexpectedly appeared with reinforcements, the South had scarcely emerged from the dugouts into which it was driven by the long barrage of moral charges ensuing from the Civil Rights Movement, desegregation, and Black Liberation. During that long siege any head lifted was promptly shot down. To explain or account for any and all of the ills that beset the black people in the Northern ghettos—deterioration of the black family, desertion of black fathers, mounting welfare rolls, soaring crime rates, increasing drug addiction, multiplying dropouts, and declining school performance—the answer was always the same: "Look away! look away! look away! Dixie Land!" It was all due to evils of long ago and far away—slavery, racism, peonage, or whatnot, way down South in the land of cotton—which, of course, could not possibly be remedied by further strains on the city budget of Boston or New York, and which could not in any reasonable way be attributed to the shortcomings of the free enterprise system and the deterioration of industrial capitalism.

But even before the recent siege, Southern historians had long cowered under a lower-keyed sniping from members of their own guild up North that intensified in the 1950s. The pattern of fire is familiar to aging survivors of that era. It did not appear planned or deliberate or even consciously malicious. Nevertheless, among a prominent school of historians, whatever appeared retrograde in national history, whether among the Founding Fathers, the Jacksonians, the Populists, the Bryanites, or the Progressives, was somehow attributable to Southern votes or influence. The tendency is familiar to any reader of the more popular books on Populism and Progressivism. As for those movements that lay clearly beyond the pale—fundamentalism, prohibition, mobism, McCarthyism—the South was assumed to be more directly responsible. To this school of historians the debit side of Tocqueville's tally sheets on democracy lay almost entirely below the Potomac. To extremists of the school the South was "marvelously useful as a mirror in which the nation can see its blemishes magnified," or "a kind of Fort Knox of prejudice—where the nation has always stored the bulk of its bigotry."[9]

Subjected to a generation or more of such treatment, with a heritage of the sort stretching even further back, Southern historians gradually acquired a vocational handicap, a permanent stance of apology and a posture of defensiveness often complicated by writer's cramp and in severe cases total paralysis. Their lectures and writings often limped along with lamentations about how bad it all was, ritual citations of Thoreau, Emerson, and Sumner, and concessions about the good intentions of John Brown. A less common reaction to the same situations on the part of a few historians was a posture of defiant bellicosity. It is hard to say which produced the more unhealthy climate for the professional welfare of historians, which shackles curtailed their freedom the more.

Then suddenly the cliometricians arrived on the scene waving an emancipation proclamation. Brushing aside questions of the legitimacy of the document, they promised to liberate the oppressed, strike off their shackles, turn the tables, throw abolitionists and neoabolitionists on the defensive, and vindicate the South. The question is how would the liberated react? Crippled by generations of bondage, were they prepared for freedom? Were they ready for equality? Might they not abuse it? Might they not interpret freedom as freedom from work, freedom from observance of the established canons of their craft, even freedom from the canons of historical evidence? Might they not acclaim the "higher law" doctrine of their liberators? What were the anarchical consequences of putting the bottom rail on top?

Before the new freedmen celebrate their Day of Jubilee prematurely, they should remember that the war that promises their liberation still rages and that the fortunes of war may change. Already serious questions are raised about the authority of the emancipation proclamation. It has been dismissed as executive fiat, lacking legislative approval and popular support, and probably unconstitutional. It undoubtedly deprives privileged classes of long-cherished rights and immunities which they will stubbornly defend and subverts the moral order that separates good and evil along established geographical lines. All these matters still await adjudication, and some call for the slow processes of constitutional change.

Finally, to abandon strained metaphors, I would simply caution fellow Southern historians against being the first to embrace the latest fashions, especially those demanding total revision. They should have observed from past instances that quantification almost invariably proves that things were not so bad before the revolution—any revolution. That is why radicals shun quantification like the plague. It is, on the other hand, a favorite resort of *ci-devant* radicals. We have enough to be grateful for from the quantifiers without uncritically accepting gifts with both hands. They have enormously enlivened and helped to rejuvenate large parts of Southern history. They have also had an important hand in lifting the fog of provincialism that had obscured the significance of the field.

Other forces have, as we have seen, contributed mightily to all these desirable ends. We have already mentioned the contributions of the Southern Renaissance in letters, the enrichment brought by comparative history, the intensified interest in black history, and the recruitment of many Northern historians of talent. The list would not be complete without mentioning the contributions of the new American school of revisionary Marxists. Renouncing with scorn the propagandistic history and vulgar determinism of the older generation of

American Marxists, the revisionists have brought the zest and independence of an Oedipal rebellion to their rediscovery of Southern history. With refreshing logic and boldness Eugene D. Genovese asks how Marxists can consistently contend that morals are determined by class interests and then withhold from planter statesmen and leaders the admiration due them for the loyalty, courage, and devotion with which they served their class. The historical works of the new American Marxists have been predominantly concerned so far with Southern history and related subjects. The whole field has profited from their intervention.

With all these windfalls and endowments from both fortuitous and inherent sources, it is little wonder that Southern history should have forged to the front in recent years and become the most active frontier of American historical scholarship. It might also be reasonably designated the most intellectually stimulating and innovative field, the one in which new techniques are most often tried and tested, where ideological skirmishing is liveliest, on which movements for racial and social justice impinge most readily, and to which Northern historians most naturally turn to escape the blandness of consensus and the drabness of homogeneity.

In full awareness of such riches, the Southern historian who is also a Southerner, white or black, has special reason for pride in his field —though none for complacency in its present state of development. Endowed with ample riches, he can afford to extend generous hospitality, even to strangers and outsiders—even if their ways are a bit eccentric and their accents rather strange. There is plenty for all down on the old plantation. Its resources are such that the historian should have no fear of exhausting them by overwork. He should feel sufficient security in his heritage never to be tempted to raise his voice in argument over its worth. As a historian with proper respect for his muse, he would never stoop to pick up ancestral polemics of the proslavery or antislavery argument. He has more important things to do. For the small domain of history he calls his own has more than its share of the triumphs and the anguish, the honor and the shame, the comedy and the tragedy that are the classic subjects of great history.

NOTES

1. C. Vann Woodward, *Origins of the New South, 1877-1913* (Baton Rouge: L.S.U. Press, 1971); see the original bibliography excluding primary works, pp. 499–515; Charles B. Dew's "Critical Essay on Recent Works," pp. 517–628.

2. David M. Potter, "The Enigma of the South," *Yale Review* 51 (1961), reprinted in his *The South and the Sectional Conflict* (Baton Rouge: L.S.U. Press, 1968), p. 3.

3. S. W. Higginbotham to C. Vann Woodward, January 3, 1975. The same editor indulges in a bit of harmless quantifying in his annual report of October 1974. While in the year 1964–65 he received 99 articles, rejected 81, and accepted 18, in the year 1973–74 he received 142, rejected 132, and accepted 7. He speaks ominously of "a large backlog, which is only gradually being reduced."

4. Rembert Patrick and Arthur S. Link, eds., *Writing Southern History: Essays in Historiography in honor of Fletcher M. Green* (Baton Rouge: L.S.U. Press, 1965).

5. Herbert S. Klein, *Slavery in the Americas: A Comparative Study of Virginia and Cuba* (Chicago: University of Chicago Press, 1967); Carl N. Degler, *Neither Black nor White: Slavery and Race Relations in Brazil and the United States* (New York: Macmillan, 1971); and Philip D. Curtin, *The Atlantic Slave Trade: A Census* (Madison: University of Wisconsin Press, 1969).

6. William R. Taylor, *Cavalier and Yankee: The Old South and American National Character* (New York: G. Braziller, 1961).

7. Alfred H. Conrad and John R. Meyer, "The Economics of Slavery in the Ante Bellum South," *Journal of Political Economy* 66 (April 1958): 95–130.

8. Robert W. Fogel and Stanley L. Engerman, *Time on the Cross: The Economics of American Negro Slavery* (Boston: Little, Brown, 1974).

9. Howard Zinn, *The Southern Mystique* (New York: Knopf, 1964), pp. 217–263.

7

Latin American History in World Perspective

Woodrow Borah

Before I deal directly with my topic, the future of the historiography of Latin America,[1] let us look at the varieties of history as they are written about Latin America now and in the fairly recent past. We must also look at the clustering of the scholars who produce such works—for, at least in the writing of history, the shape and movement of present trends are an important guide to the probable structure of the future.[2] In the chain of life there is no way that a generation can appear except as child and heir of the previous one.

One of the most striking features of the writing of history of Latin America today and in the past two centuries is that it is a truly international endeavor, pursued on three and increasingly on four continents. Unlike the study and writing of United States history, it is characteristically multilingual, and the enriching but also limiting play of school and fashion comes to bear much more imperfectly, so that Latin Americanists tend to be more general in their approach and in their command of subfields. Unlike the study and writing of European history, which is indeed multilingual and carried on on a number of continents, work on Latin America is not firmly centered on the home continent with important centers beginning to develop elsewhere. Latin American historiography, in the sense of a serious attempt to analyze or describe human experience on one segment of the planet, has had almost from its inception a strong series of centers in Europe, most notably in Spain, Portugal, France, Germany, and Great Britain. Scholarship in centers in the United States has moved from a brilliant but episodic beginning to a steady outpouring of descriptive and analytic work. The countries of Latin America have indeed contributed their share, but for long periods of time that share has been less innovative and less responsive to the twin requirements of rigorous empirical technique and command of synthesizing theory as against simplistic application of ideology, theology, or some form of philosophy. A further addition to the study and writing of history of Latin America has come since the Second World War through the increasing interest of the socialist countries in a hoped-for area of unrest and explosion. Accordingly, there have arisen sections dedicated to the writing of Latin American history within the Soviet Academy of Sciences, and the same interest is reflected in small, growing groups in the German Democratic Republic, Czechoslovakia, Poland, and Hungary.[3] In more recent years the Chinese People's Republic too has begun to study Latin America,[4] so that we may see the development in the immediate future not of one but of two or more socialist schools. Finally, I should mention the beginning of study and writing of Latin American history in Japan, still a modest effort, but one certain to grow.[5] Since it arises in institutions closely linked to American thinking and methods, it is as yet an extension of the intellectual sphere of the United States although likely rather quickly to develop distinctively Japanese approaches.

The territorial extent of a continent and a half, the international character of effort, and the need to cross the lines of national states and cultures have meant that Latin American historiography in Europe and the United States continues to have an interdisciplinary flavor that most other fields of history in these non-Latin American areas have lost and now try to regain. (What I say here applies far less to work within Latin America, where history is national and must meet another set of needs.) Among the older themes one may list rather obvious ones directly related to romanticism, *exotisme*, and the national interests of the writers. A number of generations have now poured forth works on the voyages of discovery and expeditions of exploration and conquest. The meeting of Indian and European has been another favorite theme, from mere conquest to the mixing of race and culture, the qualities of zones of frontier, and the great missionary endeavors that have made Latin America Christian. Perhaps the most notable territorial zone for such studies of penetration, mixing, and conversion has been the vast arid area of northern Mexico and the Southwest of the United States (including California), where the combined efforts of two groups of local historians supplemented by the interest of national scholars and anthropologists have led to an abundant literature with much insight. The brilliance and the drama of the shock of European civilization and the high aboriginal cultures of

Middle America have also led to a series of notable studies in history and anthropology, at their best a mingling of both disciplines. Imperial systems, their diplomatic maneuvers, their rivalries, their wars, have been another favorite theme that often reflected the national interests of the writer; it has had a continuation in studies of diplomatic and commercial relations of a Latin American country or countries with the writer's home country; or if written by a Latin American, those of his own country with others. A much pursued vein has been associated with the Wars of Independence, particularly through biographies of leading figures, such as Simón Bolívar, Francisco de Miranda, José de San Martín, Miguel Hidalgo, and José Martí. Lastly, studies of economics, politics, and social patterns, in their historical development, have been abundant but only occasionally notable.

In the last two generations, and especially since the Second World War, one may find a great diversification and enrichment of the studies combining historical dimension and anthropology. There has come into being the term "ethnohistory" to describe the best of the new output and the inextricable mingling of interest and techniques. Institutional and legal history have been pursued with greater zeal but most important of all with far better command of sources and knowledge of context. The basic impulse for legal history here came from the Spanish school centered around the *Revista de Historia del Derecho Español* and the new institutes created in Spain at the close of the Civil War.[6] Finally the vastly enlarged quantitative and analytical approach exemplified in the work of the famous VIe Section in Paris has given fruit for history of Latin America in a number of quantitative and statistical studies, of which the largest, most impressive, and perhaps most frightening is the famous study of Pierre and Huguette Chaunu, *Séville et l'Atlantique, 1504–1650*.[7] In short, there has been in Europe and the United States, despite the temporary subtraction of the formerly impressive German effort,[8] a vast outpouring of work, impressive in its exuberance, in the increasing maturity of its command of historical techniques and materials, and in its resort to increasingly sophisticated forms of analysis.

The role of Latin Americans in the post–Second World War outpouring has been somewhat different, necessarily so since Latin Americans are studying their own national histories and have different needs and purposes. They are caught in the need to create the national legend and strengthen the emerging national state; they must live in societies in which in general the supply of trained professionals is still so scant that their countries cannot afford the luxury of an independent, objective scholar nor one dedicated exclusively to writing and university teaching.[9] So they must fulfill a variety of professional, administrative, and propagandistic functions, and their choices of theme and approach are accordingly influenced or even directed. They write texts for school use, with the content conforming to the directives of the national Ministry of Education. Much of their study is concerned with creating a suitably inspiring history of the fatherland, appropriately called *historia patria*, celebrating the deeds of the great men who have created that fatherland and most of all those who were responsible for political independence (the *próceres*). A more up-to-date version extols those who have tried to build a strong independent state or achieve economic independence, especially from the United States (such as Benito Juárez, Getulio Vargas, or Fidel Castro Ruz). In this kind of writing, objectivity in approach is an impediment and contradictory evidence an impertinence. As Diego Rivera commented about the finding of a commission of scholars that the purported discovery at Ixcateopan of the bones of Cuauhtémoc, the last Aztec ruler, was undoubtedly false, there are a national verity and national imperative that lie above all historical evidence.[10] A similar attitude infuses much historical writing directed to prove the validity of ideological or philosophical positions.[11] Historiography becomes propaganda to shape the future. Almost all historiography in socialist countries is openly within this category.[12]

Nevertheless, there has always been a body of Latin American scholars who have achieved as great a measure of objectivity as their European or American counterparts, perhaps because of independent income, some quirk that placed them outside the mainstreams of preoccupation with national development, or a blessed element of simple human cussedness. Since the 1930s and increasingly since the Second World War this body has been reinforced by the slow adaptation of Latin American scholars to the newer methods and ideas developing in Europe and the United States. The Spanish refugees as university teachers have notably improved intellectual standards and performance. Further, among the newer generation, students have been sent to Europe and the United States for specialized training; especially visible have been the scholarships awarded by the French government for work at the VI[e] Section. Accordingly, there is developing a corps of scholars in Latin America, very often with foreign training but also with local training at the hands of people formed abroad, that is in touch with the wider currents of thinking and development of new techniques. As an example, I may mention El Colegio de México, in Mexico City, organized originally by Spanish refugee scholars as La Casa de España, thereafter reorganized as El

Colegio de México, with Mexican budget and increasing participation of Mexican scholars. Through the efforts of Daniel Cosío Villegas, it has organized and successfully carried through to completion a mammoth history of Mexico from 1867 to 1910[13] and has created new organs,[14] new library resources, and has trained two new generations of Mexican scholars. Throughout Latin America, the prestige of that which is most acceptable in Europe and the United States, rather than politely praised by Pan-American gatherings, strengthens the adherence of such groups to the better of the new models.

Historiography ultimately is a function of trained manpower, allocation of social resources to maintain it and to provide it with the means of acquiring data, and finally a means of dissemination of the product. The outpouring of Latin American historiography in the last twenty-five years has been based upon a notable expansion of these basic elements; one might almost talk of an explosion. In Europe and the United States expansion began with the close of the Second World War or the recovery of the early 1950s in the growth and proliferation of universities and of public resources available to students and teachers. In the United States, former teachers' colleges or new campuses erected in what were once woodland or arable have sought intellectual fields of research that could be pursued with relatively few or rapidly assembled resources. It is in these that there has been a proportionately greater emphasis on Latin American studies, of which history is a major segment. Canada in this sense is a repetition of the United States. In Europe the impulse has been more restrained, but significantly larger groups of advanced students and teachers also have entered the field, backed by relatively generous government subvention.[15] Perhaps the longest-term development, going back to the early 1940s, has been the creation of an impressive apparatus of institutes and chairs in Spain upon the victory of Francisco Franco, with the dream of reviving the influence of Spain in lands of Spanish speech.[16] The Generalísimo, if one can accept gossip, at first saw himself as a twentieth-century embodiment of Ferdinand and Isabella; later he found his truer prototype in Charles III. The result, however, for Spanish scholarship has been very substantial increases in budget and facilities for the study of Latin America, mostly of themes of the colonial past rendered more palatable by the new term, viceregal age. The current generation thus trained and given incentive for research and writing in this general expansion in Europe and the United States will have active professional lives for at least the next thirty years, that is, into the twenty-first century. Competition among them for exploitation of new themes or new aspects of old themes, for application of new methods, in short, for writing that will bring them prestige should lead to a steadily enlarging production in which the proportion of genuinely creative and analytic thinking at the least is likely to remain constant. With sharpening competition it may rise.

In Latin America there has been a comparable and perhaps greater expansion of numbers of scholars and facilities, all backed by allocations from public resources that now can be mobilized more effectively. The process was not well under way until the 1960s, but has proceeded almost like wildfire. It has involved the expansion of existing national academies, a proliferation of universities comparable to that in the United States, and the creation of new scholarly entities with budgets and staffs. In Cuba the development has been a sweeping overhaul that has left the country with an Academy of Sciences organized in imitation of the Soviet model, with a multiplicity of dependent entities dedicated to history. In many countries of Latin America, to be sure, there have been disruptions in the creation of corps of writers of what one might call serious or professional history. Argentina has twice purged its universities (1943 and 1966), presenting many of its best scholars, including historians, as a free gift to other countries. Cuba lost most of its trained faculties in the years after 1959. Chile has lost and is losing scholars, first in the tensions and political persecutions of the Allende regime and now in the deadlier persecution of its right-wing successor. Other countries, such as Brazil, have had waves of expulsion. It should be noted that the loss is mitigated by the fact that many of the scholars move to other countries, where they are able to continue their work. Whatever the turbulence engendered by political hopes and passions, there is no doubt that there has developed in most Latin American countries an impressive cadre of professional historians, either trained abroad or educated under people trained abroad. Equally there have developed cadres of technicians and skilled people in allied fields. Perhaps most important there has been a corresponding expansion of public allocation of resources to support the enlarged staffs and the facilities they need for their writing and teaching. In a country such as Mexico, public support extends to the publications of hundreds of volumes of studies in cheap, substantial editions that place the best of foreign writing and a great deal of new Mexican writing at the disposal of the reading public. Teachers and students receive free copies. [17]

Not all of the new Latin American national development can be regarded as unmixed blessing, for the development of professional cadres within each country, with good training and techniques, and aspiring both to local salary and international prestige, leads also to jealousy of the foreign scholar and political agitation to diminish his activity. At one end of the spectrum the agitation may be no more than vocal opposition to cultural imperialism, a term of highly elastic meaning but that increasingly seems to mean the study of one country by nationals of another country. At the other end of the spectrum the agitation takes the form of attempts by decree and law to curtail the studies of foreign scholars and students, to dictate the form and disposition of their findings, or in substantial measure to exclude them. [18] National resources, runs the cry, are for citizens of the nation and not for foreigners. This resort to political control of scholarly inquiry is by no means limited to Latin America; within the nonsocialist world, India may have led the way. [19] Thus far the sociologists and other social scientists, anthropologists included, have taken the brunt, but students and writers of history, inoffensive as we are in aggregate, will find access to archives and the field increasingly placed under scrutiny. Yet, the silver lining of that cloud may turn out to be substantial: relinquishment to Latin Americans of documentary publication and concentration upon better analytical use of what is available in print.

Whatever the clouds upon the horizon, Latin America, in common with Europe and the United States, now has a large body of students and writers of history in almost all countries. The manpower at work has greatly increased and has markedly improved both in capacity and command of technique. Despite the budget cuts of the past three years in Europe and the United States, the amount of funding available is impressively greater than a generation ago. To all of this must be added the entrance into the field of scholars in the socialist countries and in Japan. What I have already said about the expectancy of professional life and the pressures of production applies to the entire group of scholars, whatever their origins and locations. However, Latin Americans, since they deal in *historia patria*, have a firm base in national need and interest. It must give them possibilities of expansion of numbers and budgetary support that may in the end outweigh the greater national per capita wealth in Europe and the United States which now gives advantage to writers of history in the more developed world.

The outlook for the next thirty or forty years, then, is that substantially greater numbers of people will be studying Latin American data and writing history from those data; that they will be better trained in technique of analysis; that, whatever the fluctuations from year to year, distinctly more money will be spent in supporting those functions. Where is this increasingly larger and more able effort likely to be concentrated, and what types of investigation are likely to be the more rewarding in increase of human knowledge?

We may predict at the outset continued exploration of traditional themes and development of them in traditional forms since such thinking and writing respond to deeply felt national and regional needs. The history of the fatherland, its heroes, great moments, its institutions; the province or state, the city or town (the *patria chica* in the same terms); all will continue to excite interest and command an appreciative audience. The countries of Latin America and those of the Iberian Peninsula will continue to produce studies of the great voyages of discovery, of lesser ones, of settlement and of missionary work. For Spain and Portugal these were the golden age of contribution to human knowledge and their preponderance within the European world. They have a vested interest that will insure further research. Since there is much yet to be learned about the development of techniques of navigation, the problems of distance and profitability, modes of conquest and settlement, and most of all the nature of proselytization in an Amerindian milieu, the endeavor will not be wasted. It was only in 1962 that a perceptive study of the *hueste conquistadora* by a Chilean, Mario Góngora, opened the way to new understanding of the Spanish expeditions as ad hoc corporate entities engaged in conquest and plunder under customary rules of command and division of booty.[20] The history of settlement answers a natural curiosity in ancestors, especially prominent in societies that have grown from small groups by prolific natural increase. One further result is that such histories inevitably have an element of genealogy and prosopography since clan affiliation is all-important in the societies they describe. Religious history more often in the forms of the lives of saintly men, missionaries, and great prelates has the added dimension in Latin America of description of the endeavors that have brought a continent and a half to Christianity and have created new syncretic forms of belief and observance. The Virgin of Guadalupe will undoubtedly be celebrated in numerous new histories, as will pious belief in similar manifestations throughout the area. Some studies will move to detachment and analysis.[21] Lastly, normal national pride and interest in national performance will keep going studies of diplomatic relations, imperial rivalries and wars, and imperial systems in the older terms of episode in chronological rendering. They have given us good yarns in the past; they will do so in the future.

One series of traditional themes and treatment begins to show extension, that is the conversion of the theme of great men and preliminary movements to the needs of proletarian and revolutionary history. So the awe and adulation that have been bestowed on the *próceres* of independence now begin to be lavished on men like Emiliano Zapata, Camilo Torres, Che Guevara. Similarly, the study of the social implications of banditry, of peasant uprising and revolt, and of village wars against the hacienda open a rich new vein of study yet continue the older search for antecedent and model. One can see additional extension to the history of strikes and urban upheaval in the immediate future. All such themes exploit material that lies readily to hand, and promise fame, perhaps even fortune, to the people who write the studies since their audience will range far beyond the normal handful of scholars. They continue to fulfill a major function of historians, the creation of national legend, in this case further transmuted to suitable class legend as well. Most of this writing is likely to remain within the category of that which the French call *histoire événementielle*, although sociological urges to model building and statistical or quantitative underpinning may be adduced to shore up the narrative.

Another extension of traditional forms is the history of institutions, law, and legal theory. In general, the best of these forms in the past have dealt with the colonial period, and those written since the 1940s have tended to have Spanish inspiration. As it happens, one of the strongest traditions in Spanish historical scholarship centers around the study of law and legal structures. It has had its organ in the *Anuario de Historia del Derecho Español*, characterized by unusual rigor and understanding; and since the Civil War its paladin in Alfonso García Gallo of Madrid. Counterparts have grown up in Latin America, centered in the schools of law of the great national universities, most notably Buenos Aires, Santiago, Mexico City, and Rio de Janeiro, usually publishing similar journals. In 1966 García Gallo, Alamiro de Avila Martel of the University of Chile, and Ricardo Zorraquín Becú of the University of Buenos Aires organized the Instituto Internacional de Historia del Derecho Indiano, with a permanent secretariat in Buenos Aires. The institute, which has membership in three continents, has held three triennial congresses thus far. In them and in studies inspired by the rise in interest and communication, it has significantly opened the category of themes available in study of legal history in terms of practice, theory, and institutions. The international communication and mutual criticism it makes easier have brought greater rigor and depth to such studies, which already profit from the fact that in the Hispanic world this is traditionally an area of careful scholarship.

In Europe and the United States one of the most promising innovations in historical inquiry of recent decades has been the resort to quantitative approaches. That has meant necessarily as well turning to themes which lend themselves more readily to such treatment. In the latest innovation, embodied in the New Economic History, questions and conceptions derived from economics are applied to historical data, but that innovation has yet to reach Latin American historiography.[22] The first application of quantitative approaches to Latin American historiography have come from Latin Americanists in Europe and the United States through their proximity to other scholars applying such conceptions either in other fields of history or even in other intellectual disciplines. One need merely mention the brilliant *enfant terrible* Pierre Chaunu and the application of quantitative methods through the VI[e] Section in Paris or the group of writers in Berkeley with their connections to geography and the biological sciences. The basic need in such application is the availability of reasonably substantial, consecutive runs of material capable of being brought to similar statement and capable of statistical treatment. Latin America is in the somewhat ironic situation that the Spanish imperial system, with its steady if irregular inquiries and its insistence upon voluminous records, has left enormous deposits of material of just this nature. The Portuguese imperial system, somewhat more negligent in its recording, still has left substantial deposits. Moreover, double deposit at imperial and colonial centers has meant an unusually good chance of filling out series interrupted in one kind of deposit with material available in the other. Irremediable breaks in series are more likely to come with the beginning of independence when inquiry and recording fell into the hands of local authorities, without accountability to a central authority.

In most lands of Latin America, functioning national statistical systems have been the creation of the past century, if that much; some do not yet have them. So in Spanish America, for example, the scholar may well find excellent records for the colonial period and especially for the eighteenth century when the Bourbon reformers organized unusually effective reporting. He will find almost no national data available for a good part of the nineteenth century, and encounters fairly comprehensive recording in the late nineteenth and early twentieth centuries. The ever-lengthening period of national statistical systems in which we now live provides a relatively long term of years for historical inquiry, with far fewer problems of assembly and adjustment. Accordingly, an increasing number of scholars limit themselves to this span. Yet the gap of the nineteenth century may not be so bad as it appears at first sight if the scholar is perceptive, diligent, and loves to explore in remote places, for filling it may merely require painstaking search in local archives in order to uncover the fruits of continuing local recording. In the end, in some countries such as Mexico it is just possible that local archives, if fully explored, and some of the as yet unknown central deposits outside of the national archive may contain materials that would permit continuous series.

The themes that suit the location and analysis of runs of material are the fairly standard ones of European or United States historiography, with some regional quirks. In the subfield of historical demography, it is possible for some parts of Latin America to study movement of population over a period of four and a half centuries on the basis of parish and tribute records. I speak here of the study of changes in birth, marriage, and death rates; the way in which populations form family and household units; and the migrations of individuals and groups. One French technique, quickly picked up in the United Kingdom, is reconstitution of families through data in parish registers. Presumably the reconstitution can be continued into the era of national statistics by resort to the civil register or its equivalent. Unfortunately, this technique has not yet proved viable for Latin America because of paucity of family names and the custom of changing them rather easily.[23] What one might call another level of analysis would be the use of demographic data for study of generational change.[24] But even in Europe and the United States, studies of historical demography are just beginning, although they promise a brilliant achievement in the coming years. The ultimate hope is to put everything into computers.[25] For Latin America there is the additional problem of native numbers at the time of the coming of the Europeans, the study of which is complicated by the intense ideological passions that focus upon it. Solutions to this problem require a complex application of knowledge of environment, climate, disease, soils, technology, specific sources, and statistical techniques; much of the knowledge has yet to be developed for adequate application.[26] There is further the equally emotional problem of numbers moved in the slave trade. Philip Curtin has recently developed an ingenious suggestion for reconstruction of numbers through analysis of antecedents necessary to leave known residues.[27] It is an imaginative approach of vastly wider application to other questions.

The subfields that may be grouped as economic and fiscal history lend themselves especially to quantitative analysis, ultimately done through computers.[28] One may think here of historical studies of trade, industry in general and in terms of specific industries, general movement of the economy, economic development, per capita income, prices, and agricultural organization and production. The few studies done to date barely touch on the potential of these themes in terms of known techniques and fairly readily available materials. Jonathan V. Levin's study of the guano age in Peru,[29] although directed toward current political and economic debate, yet through thoughtful application of techniques points the way to far more perceptive historical study. In another genre, Enrique Florescano[30] has been able to write standard European price history and demonstrate the availability of data. A useful antecedent for further historical studies of quantitative approach is the preparation of a reasonably reliable series of historical statistics for each country of Latin America, perhaps on a par with *The Historical Statistics of the United States*. Such series are now in process although one cannot predict the exact measure of success or the speed of completion.[31] One major project of computerization, carried on by John TePaske and an associated group, envisages placing the data on royal treasury receipts, disbursements, and remittances to Spain for the Viceroyalty of Peru into a computer for rapid recall and assembly. Again the project is in process, and the hoped-for flow of historical writing in the future. Theoretically there is no impediment to its success except cost.

A range of themes within these subfields that desperately needs study through quantitative methods are those on land use and settlement, land accumulation, the operations of plantations and haciendas, and the functioning of labor systems on them, especially in the form of slavery and debt peonage. Emotions and ideological predispositions have seriously hampered moderately objective study here, and political rhetoric has left us with positions whose basis in evidence is questionable at best.[32] Yet readily available evidence exists in quantity in the notarial records, perhaps the best-preserved form of public record in Latin America, and in the extended runs of records of operation for large landholdings. The problem has lain in the difficulties likely to be faced by any man who followed the evidence. Again, Jan Bazant in his studies of the sale of church property in Mexico[33] and in the operations of an hacienda in San Luis Potosí[34] has successfully shown how little foundation there has been in old preconceptions, at least in what he has studied, and remains so far unscathed by political passion. The vexed question just what lay beneath peasant explosions could be settled in part by tabulation of land transfers in notarial records that are known to exist. Did Mesoamerican and Andean villages lose their lands in the sixteenth, seventeenth, eighteenth, or nineteenth century; if so, in what circumstances? Had they ever held the lands they claimed and in some instances have gained under the rubric of agrarian reform? The current equation of claim with folk memory and both with historical truth is hardly rational. In an almost totally different direction, Roberto Cortes Conde by studying land grants in nineteenth-century Argentina has demonstrated the existence of two different kinds of frontiers, in the provinces of Buenos Aires and Santa Fe, with distinct forms of settlement and society associated with them.[35]

Two subfields, historical political studies and historical sociology, lend themselves to a somewhat different mix of analytical techniques.[36] Normal quantitative methods have been applied and will be applied increasingly in the future to the attitudes and behavior of political groups, especially parties, and to inquiry into the nature and patterns of thought and behavior of the military, who are emerging as one of the most important instruments for bringing about effective change in the continent and a half. The workhorse of political studies and sociology, inquiry by questionnaire, is not easily available for application to the past. However, content analysis is a partial substitute and could be applied far more widely to such questions as the nature and development of public attitudes, the meaning of public discussion, the programs and plans of public leaders. In the deeper form of location of basic preoccupations and values, as exemplified in the inquiries of Josephine Miles for poetry in England and the United States,[37] content and language analysis offers scholars inured to monotony entrance into a vacant area of potentially brilliant and provocative yield. With the further addition of genealogical and of prosopographical inquiry, scholars can add inquiry into the intricate functioning of clan loyalties and group interests in Latin American societies.

Lastly, in the general category of quantitative and statistical approach, we come to the burgeoning subfield of historical studies of urbanism and urbanization, the one term covering the growth of cities, the other the adaptation of formerly peasant groups to their new urban environment. On the one hand, such studies link to an old genre of the history of growth of individual cities; at the other end of the range, they can be a truly innovative inquiry into historical needs and forces, patterns, and the variant ways of responding to similar pressures.[38] Of the many people now interested in the subfield, Dr. Jorge Hardoy of Buenos Aires, at one time director of the Center of Urban Studies in the Instituto Torcuato Di Tella, has brought together training as architect, city planner, social reformer, and historian for an unusual series of insights into historical process.[39] The road he opens is likely to be much trodden, increasingly with use of quantitative data and application of statistical analysis.

The styles set in Europe and the United States in recent decades have included another major category of approaches to the past of man in the form of intellectual history and history of ideas.[40] The existence of this category of forms has not been lost on Latin Americans, who, moreover, have had an agent of transmission in the Spanish refugee philosopher, José Gaos, at the University of Mexico. Under the aegis of Leopoldo Zea, the Pan-American Institute of Geography and History has sponsored a monographic series and a journal specializing on the history of ideas, the series aiming at a volume on each country. Perhaps the best of the volumes is José Luis Romero's volume on Argentina.[41] The impulse, however, has gone far beyond the Pan-American Institute to the publications of multivolume projects on thinkers, their thought, and philosophy in Latin America. The most influential writer has been Leopoldo Zea, with studies of Positivism in Latin America. In his conception Positivism moves far beyond the fairly narrow confines of what it was in Europe to become a distinctly Latin American formulation, eclectic in nature and aiming at economic as well as political independence. Zea is reported to be attempting now a similar synthesis for twentieth-century Latin American thought. The genre has evoked much enthusiasm and writing of high literary quality. It is likely to evoke a good deal more and to furnish us further with easily available texts of many Latin American and Peninsular spokesmen and writers. Its potential for genuine intellectual stimulation, however, is less clear, for there remain unsolved problems of cause and effect not of the general nature that plague all study of history but the more limited ones of demonstrating the extent to which ideas genuinely influenced policies rather than furnishing the rhetoric for political justification. The more limited theme of influence from teacher to student or agents and agencies of transmission of ideas and intellectual fashions is more susceptible to analysis based on evidence and has already yielded fine studies.[42] Beyond such studies there lies the virgin field of examination of intellectual environment, of zeitgeist, of the reservoir of conceptions, technology, and values that determine and restrict human formulation of desires and appropriate means to achieve those desires.[43] We are beginning to perceive the extent to which language, ways of thought, and technology open some channels and close off others; in retrospect burning questions turn out to have been less serious or even nonquestions; the real questions may not even have been seen. For Latin America studies of this nature have a brilliant potential if one difficult to achieve—but then that could be said of the rest of the planet.

Within the category of interest in intellectual history, one should also include anti-intellectual history, which derives much of its vigor from dissident Marxism and in part uses models from socialist countries. Many of the books and articles falling within this subcategory are characterized by more heat than scholarship. A major group of themes is periodization, in which an enormous effort is devoted to dividing human experience in one region into appropriate spans and subspans of time in terms of what is held to be the dominant force or cluster of forces. In many instances that dominant force is imperialism. Alternatively we may class as another major group of themes those that investigate the meaning and effects of imperialism. Yet a third group deals with internal exploitation, internal colonialism, and racism. With attention to evidence such studies can offer new points of view and new perceptions; they have the inestimable advantage of forcing us to reflect why we hold the points of view we do and what is our world view. In the debates of the devotees of the genre, however, it quickly tends toward a bitter politicization of all scholarly study that turns all communication into a search for the proper orthodoxy and a hounding out of deviationists. In the end, there is less and less originality. Yet in most recent years a growing amount of human effort not only in Latin America but also in Europe and the United States is being devoted to such endless and increasingly futile writing. It is the new parallel to the last centuries of scholasticism.[44]

There remain to be mentioned as imported categories of approach and treatment of historical data such genres relatively new even in Europe and the United States as the application of psychoanalytical theory and technique, the history of science and technology, in short what one might call the newer ways of the West. These have all been little applied to Latin America, sometimes for good reason. The history of Latin American science is quickly written, whatever future years may bring in contribution and innovation for a history to be written some generations from now. On the other hand, the application of psychoanalytical theory and technique and the study of technology have very considerable potential. One might continue the list by pointing out that the history of domesticated plants and animals, the spread of disease, medical and sanitary practice, and a host of similar topics will find in Latin America an extraordinarily rich source of data, very often with the variants that a tropical climate can bring to formulations based upon the temperate lands of Europe and the United States. The still to be studied epidemiological unification of the globe, first through the development of rapid navigation of oceans and more recently through the development of mass transit by air, has a particularly grim interest in the extension of Old World disease to Latin America, with a destruction that still exceeds man's best-planned achievements to date. Latin America's contribution to the Old World in the form of syphilis can hardly even the balance and has been more than outweighed by its remarkable provision of such food plants as maize, manioc, the potato, and sweet potato.

What I have said so far emphasizes that the major future developments and the major intellectual opportunities in writing Latin American history lie in the application of approaches developed in Europe and the United States for the study of their own histories. Is all work, then, to be essentially derivative; is there no promise of innovation within the study of this region? The question may be phrased more widely and differently: Within the global civilization that is now clearly coming into being on our planet, will not Latin America make genuine contribution rather than continuing an essentially passive role of recipient? In truly longer-range terms, say of centuries or even millennia, the answer is obviously an unequivocal yes. In the shorter-range terms in which we are exploring, that is, the next decades, and within the limitations of the study of history in those decades, the answer must be somewhat different. Regional innovation is likely when special circumstances favor it. Such special circumstances might be the rise in exceptional conditions of a special group of scholars, like the development of an unusually able group in Spanish medieval studies around the towering figure of Claudio Sánchez-Albornoz in Buenos Aires, favored by the unusual budgetary support of successive Argentine governments to the distinguished refugee. More usually such circumstances arise through the existence of unusually rich local materials for study. Rural and village studies of Latin America, with their richness of material easily bared, the violence of centuries-old conflicts between peasants and latifundia, among peasants themselves in the communal and racial groupings, probably have a brilliant future. Eric Hobsbawm is finding in the highlands of Peru a wealth of data, comparable with that of Sicily or Sardinia.[45] Urban history in the hands of Jorge Hardoy and a growing group of anthropologists, sociologists, and even historians so labeled, demonstrably has a potential that may carry possibility of innovation equal to that of studies of Europe but different because of differing circumstances. Relative to the United States the runs of material are far longer, covering spans of time that can be paralleled or even exceeded for Europe but not for our country.

The major innovations have come thus far, and are likely to come in the near future, in the merging of the approaches of anthropology and history called ethnohistory. For the so-called areas of high aboriginal culture—Meso-America, the central and northern Andes—there are rich and exotic masses of evidence to be uncovered through study of archaeological sites, oral tradition, native written tradition, Spanish records, linguistic evidence, and contemporary field survey. To the charms of life in picturesque villages is added the prestige of scholarship. The deciphering of the Mixtec genealogies by Alfonso Caso has been a fascinating detective story of the past generation.[46] It is more than matched by the steady but still to be rewarded attempts at reading the Maya hieroglyphs. The critical study of texts in order to detect copying and unique statement has just begun to yield us new understanding of much of what had been taken for granted rather uncritically in Preconquest aboriginal life.[47] The comparative study of oral traditions and the verification of them, in turn, against archaeological and linguistic data as well as current survivals have long been done as a matter of course where Latin America is concerned. In short, for the areas of high culture much of the kind of fusion of approaches that has been possible for the Old World can be duplicated but in different circumstances and for differing cultures. One of the more fascinating possibilities, yet to be explored, is the evolution of parallels and differences as two segments of mankind, separated since the Lower Paleolithic, went their divided cultural ways yet had to meet essentially similar problems of need for increase in food supply, propitiation of the unknown and elemental, and organization of increasingly complex political forms. The writing of history for the areas of low culture—the temperate south, the Atlantic coast of South America, and Amazonia—awaits the development of new techniques and their associated conceptions both in anthropology and history. For both sets of areas there exists further the potential of studies of the frontier, less as a zone of confrontation of two races and cultures than as a zone of mingling of races and the creation of mixed cultures shading from the European, through mestizo and invigorated aboriginal, to the remoter and untouched Indian.[48]

With the exceptions I have indicated, writing on the history of Latin America is likely to be derivative in ideas and techniques. Ideas and techniques, however, must be clothed in flesh, and that flesh in turn must come from the continent and a half that we call Latin America. The terrain is different; the people, because of their diverse racial and cultural antecedents, also show substantial variation from Europe and even from the melting pot of the United States. Those differences of terrain and climate, that variation in race and culture mean that the accidents, the episodes, that will clothe the more abstract must take on a richness of local color. In the end, a mango is not an apple, nor is a Chilean a European or North American. So the flavor will be different. The Latin American will be writing his national history, the adventures of the national entity reaching for a unique identity; the European and North American will be embarking upon exploration of an alien entity, imperious, alluring, and full of delight.

NOTES

1. In preparing this paper I have had a great deal of help and critical advice from my colleagues Eugene Irschick, Tulio Halperín Donghi, and Luis Monguió. I take this opportunity to acknowledge my debt and thank them.

2. As in most other fields of history there is a steady publication of bibliographical guides and comments to keep scholars abreast of new writing in Latin American history. The *Latin American Research Review* has had an especially notable series of articles: M. S. Al'perovich, "Soviet Historiography of the Latin American Countries," 6, no. 1 (1970): 63–70; Charles W. Bergquist, "Recent United States Studies in Latin American History: Trends since 1965," 9, no. 1 (1974): 3–35; Harold Eugene Davis, "The History of Ideas in Latin America," 3, no. 4 (1968): 23–44; William P. McGreevey, "Recent Research on the Economic History of Latin America," 3, no. 1 (1968): 89–117, and "Recent Materials and Opportunities for Quantitative Research in Latin American History: Nineteenth and Twentieth Centuries," 9, no. 2 (1974): 73–82, also published in somewhat different form as chap. 10 of Val R. Lorwin and Jacob M. Price, eds., *The Dimensions of the Past; Materials, Problems, and Opportunities for Quantitative Work in History* (New Haven and London: Yale University Press, 1972), pp. 477–501; Thomas F. McGann, James Lockhart, Karen Spalding, and Frederick P. Bowser, "The Social History of Colonial Spanish America," 7, no. 1 (1972): 5–94; Magnus Mörner, "The Study of Latin American History Today," 8, no. 2 (1973): 75–93; Richard M. Morse, "Trends and Issues in Latin American Urban Research, 1965–1970," 6, nos. 1 and 2 (1971): 3–52 and 19–75 respectively; John V. Murra, "Current Research and Prospects in Andean Ethnohistory," 5, no. 1 (1970): 3–36; T. Lynn Smith, "Studies of Colonization and Settlement," 4, no. 1 (1969): 93–123; Victor V. Sol'skii, "The Study of Latin America in the U.S.S.R.," 3, no. 1 (1967): 77–87; and many others.

The *Hispanic American Historical Review* has systematically tried to print articles reviewing recent historiography by country; the articles are especially good for more conventional types of writing within each country. Their stated purpose is to survey historiographical trends since 1830 with an emphasis on materials that have appeared since 1920—Joseph R. Barager, "The Historiography of the Rio de la Plata Area Since 1830," 39, no. 4 (1959): 588–642; Stanley J. Stein, "The Historiography of Brazil 1808–1889," 40, no. 2 (1960): 234–78; William J. Griffith, "The Historiography of Central America since 1830," 40, no. 4 (1960): 548–69; Robert A. Potash, "Historiography of Mexico since 1821," 40, no. 3 (1960): 383–424; Charles W. Arnade, "The Historiography of Colonial and Modern Bolivia," 42, no. 3 (1962): 333–84; Robert Freeman Smith, "Twentieth-Century Cuban Historiography," 44, no. 1 (1964): 44–73; and Adam

Szaszdi, "The Historiography of the Republic of Ecuador," 44, no. 4 (1964): 503–50.

In Europe the Institute of Latin American Studies, London, publishes an annual listing of work published and under way for the United Kingdom; for France there is now an attempt at such annual listing in the *Cahiers des Amériques Latines, Série Sciences de l'Homme*, published by the Association Marc Bloch and the Institut des Hautes Études de l'Amérique Latine; previously there have appeared fairly frequent *comptes rendus* in the *Revue Historique* and *Annales: Économies, Sociétés, Civilisations*. A number of publications in Spain also attempt to keep the reader abreast of current bibliography and past developments, not merely of work done in Spain but throughout the learned world, especially for the Preconquest and Colonial Periods. Most notable are the *Indice Histórico Español* and the *Historia y bibliografía americanista*, published as a section within the *Anuario de Estudios Americanos*, Seville, until 1971 and subsequently as a separate journal issued three times a year. For many countries of Latin America there are equally annual bibliographies and occasional stocktaking.

One should mention further Lorwin and Price, eds., *The Dimensions of the Past*, cited above, which has a chapter by John J. TePaske, "Quantification in Latin American Colonial History," paralleling the one by McGreevey on the later period; Robert S. Byars and Joseph L. Love, eds., *Quantitative Social Science Research on Latin America* (Urbana, Chicago, and London: University of Illinois Press, 1973), with a chapter on history by Peter H. Smith (pp. 14–61) but useful throughout; and the long series of papers *La historia económica en América Latina* (2 vols.; Sep-Setentas, 37 and 47, Mexico City, 1972), which are the symposium held under the auspices of the Consejo Latinoamericano de Ciencias Sociales (CLACSO) at the XXXIX International Congress of Americanists, Lima, 1970. These are only some of the more recent and notable guides, and essays of stocktaking. A somewhat older but thoughtful survey is the papers of a seminar held at Stanford University in 1963 under the auspices of the Committee of Latin American Studies of the Social Science Research Council; they have been published in Charles Wagley, ed., *Social Science Research on Latin America* (New York and London: Columbia University Press, 1964). Much of what I write in this essay is based, in turn, upon listings and discussions in these works.

3. The German Democratic Republic has a number of centers in East Berlin, Leipzig, and Rostock, and is after the Soviet Union the most important Socialist country in Latin American studies. Czechoslovakia has a center in Prague, publishing a yearbook of Hispanic studies. Poland has a parallel center in Warsaw, also publishing a yearbook. Hungary has had one scholar of note, who has recently died.

4. Reported by Manfred Kossok of the University of Leipzig.

5. There is an Institute of Latin American Studies at Sophia University, Tokyo.

6. One might list the Escuela de Estudios Hispano-Americanos, Seville; the Instituto "Gonzalo Fernández de Oviedo," Madrid; the Instituto "Santo Toribio de Mogrovejo," Madrid, specializing in the history of the Church and its missions; and a series of other institutes and groups in Barcelona, Pamplona, Valladolid, etc.

7. 8 vols. in 11 parts; Paris: A. Colin, 1957–59.

8. Some of the gap has been filled through the efforts of the group centered around Richard Konetzke at Cologne, which publishes the *Jahrbuch für Geschichte von Staat, Wirtschaft und Gesellschaft Lateinamerikas*. There are now plans to revive the long-suspended *Iberoamerikanisches Archiv*, issued by the Iberoamerikanisches Institut in West Berlin.

9. Even for university posts, the councils of selection usually have a substantial component of students, who are usually plumping for partisan, activist teaching and writing.

10. See the report of the interview with Diego Rivera in *Excelsior*, October 19, 1949, p. 13, and the report of a speech by Diego Rivera in the Faculty of Filosofía y Letras of the Universidad Nacional Autónoma de México, *Hispano*, October 28, 1949, in section *Jornadas Nacionales*, p. Ib.

11. An example of such writing: Federico Brito Figueroa, *Historia económica y social de Venezuela*, 2 vols. (Caracas: Universidad Central de Venezuela, 1966).

12. See the very careful analysis by Juan A. Ortega y Medina, *Historiografía soviética iberoamericanista (1945–1960)* (Mexico City: Universidad Nacional Autónoma de México, 1961) and, *inter alia*, the articles in the *Hispanic American Historical Review* on Soviet historiography of Latin America: Warren Schiff, "An East German Survey concerning Recent Soviet Historical Writings on Latin America," 40 (1960):70–71; Russell H. Bartley, "A Decade of Soviet Scholarship in Brazilian History: 1959–1968," 50 (1970): 445–66; and Edward B. Richards, "Marxism and Marxist Movements in Latin America in Recent Soviet Historical Writing," 45 (1965): 577–90.

13. *Historia moderna de México*, 9 vols. (Mexico City: Editorial Hermes, 1955–72). The period since 1910 is considered *historia contemporánea*.

14. Most notably *Historia mexicana* (1951–   ) and *Bibliografía histórica mexicana* (1967–   ).

15. The development is easily traceable in the rise of regional associations for Latin American history or Latin American studies in Europe and the United States. Our country is at the point of having one for each region, each holding meetings. In Europe activities are now coordinated informally by an Association of European Latin Americanists.

16. See n. 6.

17. Most notably in the Sep-Setentas series.

18. The wave of the future may be recognized in the recent regulation of the Instituto Colombiano de Cultura, July 2, 1973, which requires written license for all anthropological field work in Colombia, to be obtained upon registering a project, paying 30 percent of the budget of the project to the Instituto Colombiano de Cultura, arranging for a Colombian supervisor and providing a parallel fellowship for a Colombian in the United States if the project is to prepare a doctoral dissertation, turning over a report in Spanish before leaving the national territory, giving copies of all subsequent publications on the work, and agreeing to allow the Instituto Colombiano de Cultura to publish or authorize publication of Spanish translations without royalties and at its own discretion. The regulation is published in full in *El Mensajero, Newsletter of the Latin American Anthropology Group, American Anthropological Association* 3, no. 1 (June 1974): 5. Private conversations I have had with European and North American Latin Americanists and Latin Americans indicate to me a large reservoir of resentment.

19. *New York Times*, September 26, 1973, p. 7; see the editorial in *The Hindu*, Madras, September 7, 1973, protesting the drastic limitation to twenty a year of visas to U.S. scholars.

20. *Los grupos de conquistadores en Tierra Firme (1509–1530): fisonomía histórico-social de un tipo de conquista* (Santiago: Universidad de Chile, Centro de Historia Colonial, 1962). A further development may be found in James Lockhart, *The Men of Cajamarca. A Social and Biographical Study of the First Conquerors of Peru* (Austin: University of Texas Press, 1972).

21. What may well be the outstanding work in the religious history of Latin America is now over forty years old—Robert Ricard, *La "conquête spirituelle" du Mexique. Essai sur l'apostolat et les méthodes missionaires des Ordres Mendiants en Nouvelle-Espagne de*

1523–24 à 1572 (Paris: Institut d'ethnologie, 1933). It is available also in a sensitive translation by Lesley Byrd Simpson, *The Spiritual Conquest of Mexico* (Berkeley and Los Angeles: University of California Press, 1966). Manpower and budget do not always provide genius.

22. See McGreevey, paper of 1974, cited in n. 2.

23. See Woodrow Borah and Sherburne F. Cook, "La demografía histórica de América Latina: Necesidades y perspectivas," in *La historia económica en América Latina, II. Desarrollo, perspectivas y bibliografía* (Sep-Setentas, 47, Mexico City, 1972), pp. 82–99. The English original, given as a paper at the XXXIX International Congress of Americanists, Lima, 1970, is yet to be published in the Proceedings.

24. As has been done by Daniel S. Smith in a sophisticated analysis of demographic data in his doctoral dissertation, still in manuscript.

25. See the proposal for computerization of the 1777 counts in D. J. Robinson, M. M. Swann, and M. D. Miller, "Distribution and Structure of the Population of Spanish America, 1750–1800: A Framework for Computer Analysis," a paper given at the XLI International Congress of Americanists, Mexico City, September 2–7, 1974, to be published in the Proceedings. The project is a joint one of the universities at Syracuse, New York, and Oxford. The problems of reconciling terminology over a continent and a half will create obstacles, but there can be no doubt of a brilliant field for future work here.

26. Woodrow Borah, "The Historical Demography of Latin America: Sources, Techniques, Controversies, Yields," in *Population and Economics; Proceedings of Section V (Historical Demography) of the Fourth Congress of the International Economic History Association, Indiana University, Bloomington, Indiana, U.S.A. September 9–14, 1968*, ed. Paul Deprez (Winnipeg: University of Manitoba Press, 1970), pp. 173–205.

27. *The Atlantic Slave Trade: A Census* (Madison: University of Wisconsin Press, 1969).

28. McGreevey's two papers and that by TePaske, cited in n. 2, are guides for what follows.

29. *The Export Economies. Their Pattern of Development in Historical Perspective* (Cambridge: Harvard University Press, 1960).

30. *Precios del maíz y crisis agrícolas en México (1708–1810)* (Mexico City: El Colegio de México, 1969). The records of tithes, municipal granaries, convents, and hospices probably give Latin America as good runs for history of prices as are available in Europe.

31. Thus far there have been published Miguel Urrutia Montoya and Mario Arrubla, eds., *Compendio de estadísticas históricas de Colombia* (Bogotá: Universidad Nacional de Colombia, 1970), and Miguel Izard, ed., *Series estadísticas para la historia de Venezuela* (Mérida: Universidad de los Andes, Escuela de Historia, 1970). Obviously one such volume is needed for each country, and coverage within the volumes will have to become more comprehensive.

32. See the preliminary pages of Paul Friedrich, *Agrarian Revolt in a Mexican Village* (Englewood Cliffs, N.J.: Prentice-Hall, 1970), on both passion and position.

33. *Los Bienes de la Iglesia en México (1856–1875): Aspectos Económicos y sociales de la Revolución liberal* (Mexico City: El Colegio de México, 1971); published in English as *Alienation of Church Wealth in Mexico: Social and Economic Aspects of the Liberal Revolution, 1856–1875* (Cambridge: At the University Press, 1971). Bazant demonstrates how unrealistic were Liberal ideas of wealth locked in mortmain.

34. "Peones, arrendatarios y aparceros en México: 1851–1853," *Historia mexicana* 23 (1973–1974): 330–57; "Peones, arrendatarios y aparceros, 1868–1904," ibid., 24 (1974–1975): 94–121.

35. "Algunos rasgos de la expansión territorial en Argentina en la segunda mitad del

siglo XIX,"*Desarrollo económico*, no. 29 (April–June 1968), pp. 3–29. The possibilities in this line of inquiry were further demonstrated in a series of papers given at the IV International Congress of Economic History, Bloomington, September 1968, and published in Alvaro Jara, ed., *Tierras nuevas. Expansión territorial y ocupación del suelo en América (siglos XVI–XIX)* (Mexico City: Colegio de México, 1969).

36. See McGreevey's paper of 1974, *Latin American Research Review* 9, no. 2 (Summer 1974): 77.

37. *Renaissance, Eighteenth-Century, and Modern Language in English Poetry. A Tabular View* (Berkeley and Los Angeles: University of California Press, 1960).

38. See the long assessment by Richard M. Morse, cited in n. 2.

39. Hardoy and Carmen Aranovich, "Urban Scales and Functions in Spanish America toward the Year 1600: First Conclusions," *Latin American Research Review* 5, no. 3 (Fall 1970): 57–92; also published in the original Spanish as "Escalas y funciones urbanas en América Hispánica hacia el año 1600. Primeras conclusiones," in XXXVII International Congress of Americanists, Mar del Plata, 1966, *Actas y Memorias* 1, pp. 171–208; Hardoy and Diana Mosovich, "Un ensayo de interpretación del proceso de urbanización de América Latina," *Revista Interamericana de Planificación* 7 (1973): 95–134.

40. See the article by Harold Eugene Davis, cited in n. 2. Much of what follows relies on Davis. The appreciations are mine.

41. *El desarrollo de las ideas en la sociedad argentina del siglo XX* (Mexico City and Buenos Aires: Fondo de Cultura Económica, 1965).

42. As for example in Luis Monguió, *Don José Joaquín de Mora y el Perú del ochocientos* (Madrid: Editorial Castalia, 1967).

43. The possibilities of this kind of intellectual history may be seen in Jacques Lafaye, *Quetzalcóatl et Guadalupe. La formation de la conscience nationale au Mexique (1531–1813)* (Paris: Gallimard, 1974). Lafaye has written a history of ideas, but ideas that lie at the basis of national identity. Another work, on concepts of America, is Antonello Gerbi, *La disputa del Nuovo Mondo* (Milan: R. Ricciardi, 1955), translated into Spanish as *La disputa del Nuevo Mundo* (Mexico City and Buenos Aires: Fondo de Cultura Económica, 1962), and into English in a revised and enlarged edition as *The Dispute of the New World* (Pittsburgh: University of Pittsburgh Press, 1973).

44. Much of what I have to say here may be seen in Andre Gunder Frank, *Lumpenburguesía: lumpendesarrollo* (Santiago, Chile: Ediciones Prensa Latinoamericana, 1971), translated into English as *Lumpenbourgeoisie: Lumpendevelopment. Dependence, Class, and Politics in Latin America* (New York: Monthly Review Press, 1972).

45. "Peasant Land Occupations,"*Past and Present*, no. 62 (February 1974), pp. 120–52.

46. The book that incorporates Caso's work of nearly forty years fortunately was written before his death but is still in press.

47. At the Instituto de Investigaciones Históricas of the National University of Mexico, a group of scholars, under the direction of Dr. Miguel León-Portilla, are preparing critical editions of texts such as the chronicle of Juan de Torquemada, with special attention to sources. It is the kind of study that has given substantial reward in European history.

48. A notable work in this direction is Edward H. Spicer, *Cycles of Conquest: The Impact of Spain, Mexico, and the United States on the Indians of the Southwest, 1533–1960* (Tucson: University of Arizona Press, 1962).

8

Japanese History
in World Perspective

John Whitney Hall

Since Japan's remarkable recovery from the devastation of World War II, and particularly as Japan's gross national product outstripped that of England, France, and finally West Germany, Japan has emerged as one of the great powers—a major participant in world affairs. Yet while we permit ourselves to be persuaded by "futurologists" like Herman Kahn into thinking of Japan as a potential superpower of the twenty-first century, most of us give scant consideration to what Japan was like prior to modern times.[1] The assumption that Japan before it became a military or economic competitor of the Western world had little direct relevance to world history has remained strong. There is common agreement, to be sure, that Japan's history is a necessary subject of study if we wish to understand the present and future of that country, but aside from that, the content of Japanese history is judged not of sufficient concern to be given a place in our intellectual and educational institutions commensurate with its present world economic status. The fact that Japan's history is locked away in a most difficult and unfamiliar language is only part of the problem.

Twenty-five years ago G. B. Sansom, the foremost Western historian of Japan, delivered a series of lectures in Tokyo entitled "Japan in World History." The wisdom he expressed in these lectures was ahead of his time. He started with the admission that until recent times Japan had not played a visible part in world history, but, he pointed out, neither had England until the end of the Middle Ages. He then went on,

But it is not in that sense that I am using the expression World History. What I have in mind is something much wider, because I am thinking of the history of all human societies, however separate in time and place. In *that* sense the behavior of men in communities is the true material of history, the proper study of mankind. It is my purpose to suggest that the national history of Japan is an important part of the history of the aggregate of human societies, a part which has so far been neglected by Western scholars, and which, I suspect, needs from that point of view some further attention by Japanese scholars.[2]

Then, by way of illustrating what he meant, he discussed a number of features of Japanese and English society which could be illuminated by means of comparison: for instance, the implications of the fact that Japan retained a rice economy while England shifted to sheep raising and the accumulation of commercial capital, or the reasons why England gave rise to a liberal tradition in politics and a strong commitment to individual rights while Japan condoned authoritarianism in government and submerged the individual in family and community. To put Japanese history into world perspective, or as Sansom suggested, to add Japanese history to that of the "aggregate of human societies," is not something that can happen automatically; it requires conscious effort on the part of the historian and a systematic handling of historical data and the methodology of comparative analysis.

The requirements in this effort are obvious enough. There is first the need for the recovery and preservation of the historical evidence and second the interpretation of that evidence in a language which can make it comprehensible not only to contemporary Japanese but beyond Japan to a world audience. Fortunately, these preliminary requirements have by now been met in full through the combined efforts of Japanese and Western historians.

The Japanese are clearly a historically minded people. In the last hundred years they have opened up for themselves and for the world at large the content of their national history purposefully and with great determination. The establishment in 1869—the second year of the Meiji government's existence—of an office for the Collection of Historical Materials and the Compilation of National History marked the beginning of a national effort to preserve and interpret the country's past and to write its history in a way that would both serve the state and place the Japanese historic record in world context. The creation in 1889 of a department of Japanese history at Tokyo Imperial University and the employment of the German historian Ludwig Reiss as professor of history confirmed the intention of the Japanese scholarly world to base their historical profession on the historiographical methods of the West. Today history is one of the best served of the academic disciplines in Japan.[3]

As a way of getting a sense of the magnitude of the achievement of Japanese historians, let me cite a few scattered figures. There are today in Japan at least six major national associations of historians. The oldest, the Shigakkai of the University of Tokyo, has been in continuous existence since 1889. The more popular Nihon Rekishi Gakkai has a membership of 4,000 and its journal a readership of 8,000. Between 1946, when it first started publishing, to 1974, over 1,300 individuals have placed articles in this journal.[4] All told, there are over a hundred professional journals devoted substantially to history. The annual commercial production of history titles numbers over a thousand items.

Today the professional Japanese historian has at his command great stores of archival and printed source materials. The Historiographical Institute of the University of Tokyo, successor to the government historical office created in 1869, in just two of its many series has published some 360 volumes of source materials covering Japan's political history from the ninth century to the Meiji Restoration. The Institute is at this point probably less than halfway through its ambitious compilation program. Another compilation, *The Historical Documents of the Prefectures of the Early Meiji Era* (the original of which is lodged in the Cabinet Library in 2,166 volumes running to 671,600 pages), is available in 378 microfilm reels.[5] More significant is the range of historical materials now available, for these cover the gamut from diaries of court nobles to village tax records.

Finally, the historical profession is served by a comprehensive and sophisticated apparatus of reference works. The Kawade Shobō's *Encyclopedia of Japanese History* runs to 22 volumes. The Heibonsha's *Encyclopedia of World History* covers the world in 25 volumes. The massive 1,900-page *Handbook for Historians* contains Japanese chronological tables, genealogies, roster of officeholders, and indexes to documentary collections. There are annual bibliographies and annual reports on the state of the field.[6] An example of such reporting can be seen in the extensive and carefully compiled reports presented by the Japanese National Committee of Historical Sciences since 1960 for the periodic meetings of the International Congress of Historical Sciences.[7]

So much for the apparatus; what of the content? How have modern Japanese written their history? The Japanese interpretation of their own history has evolved through numerous phases during the last hundred years, from the antiquarian approach to the Marxist, from the nationalistic to the world-centered. Perhaps the most important feature of the Japanese effort at writing their own history has been the absorption into it of a vocabulary which links their work to the community of historians working in the Western tradition. Before reaching the present state in which Japanese historical studies can communicate directly to Western historians through the simple technique of translation, there had to be a prior transformation of the conceptual vocabulary used by Japanese scholars. This was brought about in part as the result of a growing familiarity with the works of Hegel, Marx, Lenin, or Weber, and also as a result of the necessary coining of new words which were not in the lexicon of premodern Japanese historians. What would the Japanese historian today do without such newly coined words as *kokka* (nation), *kokka-shugi* (nationalism), *jiyū* (freedom), *minshushugi* (democracy), *shakaishugi* (socialism), *nōdo* (serf), *burujowa* (bourgeoisie), *kenryoku kōzō* (power structure), *fuashizumu* (fascism), *zettai shugi* (absolutism), *kindaika* (modernization), and *shihonshugi* (capitalism)?

The creation of a modern school of historical study in Japan has been a remarkable achievement—all the more so because the effort has been directed for the most part inwardly to satisfy a national need. In other words, the chief interest of Japanese historians has been to interpret their own history to their own people with the use, when necessary or advantageous, of concepts derived from the West. Although a few books by Japanese historians have been written for translation into English in order to gain world attention, these have been addressed in the main to popular audiences. Ironically, it has been primarily through the efforts of Western scholars that Japanese history has been introduced to the world audience.

Prior to World War II the prime center for Japanese studies by Westerners was Tokyo, where an international community of scholars and diplomats wrote for the *Transactions of the Asiatic Society of Japan*. The most respected historian writing in English was George Sansom, who was strictly speaking an amateur scholar although a very good student of Japan. The war and subsequent Allied Occupation had the effect of transferring the center of Japanese studies in the West to the United States. It gave rise, first of all, to enough Japanese language specialists to do for a generation of active scholarship. On top of this, the postwar boom in area programs in colleges and universities stimulated an explosive increase in academic positions for Japanese specialists in the United States. Within a decade there was created in this country the whole complex support system of language programs, libraries, research centers, and publication facilities needed to make Japanese studies a recognized field of academic endeavor. The result was a dramatic multiplication of college- and university-based historians of Japan and an accompanying flood of monographs and translations dealing with Japanese history.[8]

At the close of the Pacific War there was but one book on premodern Japan suitable for use as a college history text—Sansom's *Japan's Short Cultural History*.[9] Today we have the choice of three or four, and in addition many aids in teaching, such as source books and syllabi. Before the war there were perhaps eight academic institutions which offered training in the Japanese language, and that on only a limited basis. Today no major center is without a full-scale program in Japanese language and literature, and many less well staffed institutions are able to teach the language through the use of newly developed language lab techniques. Aside from the establishment of the Ford Foundation Foreign Area Fellowship Program and the government-supported programs under the National Defense Education Act, the most significant development has been the creation of the Inter-University Japanese Language Center in Tokyo, a half-million-dollar-a-year facility for intensive study. There are today over 200 professional historians of Japan working in American colleges and universities. They are, for the most part, well trained both in history and in the Japanese language.[10]

An important feature of the current state of Japanese studies in this country is the high degree of communication that is taking place between the Japanese and American professional communities. Although few Japanese historians of note have taught in the United States, many have visited our campuses on research grants or to attend academic conferences. A fair number of their works have been translated into English, as for example, the distinguished works of Professor Maruyama Masao. More important, American scholars now almost routinely travel to Japan to work with or learn from Japanese scholars. Thus the works of American historians of Japan have as their minimum requirement the expectation that they reflect the highest level of Japanese scholarship. To this extent they serve as the prime means of export of Japanese scholarship to the Western world.

These parallel and interrelated developments in Japan and America (and increasingly in Britain, Australia, Europe, and Mexico) are of enormous significance. Japanese history is now more accessible than that of any other non-Western nation and thus is capable of being assimilated into the "aggregate" of world history. But the process of assimilation has yet to be pursued systematically, and this for obvious reasons. The idea of universal history is, in fact, a very recent invention, still inadequately formulated by its proponents and vigorously rejected by its opponents.

In actual practice attempts to place Japanese history into world context have taken three forms. Western, and even some Japanese, scholars, starting with the premise that the mainstream of world history is that which flowed from Greece and Rome to western Europe and now to America, have interpreted Japanese history in the context of "Westernization." To them Japan remained outside the mainstream until the middle of the nineteenth century, when the Perry expedition lured the Japanese out of national seclusion. Thus it was the "impact of the West" that was the critical factor in placing Japan onto the road toward world involvement. Japan's modern history, they believe, must be comprehended in terms of the effort of the Japanese people to catch up with the advanced Western states. Premodern history becomes prelude to this process. That the Japanese people, by and large, have acquiesced to this interpretation is revealed in the statement issued by the Japanese government committee for the celebration of the Japanese Centennial in 1968. Japan, it stated, having run the race since 1854, had come to a point when it could proudly say that it had caught up with the West and could now chart its own course.[11]

All through Japan's modern century there were Japanese who kept alive an alternative view of the relation which their country had to the rest of the world, one which placed Japan at the center of the historical stage. This view, which had its start in the Shinto revival movement of the nineteenth century, reached its ultimate expression in the propagandistic writings brought out between 1938 and 1945. They claimed for the Japanese a unique position in world history as the one people capable of bridging the differences between Western individuality and Eastern community-based morality. It was the presumed destiny of the Japanese emperor to unite the world under his benevolent rule.[12] Defeat in World War II laid this argument to rest, though there are still those who see Japan as the ultimate synthesizer of Eastern and Western cultures.

Between, or beyond, these two ethnocentric extremes have been the attempts to devise universal, or world history, conceptions that could transcend or embrace individual national histories. Of these, the Marxist is the most widely known, and in the case of Japan the most broadly applied. In one way or another, Marxist theory has touched nearly every aspect of Japanese historiography in the twentieth century. The reason for this is twofold. First, Marxism has offered to Japanese historians the only fully formulated system of historical analysis that provides a world framework into which their history could be placed. Second, Marxist theory, by focusing on social and economic change, has served an important methodological purpose by drawing the attention of Japanese historians away from their early concentration on political history at the elite level. Most Japanese historians today adopt the Marxist form of periodization, dividing Japan's past into blocks of time labeled ancient, feudal, and capitalistic. And through such periodization, Japanese history is placed alongside the presumably comparable histories of Europe and China, forming a unified context of comparison.

Fifteen years ago I led a group of Americans to organize a meeting with Japanese scholars on the theme of "modernization" in Japan. An effort was made on that occasion to establish a presumably "value-free" conception of modernization which would transcend both Marxist theory and the common Western habit of equating modernization with progress. The occasion was the Hakone Conference, which was to loom so large in the intellectual discourse between American and Japanese historians in the last decade and a half. What we learned at that time was the basic incompatibility of two approaches, one ideological the other methodological. The underlying purpose of the American scholars at Hakone had been to move out from under any unicausal or "grand design" conception of historical change and to work instead with the more limited theories and hypotheses advanced by the various social sciences.[13]

By putting aside the assurance that history has been shaped by some ascertainable grand design, however, the historian opens up the question of whether there is anything more than unlimited diversity and randomness in his data. And if that is the case, how is Japanese history to be studied other than as a completely separate strand in human affairs? The anthropologist Clyde Kluckhohn gives us an answer when he writes: "Each human being is unique in his concrete totality, but he resembles other human beings in certain respects and some particular human beings a great deal."[14] The search for patterns and uniformities in human organization and behavior rests on the premise that basic structures are limited and classifiable, and that human motivation is rooted in common psychological traits. Language, for all its diversity, falls into a finite number of categories of classification; so do techniques of agriculture and systems of family organization. Institutions, technologies, systems of belief, these are the levels at which historical comparison can most properly take place. The emphasis must be on limited cross-cultural comparisons and analyses, not on some grand design. And if Japanese and European data are to be pulled together for comparative analysis, this can only be done through the development of a common conceptual vocabulary at these more manageable levels.

Historians have yet to proceed very far in the creation of a uniform vocabulary of cross-cultural analysis. What is called for is best illustrated in some of the more methodologically sophisticated social science disciplines. Economists, especially those involved in the study of economic development, now find increasingly that they cannot omit Japan from their computations. Students of political behavior have accepted the lack of any absolute historical norm by developing the concept of "political culture." Increasingly it becomes possible in these spheres to expect the use of a data base which extends across cultures and a uniformity of vocabulary and theory which transcends cultural or chronological boundaries.

We as historians working out of the Western historiographical tradition have had a particular problem in the assimilation of Japanese history into a pluralistic world perspective because of the dominant role which our Western-based analytical concepts have played not only in our own thinking but also in the thinking of Japanese scholars. The actual assimilation of Japanese historical data into our historical consciousness and into our educational system has been slow and incomplete. Yet the effort is being made with considerable success in the years since World War II.

The first essential for the kind of assimilative approach to Japanese history described above is a matter of basic attitude. It starts with a commitment to avoid exoticism and the enigmatic explanation. It cultivates a humility which claims no more for our own culture than for the Japanese. It rests on a belief in the basic unity of the human experience as well as the inevitable diversity of the human response.

From this position the first and most fundamental requirement is that we, as outsiders, strive continuously for the creation of "contexts of understanding" or, in the Japanese case, "contexts of plausibility" which will eliminate the mystery and exoticism from our telling of the Japanese story. The important thing is to be able, for each period or each situation in Japanese history, to demonstrate its own integrity, its own inner coherence, in the process of explaining away what may seem enigmatic and contradictory from an outsider's point of view. This may seem easy to do. But for those who have limited acquaintance with Japanese culture, the temptation is to accept familiar Western behavior as the norm and to explain Japanese deviation from that norm as being "unique" or "oriental" and hence inexplicable.

Let me cite a few examples of what I mean. One of the eras of

Japanese history most subject to exotic treatment is the late Heian period, that period in the eleventh century when the Japanese aristocracy reached a peak of affluence and creative capacity. The *Tale of Genji*, written at this time and translated so beautifully into English by Arthur Waley, told of a court society of almost pure aesthetes. G. B. Sansom in his early writings created a picture of an effete aristocracy based in large part on his readings of the *Genji* and diaries of court ladies. Yet as a practical historian he realized that a playboy aristocracy could hardly have governed Japan in peace, as indeed it did, for over three centuries. He himself in his later work corrected his "context of understanding" for Heian Japan by adding new materials from the writings of some of the more diligent court nobles. He thereby showed their concern for practical administrative matters. [15]

To take another example from a slightly later period, there was a political situation in the early thirteenth century which is often cited as the height of Japanese institutional irrationality, something which could have existed only in Japan. At that time political power in Japan was held by the Hōjō family, regents of the Kamakura shogun who, in turn, had grasped power from the imperial court. This resulted, in Sansom's words, in "the astonishing spectacle of a state at the head of which stands a titular emperor whose vestigial functions are usurped by an abdicated emperor, and whose real power is nominally delegated to a hereditary military dictator but actually wielded by an hereditary adviser of that dictator." [16] How devious can the Japanese be, and how irrational their use of behind-the-scenes political arrangements? But if we understand that this situation developed at a time when legitimacy was vested in family lineages, the use of elaborate kinship step-downs to justify delegation of power is in reality no more mysterious than, say, the complex structure of corporate entities in a modern financial combine.

To cite yet another example, the gruesome practice of seppuku, which so shocked Western observers, can be explained if we realize that for the samurai caught in an infraction of the law, ritual suicide became the only way of assuring the continuance of his family name, property, and status beyond his death. Execution as a common criminal automatically resulted in the complete extinction of his family line and its patrimony. The things men give their lives for differ from culture to culture. And we do an injustice to both the samurai of medieval Japan and the kamikaze pilots of a later age if we explain their actions simply by saying that they held their lives cheaply. Their actions reflect profoundly different but reasonable relationships among individual, family, society, and government.

One could go on with such examples, but enough has been revealed to explain what I mean by "contexts of understanding." The foreign historian of Japan is faced with problems of cross-cultural explanation and interpretation at almost every turn. The mere fact of translation from the Japanese requires a selection of terminology which either explains or obfuscates Japanese historic behavior. Is it proper to call the Japanese *tennō* emperor? Is a *shō* a manor or an estate? Is a *han* a fief or a domain? Is a *hyakushō* a peasant, a serf, or a farmer? The perfection of an accurate and purposeful vocabulary for problems of this sort has been the main advance which contemporary historians, both foreign and Japanese, have achieved in their handling of Japanese history in a world context. They have come a considerable distance in their capacity to tell Japanese history in such a way that its main actors, their motivations and actions, are made plausible to audiences outside of Japan.

But the attainment of plausibility is simply the first level of what is meant by assimilation. The next level inevitably moves into the risky terrain of comparison. Comparison is the essence of assimilation. The urge to compare Japanese history with that of Europe is particularly strong, not only because of the close intellectual contact between contemporary Japanese and Western historians but because of many very real or apparent similarities that exist. Sansom's writing abounds with comparative observations, many of them quite provocative. But are they valid? Are comparable things being compared? And are the right conclusions being drawn? We again confront the problem of contexts, this time "contexts of comparability." Sansom shied away from the theoretical and definitional problems which underlay his comparisons. But in making comparisons between Tudor England and Tokugawa Japan, he obviously assumed a framework of comparability, and behind such an assumption was an implied set of criteria which made his comparisons legitimate. Chronological equivalence is not in itself sufficient justification.

It is now virtually impossible to conceive of the history of Japan from 1500 to 1900 without meeting head on the question of comparison with Europe. For the Marxist historian this chapter in Japan's history is explained in terms of the universal process of passage from feudal to capitalist society. For others the issue of comparability comes down to the definition of two complex concepts: feudalism and modernization. These two approaches, one based on a universal concept of historical change, the other seeking to define and apply theoretical models in the manner of Max Weber, remain basically in conflict.

The utility of the ideal type model is that it permits comparisons to be made without committing the historian to the acceptance of a specific and inevitable sequence of events. What the model does is to identify the variables the historian chooses to recognize as being essential if comparison is to be considered valid. In other words, it becomes the historian's statement of how many similarities there need to be between two societies or two historical situations before comparisons can legitimately be made.

Comparison illuminates both by analogy and by clarification of differences. Between feudal Europe and post-1500 Japan parallels abound. The Japanese samurai equates with the European knight. In Japan there were castles and fiefs, oaths sworn in blood, and peasants treated as serfs. Yet there were numerous and profound differences which illuminate the deepest social and religious contrasts between feudal Europe and feudal Japan. The relationship between lord and vassal, for instance, was conceived of in family terms in Japan. The vassal was called the "houseman" or "child" of the lord. The vassal's pledge of loyalty was absolute and made no reference to his own rights with respect to the lord, although the lord did guarantee protection of the vassal's possession of his fief. In Japan neither the church nor the law was above political authority vested in the feudal lord.

Japan was clearly a society which bore great superficial resemblance to that of medieval Europe, and yet it was based on legal, philosophical, and religious principles quite different from those of Europe. By comparison with the rest of Asia, China in particular, however, the similarities seem at least as significant as the differences. The late Kan'ichi Asakawa was the first to suggest that Japan's "feudal heritage" might have had something to do with the manner in which the Japanese people reacted to their confrontation with the West.[17] For it may well be that the samurai as militant men of action, the lord-vassal ethic, and the social class categories which contrasted so much with those of China provided the fundamental elements which made possible Japan's detachment from the Chinese world view and provided the activating force in Japan's rapid acquisition of the sense of national identity which so eased the transition into modern nationhood.

Once questions are raised about the relationship between Japan's feudal background and the process of modernization in Japan, we are in the thick of still another definitional problem. The historian's interpretation both of the Tokugawa era and of the Meiji Restoration era depends to large extent on his conception of what is meant by "being modern." Here again two different lines of analysis have characterized the work of Japanese and American scholars. Marxists have concentrated on evidence of social tension, peasant violence, political oppression, and ideological conservatism. Their search has been for the roots of "absolutism" in Tokugawa society. Meanwhile the recent work of American scholars, based on the premise that modernization is defined by certain rates of urbanization, literacy, social mobility, bureaucratization, and nationalism, has been characterized by the search for antecedents of "modernization" in the Tokugawa past.

Whichever approach to modernization is taken, however, the chief interest of historians writing about the Meiji Restoration today has been to put the event into the context of other major modern revolutions like those of Russia, France, England, and the United States on the one hand, and of China, India, Mexico, Turkey, and Egypt on the other. What used to be told simply as a story of Japan's adaptability to the "Western impact" has taken on new dimensions. It is now assumed that Japan, like the countries of Europe, struggled with universal problems of modernization, confronted dilemmas of balancing national unity against mass political participation, attempted to deal with the social effects of industrialization and urbanization, and above all, faced the choice of whether or not to use warfare in national policy. No period in Japanese history has been more thoroughly studied in comparative terms than that of the Restoration. And no event in Japanese history has depended for interpretation so directly on general theories of social change and on comparison with other societies.

The use of general models is a useful means of structuring the historian's efforts at comparative analysis. In all of the instances cited so far, however, the models have been derived in the first instance from Western data. The norms, whether explicit or implicit, are consequently identified with the West. But the reverse is conceivable as well. Could not models be fashioned out of Japanese data and applied to other societies, even our own? Should not the historian who aspires to a balanced world perspective consider his models to be hypothetical until the Japanese dimension has been put into his calculation? Are there not instances in which the critical judgment should assume Japanese norms as being more universal, and contrasting European conditions the deviations? The answer, of course, is yes, and it is increasingly evident that "reverse judgments" of this sort are being made as an ultimate step in the assimilation of Japanese data into our historical consciousness. In the existing historical literature I find examples in four different analytical categories.

In the first place, there is the category of differing concepts of periodization. The question of whose historical calendar to adopt, ours or theirs, is well brought out in the case of the so-called "Christian century." As an exercise in comparative historical periodization, we discover that for Western historians the years between 1540 and 1640 constitute a distinct and important period in their conception of Japanese history by virtue of the presence of Christian missionaries in Japan at that time. From the Japanese point of view, however, these hundred years have no significance at all as a special period. To the Japanese of the time, as well as to modern Japanese historians, the great event of that century was the reunification of the country which occurred between 1568 and 1614. The term "Christian century" is clearly a Western conceit.

Second, there are those obvious lessons in the field of foreign relations—situations in which national interests are in conflict. The causes of Japan's war with the United States, for instance, when studied objectively, afford a sobering exercise in national self-evaluation. Japan, as the only modern nation to attack the United States frontally, forces American introspection. For if we accept, as we must, the fact that Japan did not attack the United States out of sheer madness, then it becomes possible to imagine situations in which other nations rationally driven to extremities might find peaceful coexistence with the United States impossible or at least unbearable.

Third are those many instances in which differing cultural values lead to different interpretations. The Occupation era in Japan is a virtual storehouse of issues which demonstrate the relativity of national interests, historical interpretations, and cultural values. What were the basic principles of government, society, and morality which the United States attempted to export to Japan? And why did some reforms take effect and others not? What is the difference between democracy (our term), *demokurashi* (their effort to pronounce our term), and *minshushugi* (their word for democracy)? On what basis did one country invoke a superior morality and thereby send to death for war guilt the wartime leaders of a defeated Japan? How is it that the principle of nonresort to warfare which the United States wrote into the so-called Showa Constitution is now clung to by the Japanese, while our government finds the clause at odds with its desire to see Japan, as the phrase goes, carry its burden of security in the Pacific?

Fourth, and finally, there are the possibilities of generating true alternative models. The kind of questioning I have just suggested helps to create the intellectual environment in which we, as Americans, can accept the Japanese in their own right and on their own terms. Once this is done, the possibilities are enormous and exciting. For just at the time that we ourselves are questioning many of our inherited values or our capacity to cope with the "postindustrial world," Japan offers new ways of looking at life which are not simply retreats into an exotic escapism. Japanese culture provides evidence of different life values, different political and social concepts, and different religious attitudes which contrast fundamentally with those which we in the Western tradition have come to believe as immutable—models which may well prove more useful for those who would live in peace in the mass-industrial future which lies ahead. From their Confucian-Buddhist religious tradition, the Japanese have always looked with skepticism upon the extreme accent on individualism which has been so admired in the West, particularly in the United States. Yet we ourselves are finding our faith in individualism shaken by contemporary conditions. Will the Japanese with their more collectivist ethic prove themselves better equipped than we to handle the conditions of mass-industrial society? Can Japanese history be studied, not simply to explain Japan, but to learn from it?

As I survey the work of scholars outside of Japan during the last decade, particularly through the evidence of papers delivered at international congresses (for instance, the Japan P.E.N. Club meeting of 1972 in Kyoto)[18] or in the research designs submitted to foundations (particularly the Japan Foundation), I find remarkable evidence of a new trend in intellectual approach. Where American scholars heretofore were concerned mainly with explanatory research (the attempt to make Japanese institutions or events understandable to non-Japanese), this recent trend seeks to use Japanese data for creative purposes. The evidence is particularly strong in the humanistic disciplines, where one may find a writer wishing to study in Japan in order to find inspiration for a new form of poetry, or a dramatist who wishes to study Kabuki for new theatrical techniques applicable to the American stage. There are musicians who seek to explore Japanese music as a way to gain new theoretical insights into the use of sound. The influence of Japanese architecture or ceramic technique in the United States is visible nearly everywhere. Institutions are less easily seen as holding possible alternatives. But the current interest in Japanese managerial systems comes from a practical recognition of Japanese business successes in a competitive world market.

We, as historians, also work in a world market of ideas. Japanese history has much to offer on this world market, but the process of assimilation or universalization has only begun. The process, as we have noted, has operated at four different levels. First is the straightforward but basic matter of the collection and classification of historical evidence. Second comes the task of communication beyond the shores of Japan. This begins with the establishment of contexts of plausibility which would make possible the explanation of Japanese history in ways that carry meaning to non-Japanese. Third is the creation of contexts of comparability, which are necessary preludes to certain kinds of cross-cultural analysis and to the inclusion of Japanese data into universal systems of analytical study. Fourth, and finally, there remains the still largely unexplored areas in which Japanese historical experience can offer alternative models of behavior or attitude. We in America have had a hand in carrying forward each of these levels and have begun in the last few years to take seriously the thought that Japan, its historical record and present constitution, may have lessons for us to learn.

NOTES

1. Herman Kahn, *The Emerging Japanese Superstate: Challenge and Response* (Englewood Cliffs, N.J.: Prentice-Hall, 1970).

2. Sir George B. Sansom, *Japan in World History* (New York: International Secretariat, Institute of Pacific Relations, 1951), pp. 5–6.

3. See Jiro Numata, "Shigeno Yasutsugu and the Modern Tokyo Tradition of Historical Writing," in *Historians of China and Japan*, ed. William G. Beasley and E. G. Pulleyblank (London: Oxford University Press, 1961), pp. 264–87. Also, John W. Hall, "Japanese Historiography," in *International Encyclopedia of the Social Sciences* (New York: Macmillan, 1968), 6:413–20.

4. *Nihon Rekishi*, special issue (April 1974).

5. See the catalogue of Yushodo Microfilm Publications for 1967–68.

6. See John W. Hall, *Japanese History: A Guide to Japanese Reference and Research Materials* (Ann Arbor: University of Michigan Press, 1954).

7. The latest such bibliography was prepared for the XIV International Congress of the Historical Sciences in San Francisco, 1975: *Bibliography of Japanese Historiography (1969–1973)*, ed. The Japanese National Committee of Historical Sciences (Tokyo, 1975).

8. John Whitney Hall, *Japanese History: New Dimensions of Approach and Understanding*, Service Center for Teachers of History Publication No. 34, 2d. ed. (Washington: American Historical Association, 1966).

9. Sir George B. Sansom, *Japan, A Short Cultural History* (New York: The Century Co., 1931; rev. ed., New York: D. Appleton-Century Co., 1943).

10. For a thorough description of the field of Japanese studies in America, see *Japanese Studies in the United States* (New York, 1970), a report prepared by the SSRC-ACLS Joint Committee on Japanese Studies.

11. See the statement of the Japanese government committee for the Meiji Centennial in John Whitney Hall, "Reflections on a Centennial," *The Journal of Asian Studies* 27, no. 4 (August 1967): 713.

12. Among the prewar KBS (Society for International Cultural Relations) publications

is Kenzō Akiyama's *The History of Nippon* (Tokyo: Kokusai bunka shinkokai, 1941), which stresses this theme.

13. See John W. Hall, "Changing Conceptions of the Modernization of Japan," in *Changing Japanese Attitudes toward Modernization*, ed. Marius B. Jansen (Princeton: Princeton University Press, 1965). The most extensive discussion of the so-called "modernization controversy" from the Japanese point of view is Kimbara Samon, *Nihon "kindaika" ron no rekishi zō*, rev. ed. (Tokyo, 1971).

14. Clyde Cluckhohn, "Common Humanity and Diverse Cultures," in *The Human Meaning of the Social Sciences*, ed. Daniel Lerner (New York: Meridian Books, 1959), p. 280.

15. Although he still played down the functional importance of the Heian courtier's attention to administrative matters, Sansom balanced his picture of Heian court society in his chapter on "The Rule of Taste," in *A History of Japan to 1336* (Stanford: Stanford University Press, 1958), pp. 177–96.

16. Sansom, *Japan*, p. 247.

17. Asakawa, while still a student at Dartmouth College, wrote in 1899 a paper entitled "A Preliminary Study of Japanese Feudalism," in which this point is made.

18. The Japan P.E.N. Club, ed., *Studies on Japanese Culture*, 2 vols. (Tokyo: P.E.N. Club, 1973).

9

Periodization in History: Renaissance and Reformation

Lewis W. Spitz

Paul Valéry describes history as the most dangerous potion ever concocted in the laboratory of the human mind. To reflect on the future of history is indeed not to be undertaken lightly without concern for the implications of that very act. Christopher Dawson once observed that it is unfortunate for a civilization to have sociologists and historians, for when they begin to grow self-conscious, they are nearing their end. Nicholas Berdyaev, in *The Meaning of History*, described the four stages in the growth of civilizations—barbarity, vigorous growth, culture, and civilization, the final cultivated age in which self-conscious intellectuals speculate not only on the future of the world but on the future of their discipline. Arnold J. Toynbee, of course, considers the wars of religion as the onset of our "time of troubles," and that even this time is running out. André Malraux observes that "Western Civilization has begun to doubt its own credentials." We cannot, therefore, naively or innocently return to examine the *incunabulum* or cradle of modernity, the "twin sources" of our present age, without an acute awareness of what that very intellectual enterprise may itself imply.

It was the great historian of the Reformation, Lord Acton, who pronounced the dictum that history should concentrate on problems and not on periods. But periodization is itself a problem, for historians know full well that any division of time into carefully defined periods is merely a convenient device for conceptualization, an instrument for grappling with the continuum of the "seamless web of history" on one hand and the chaotic mass of particulars, the shards and fragments of the past, on the other. They are acutely aware of the complexities of every age, the cross currents and new dimensions

189

constantly being discovered and explored in research, and yet they need general concepts in order to impose order and give meaning to their account of past actuality. The extent to which those concepts identify the peculiar or unique characteristic of our age, point to its cultural center of gravity, or assist in mentally relating its multifaceted aspects and variegated components, determines their validity. The historian, Hermann Hesse mused in his *Magister Ludi*, must expose himself to chaos while retaining a faith in order and meaning.

The great Annalist, Fernand Braudel of the Sixth Section, whose masterpiece on the Mediterranean world in the age of Philip II has at last appeared in English, observed that historians first create concepts, then glue them as labels on their precious bottles, and end up giving the labels authority over their contents.[1] The label, to be useful, must reflect as accurately as possible the contents of the age, and that is the point at which the discussion must start rather than end. Historians as masters of the millennia do enjoy their privileges. "To give an accurate description of what has never occurred is the inalienable privilege and proper occupation of the historian," Oscar Wilde observed in *A Woman of No Importance*. But mislabeling their Grecian urns can only multiply confusion.

The poet e.e. cummings is impatient with any temporal divisions. "As for a few trifling delusions like the 'past' and 'present' and 'future,'" he exclaimed, "of quote mankind unquote, they may be big enough for a couple of billion supermechanized submorons but they're much too small for one human being." But for all human beings taken collectively, which constitute the near "infinite subject matter of history," to borrow Schopenhauer's phrase, temporal categories are necessary, and that is where the problem of periodization begins. It is not true of the major periods that historians have arbitrarily concocted labels and applied them, for the process has been far more interesting than that. A certain notion of the meaning of an age is born usually in the minds of the elite of the time or of the time immediately succeeding. The meaning is discussed, argued, simplified, reduced to a formula, a phrase, a term, and is then adopted by the historians, canonized in their books and institutionalized in university curricula.

The tripartite division of Western history into ancient, medieval, and modern developed in that very way. The *trecento* and increasingly the *quattrocento* humanists became disdainful toward and demeaning of the centuries preceding their own times. The Protestant reformers, magisterial and radical alike, took up the theme of the dark ages that contrasted so badly with the golden age of Augustus and with the pristine purity of New Testament Christianity. Their own times seemed, as both Erasmus and Luther expressed it, to be the dawn of a golden age. The concept of a long cultural caesura between antiquity and present days, a thousand years without a bath, with Dante as "the voice of ten silent centuries," gathered momentum. Gradually the overall reading of history changed under pressure from the new view. The time-honored account of universal history based upon the four kingdoms, with the *translatio imperii* serving to assure the legitimacy and permanence of the Holy Roman Empire which was to last to the end of time, gave way to the tripartite division in which the centuries between antiquity and the Renaissance came to be viewed as merely a *medium aevum*, a Middle Age, a moratorium or, dynamically conceived, as an age of transition to the new. The tripartite division was finally enthroned by Christoph Keller or Cellarius, a Lutheran with a humanistic education, about 1688 in a widely used textbook, a history of the *medium aevum* from the times of Constantine the Great to Constantine XI (1453). Despite the fact that the four kingdoms or empires reading of history was strongly entrenched in the German university curricula and persisted in church history writing, according to Karl Heussi, down to the end of the eighteenth century, the new threefold division of universal history—for until the end of the seventeenth century European history was considered to be universal history—gradually over several decades made its way into the books and universities. Werner Kaegi points to Voltaire's *Essai sur les mœurs* (1757) as the terminus of the four kingdoms reading of history and the triumph of the "great ages" view—two ancient (Athens and Rome) and two modern (the Italian Renaissance and the age of Voltaire), with the dark Middle Ages in between. Despite some brave beginnings by Lucio Varga, Luigi Sorrento, and Giorgio Falco, no analysis or history of the concept *medium aevum* exists similar in scope and depth to Wallace K. Ferguson's *The Renaissance in Historical Thought*.[2]

The French historians refined *histoire moderne* by introducing *histoire contemporaine*, beginning, of course, with the French Revolution. The German historians, judging from the review division of the *Historische Zeitschrift*, prefer to move directly from *Mittelalter* to *Reformation*. American historians speak of "recent U.S." or "contemporary Europe" and even use the paralogistic term "current history." Dietrich Gerhard has made a very intelligent plea for reperiodization, substituting the era of "old Europe" from the eleventh to the eighteenth century and modern Europe as the eighteenth century to the present, beginning with the Enlightenment, the scientific, industrial, and the French revolutions. Moreover, with the eighteenth century, European history becomes increasingly enmeshed with world history throughout the globe.[3] His perfectly reasonable suggestion will remain stillborn, however, until the pressures of history itself lead historians to adopt it, perhaps some time far down the road of the future when the centuries since the eighteenth century have multiplied and this new triad will have achieved chronological symmetry. But the historian, said the philosopher Friedrich von Schlegel, is a prophet looking backward, so we must turn again to look at what is and has been rather than at what may well be in the future.

Within the large chronological and geographical limits and divisions of history, historians must devise subdivisions in which, as Delio Cantimori has argued, the two objectives are achieved of (1) corresponding to a general conception of historical development and (2) permitting the stabilization of the peculiar characteristics of every period and of making clear the connection with the different forms of historical development. Periodization also undertakes to order the historiographical material and to connect it with the fundamental general tendency of human society of a particular period, which presupposes something called interpretation.[4] Historians can more easily make a case for the subdivisions of history than for the major divisions, though not a single one of these periods or tags for the period stands unchallenged, and some are still the center of stormy controversy whether it be the age of the Enlightenment, Baroque, Nationalism, Feudalism, Hellenism, or Renaissance and Reformation. Wallace K. Ferguson has called the Renaissance "the most intractable problem child of historiography."

The very terms Renaissance and Reformation have been protean concepts used in many different contexts and only gradually attached with specific connotations to an era of European history which we are conditioned to consider the birthplace of modern times. It will be instructive (1) to review the history of the concepts themselves, (2) to consider the interior cohesiveness of the period itself, (3) to reflect on appropriate chronological limits, and (4) to review the present trends and future possibilities of historical research as they bear upon the problem of periodization. That is a tall order for a short paper and it will have to be done more by suggestion and implication than as a definitive statement. In 40 B.C. the Roman historian Sallust wrote: *In primis arduum res gestas scribere*, the writing of history is among the most difficult things to do.

1. *History of the Concepts*

The Renaissance denotes a well-known but indefinite space of time and a certain phase in the development of Europe. As John Addington Symonds already asserted, it denotes the transition from the period of history we call the Middle Ages to that which we call modern. On the other hand, it implies those changes in the intellectual and moral attitude of the Italian and non-Russian European nations by which the transition can be characterized. The metaphor of rebirth may suggest that the peoples of central and western Europe, beginning with Italy, entered upon a fresh stage of vital energy in general, implying a fuller consciousness and a freer exercise of faculties than they had previously employed. Or the metaphor may imply simply the resuscitation of intellectual activities stimulated by the revival of classical learning and its application in art and letters. Whichever emphasis is adopted will determine not only what range of social as well as cultural phenomena are to be included and integrated, but also how the Italian and the trans-Alpine manifestations of renaissance are to be related.

The word "renaissance" itself had a long and fascinating history. The Romans borrowed poetic imagery from the renewal myths of the ancient Near East. Martial used the symbol of the phoenix as a vitalistic metaphor for the renewal of Rome, the idea of *Roma renascens.* The longing for a rebirth was associated with the hope for a return of the "Golden Age" under the aegis of Saturn. The best-known expression of that hope was the passage in Vergil's fourth *Eclogue* which was interpreted in the Christian era as a prophecy of the virgin birth and the new spiritual age.[5] The term *restitutio* for renewal was used in Roman law in antiquity and received currency with the revival of Roman law from the twelfth century on and especially during this period.

During the medieval period the connotation was usually that of a spiritual regeneration, as in the Scriptural passage John 3: 3, "Except a man be born again, he cannot see the kingdom of God (*nisi quis renatus fuerit denuo*). Through Christ man experiences a *renovatio ad imaginem et similitudinem Dei.*[6] The idea of the rebirth of Rome was alive and surfaced vigorously though futilely from time to time with Arnold of Brescia and a few others. Ecstatic prophetic movements arose such as that of the Spiritual Franciscans, inspired by Joachim of Flora, in which the year 1260 was expected to begin a new age of the Holy Spirit. Cola di Rienzo, the "last of the Roman tribunes," as Richard Wagner dubbed him, who sought to revive the Roman republic in 1347, was himself influenced not only by Livy and antique sources but by Joachimite ideas. In his *History of Florence*, Machiavelli said that under Rienzo, "the ancient provinces, seeing Rome arise to new life, again raised their heads."[7]

Although the term *rinascita* was first introduced and gradually adopted only during the sixteenth century in the sense in which historians have come to use it, already during the fourteenth and fifteenth centuries the ideas of a cultural rebirth replaced Cola's notion of a political rebirth. As early as the beginning of the fourteenth century, Benvenuto Campesani of Vicenza entitled an epigram on the discovery of a Catallus manuscript *Versus . . . de resurrectione Catulli poete Veronensis*. In *The Decameron*, Boccaccio hailed Giotto as the artist who had restored painting to its original glory:

> Now he [Giotto] who brought back to light that art which for many centuries had lain buried under errors (and thus was more fitted to please the eyes of the ignorant than the minds of the wise), may rightly be called one of the shining lights of Florentine glory. And the more so since he performed it with the greatest humility, and, although the master of all painters living, always refused to be called master.[8]

This view of Giotto as the restorer of the fine arts became standard during the following centuries. Filippo Villani, Matteo Palmieri, Lorenzo Ghiberti, and many others shared this assessment of Giotto as the pioneer of a new period in art. Around 1550, Giorgio Vasari (1511–1574), author of the *Lives of the Painters*, characterized the preceding two centuries as a period of *rinascita* in the fine arts. He considered the period from Giotto (1266–1337) with his naturalism in style to Michelangelo (1475–1564) to represent a new age in art, just as a new day had dawned in letters beginning with Petrarch (1304–1374) and reaching to Erasmus (1469–1536). Vasari was the first historian of art to use the threefold characterization of *maniera antica, maniera vecchia,* and *maniera moderna,* the period of the *rinascita* of the arts from the mid-thirteenth century on. Aeneas Silvius, too, linked the revival of letters with that of art.[9] Paolo Giovio, in his *Eulogies of Famous Men of Letters*, applied the word *rinascita* to literature. In 1553, Pierre Belon (c. 1518–1564), the French natural scientist, substituted his French word *renaissance* for *rinascita*. The sciences would be reborn, he wrote, after a long slumber in the darkness of ignorance just as the plants awaken at the end of winter and begin to grow under the warm rays of the spring sun. The French word stuck, often reflecting Belon's consciousness of an historical epoch which, as he mistakenly saw it, began in Florence and spread through Italy and Europe in the sixteenth century.

In providing a term for an epoch in Italian and European history gradually taken over into historiography, the men of the sixteenth century were reflecting a self-conscious assessment of the age by its leading protagonists and participants, the humanists and artists. The term gradually came to be applied not only as they intended it to the rebirth of culture and the rebirth of classical culture, but to nearly all aspects of society and culture in terms of economic, political, and social life. The consciousness of living in a newly reborn age grew steadily over three centuries. The fourteenth-century Florentine chronicler Giovanni Villani (c. 1276–1348) made no distinction at all between the medieval period and his own times. Francesco Petrarch (1304–1374) felt acutely the difference between the *tempora antiqua* (ancient) and *tempora nova* (modern), by which he meant the dark ages from which he was struggling to free culture and restore antiquity. Giovanni Boccaccio, in his *Vita di Dante* (1313–1375), pronounced that poet to have been the first since the Romans to prepare the way for the return to Italy of the exiled Muses, and declared that Dante had called the dead art of poesy back to life. Salutati, G. Villani, and Polenton all echoed this tribute to Dante. Guido da Pisa, an early commentator on Dante, celebrated him as the reawakener of dead poesy, "For through that poet dead poesy was resuscitated. . . . He truly brought poetic knowledge back to life and caused us to recall the ancient poets to our minds."[10] Writing about 1400, Filippo Villani saw the revival of the plastic arts not so much in a reversion to antiquity as in a reversion to nature, from which they "had strayed away in a childish fashion through the ignorance (*inscicia*) of the painters." Leonardo Bruni, in his *Dialogi ad Petrum Paulum Histrum*, praised Petrarch as the man who "restored the *studia humanitatis* which had become extinct and opened the way for us." Bruni developed the theme of the battle of the ancients and moderns which was to reverberate in the salons down to the days of Jonathan Swift. Lorenzo Valla (1405–1457), whom Leibniz considered to be together with Cusanus the most brilliant mind of the Renaissance, predicted a general reawakening of learning. Near the end of the *Quattrocento*, Marsilio Ficino (1433–1499), the Neoplatonic philosopher, saw all the *disciplinae liberales* and especially Platonic philosophy undergoing a renewal. He ascribed the dawn of a golden age not only to the revivification of the liberal arts, of grammar, poetry, and rhetoric, but also to that of painting, sculpture, architecture, and music.[11] In art, Leonardo da Vinci (1452–1519) associated the *maniera nuova* with the *maniera antica* as opposed to the *maniera vecchia*, linking nature and verisimilitude and mathematical foundation. In politics, Flavio Biondo (1392–1463), in his *Italia Illustrata*, saw a fresh turning point in the innovations of the fourteenth century. And in a way Machiavelli (1469–1527), for all his historical pessimism, included political thought within the overall consciousness of renewal.

In the North a consciousness of an epochal renewal was gradually building up during the fifteenth century and is clearly articulated at the end of the century and beginning of the sixteenth.[12] Conrad Celtis (1459–1508), the German archhumanist, in an *Ode to Apollo* summoned the god of the poets northward. Guillaume Budé (1467–1540) saw learning saved from a deluge of mud lasting a thousand years. Albrecht Dürer (1471–1528) spoke of the *Wiedererwachung* or reawakening of culture. Ulrich von Hutten (1488–1523) could exclaim, "What a century! What Scholarship! It is a sheer joy to be alive, even though not yet in tranquillity. Learning flourishes, men are spiritually quickened. O Barbarism, take a rope and prepare for extinction!" Erasmus in a letter to Wolfgang Capito wrote in 1517: "I anticipate the near approach of a Golden Age!" For Erasmus the word *renascentia* had a heavily Christian connotation. His Christian humanism aimed at the "restoration of a well grounded human nature" and pointed toward the religious enlightenment and evangelical movement of the reformers. If the Renaissance represented primarily a return to classical antiquity, the Protestant reformers considered their movement to be that, and beyond that a return to Christian antiquity. Luther, who hailed the dawn of a golden age, saw the revival of learning as a John the Baptist heralding the coming of the evangelical renewal. The Reformation was generally viewed by the younger humanists as a renewal of theology, completing the work of the Renaissance. It is that thesis which was carried by humanism into the Reformation and transmitted to Christoph Keller in the late seventeenth century and thus became a part of our mentality, virtually a historical cliché.[13]

It would be interesting to trace the concept through the centuries, the rationalist tradition of the eighteenth century, the romantic reaction, Jacob Burckhardt's masterpiece, the Burckhardtians, the revisionists, the revolt of the medievalists, the root stretchers finding renascences before the Renaissance, the theorists of decline, the Neo-Burckhardtians, transitionists, and synthesizers. But there is no need to follow through on the story, for Wallace K. Ferguson has done a near saturation job in his volume *The Renaissance in Historical Thought* (Boston: Houghton Mifflin, 1948).

Less well known is the history of the word "reformation" in its various historical modalities. A major work on "The Reformation in

Historical Thought" remains to be done. The Whig historian James Froude spoke of the Protestant Reformation as "the hinge on which all modern history turns." Although the word reformation is associated in the popular mind nearly exclusively with the Protestant movement, the term is one of great antiquity and complexity. It must be differentiated from conceptions of renewal and renaissance which are deterministic, naturalistic, or supernaturalistic, for reformation involves man's evocative and creative effort to restore an improved or more perfect condition to the life of a single person, to the church, the state or society. Though emphasizing recovery and restoration and thus in a romantic way looking backward perhaps to a golden age, the reformer in some cases views the eradication of defects and restoration as an essential preliminary to further advance. Historically the return to a golden age has thus at times been linked to the eschatological expectation that reform might hasten the coming of the kingdom of God. A reformation may be defined, then, as a free act or a series of actions which are intended to recover, augment, and perfect certain essential values which at one time existed or at least were thought to exist but which subsequently were lost or impaired by neglect and evil intent or as a result of a general decline.

The terms reformation and reform are interchangeable in certain contexts when they are employed in the general sense of improvement or the restoration of a better condition. The word reformation, however, has come to be preferred in historical literature for a movement which has produced significant change or improvement in morals or in religious teaching and practice. The word reform is reserved for efforts to eliminate abuses, correct corrupt practices, and initiate change for the better in any way. The term reform can be applied to a specific political or legislative act or to a legal amendment in a way that reformation can not.

In Western intellectual history the idea of reformation was essentially a Judeo-Christian conception. It was associated first of all with personal regeneration and the reformed life of an individual, secondly with the restoration within monasticism of an ideal community life, and thirdly with the Gregorian reform drive to restore "the right order of things" in the world. At no time in history did the advocates of individual, institutional, and social reform sound out more loudly than during the sixteenth century. Their calls have echoed down to the very present. The Christian idea of reformation had antecedents in pre-Christian literature, in Greco-Roman, and already in preliterate religious belief. The more general renewal ideas which must be distinguished from reformation and reform may be categorized as the cosmological, vitalistic, millenarian, and conversion ideologies.[14] Cosmological renewal ideas are derived from and remain closely related to the cyclical patterns of diurnal and seasonal change and the life, procreative, and death sequence of organic beings. The cyclical aspect reflects the myth of the eternal return.[15] Vitalistic renewal ideas are generically related to the biological processes of procreation and growth. Millenarian renewal ideas, utopian and messianic, look forward to a period of perfection, not necessarily as a rationalist or reformer might press toward a future utopia but more in an eschatological sense of expecting a reign of peace at the end of time. Conversion renewal ideas are identified with intervention by the Holy Spirit or rebirth through baptism, which is a "washing of regeneration and renewing of the Holy Ghost."

Even though renewal ideologies with their deterministic and cyclical aspects were out of phase with the linear conception of history characteristic of the Christian tradition, certain aspects of renewal ideologies were adapted to and fused with reformation ideas. Moreover, the terminology used for reformation was not always clearly distinguished from the language of renewal ideologies, so that in each historical instance it is necessary to examine the essence of the concept and the program for its realization in their historical context before venturing a judgment as to whether a movement in question constituted a reformation, a renewal, or a combination of both. Medieval linguistic usage employed the words *reformare* and *reformatio* in a way parallel to such words as *regenerare* or *regeneratio*, παλιγγενεδια, *renovare*, *innovare (nova vita)*, *suscitare* or *resuscitare*, *restituere*, *instituere*, *surgere*, *renasci*, *reviviscere* (to revive), *revirescere* (to grow green again).

The leisurely rhythm of establishment, decline, and reform which characterized the long centuries of the Middle Ages yielded in the final medieval centuries to phrenetic action, hysterical reaction, and a cacophony of shrill and strident calls for reformation. The angry or anguished responses to the "Babylonian Captivity" of the church and the divided authority during the schism were more desperate and urgent. William Durand called for a *reformatio in capite et in membris*, a reformation in head and members. The conciliarists blamed the papacy and *curia* and worked for constitutional and administrative change. In his treatise *De modis uniendi et reformandi ecclesiam in concilio universali* (1410) on ways of uniting and reforming the church in a universal council, Dietrich von Niem declared that the reunion of the church had to be accompanied by the cleansing of the church.

The "forerunners of the Reformation" found themselves more often in agreement as to the nature of the ills of the church than they did as to the best program for reform.[16] There was still general agreement that reform must be the work of God himself, acting through spiritual men, but there was less consensus as to which spiritually quickened members should lead in the reform and what shape it should take. Marsilio of Padua in the *Defensor Pacis* criticized abuses and proposed constitutional changes which would introduce representative principles. William of Occam joined the Spiritual Franciscans in the cry for "evangelical poverty." John Wyclif urged Christian laymen and worthy secular rulers to shoulder the task of reform and to depose and dispossess unworthy clergy. John Hus cried out, "O Christ, it will take a long time before the proud priests will become so humble as to subject themselves to the Church for sin, as thou, being innocent, has subjected thyself."[17] Wessel Gansfort, who conceived a reform as a spiritualizing of rites and dogmas, had a direct influence upon Luther.

During the fifteenth century a widely circulated treatise, the *Reformatio Sigismundi*, supposedly an account of a vision which the Emperor Sigismund had as he lay dreaming on his bed near the dawn, fused the religious idea of reformation with the concept of the sacramental kingship. The emperor was commissioned to prepare the way for the coming of the divine order. The document foretold the coming of the priest-king Frederick who would realize God's own order by promoting a spiritual and secular reform program.[18] During the fifteenth century, however, the concept of reformation was given an immediately practical technical meaning. At every Diet throughout the century the *gravamina* or grievances of the Empire were presented, usually conjoined with appeals to the "good old law" and with references to the happier days of old. The Diet of Eger in 1436 "reformed" laws governing feuds and coinage. The restoration of "good old laws and customs" was an important part of the program in the reform of city ordinances such as the reform in Nuremberg (1479), Worms (1498), Frankfurt (1509), and the like. In the 1518 "modernization" of Bavarian territorial law the term reformation was given a legal application. In 1442 Emperor Frederick III codified a "reformation of the territorial peace."[19]

The term reformation, then, had appeared in varying modalities during the long centuries before that historical epoch which has come to be known as the Reformation period. That the term came to be associated almost exclusively in historical literature with a development within church history and as a term for an entire era of general European history poses a fine problem for historiography. Luther, surprisingly, did not apply the word to his movement as a whole. He used it in the old legal sense, not in a utopian, apocalyptic sense. He used the term as the creation of something new only with reference to the reform of the university, the curriculum and faculty, as in the Wittenberg university reform of 1518. He seldom referred to himself as a reformer and innovator but thought of himself rather as an instrument which God was using to reform the church. His most comprehensive early statement about "reformation" is his *Resolution to Thesis 89:* "The Church is in need of a reform—which is not the duty of one man, the pontiff, or of many cardinals (as the most recent council has proved both points), but of the whole world, even of God alone. But the time of this reform is known to Him alone who has founded the times."[20] Luther believed himself to be evangelizing a part of the *una sancta*, hoping the gospel would be revitalized throughout the whole Christian Church.

As the new territorial church orders developed, the concept of the "reformation" of the church in the Protestant lands crystallized. With the adoption of the new evangelical *Kirchenordnungen* or church orders the word "reformation" was specifically used, as in the "Cologne Reformation" of 1543. Melanchthon was always hesitant about using the term reformation even in the old legal sense, even though he had a vision of Luther standing in the long line of prophets, apostles, evangelists, church fathers, and doctors of the church. Luther had led Christendom to light, to the true and necessary doctrine, when the densest darkness existed regarding the doctrine of repentance.[21] The superscription *De iure reformandi* in the key document of the Schmalkald Diet of 1537 is an addition by another hand. Only when Emperor Charles V in his proposal of 1544 announced a Christian reformation did the Saxons feel justified in referring to their reform proposals the following year as the "Wittenberger Reformation." Three years later the Diet of Augsburg achieved a "Reformation guter policey." Pfeffinger and Flacius Illyricus, waging the battle of conservative Lutheranism against the Emperor's Leipzig Interim, undertook the "reformation" of various rites such as confirmation.[22] Flacius agreed with Melanchthon's reading of Luther's place in church history. In his major works *The Witness of Truth* and the *Magdeburg Centuries*, he followed the conservative tradition of referring to the medieval reformations in the old legal sense of restoration of the good old original condition and law, and he viewed the reform ordinances of the preceding centuries as foreshadowing Luther's work.

The first serious, self-conscious, and consistent use of the term reformation for Luther's religious movement came only in the seventeenth century with the histories of the famed Lutheran historian, Veit

Ludwig von Seckendorf. Seckendorf's *Historia Lutheranismi* (1688) or *Commentarius historicus et apologeticus de Lutheranismo*, which served as a response to the attack of the French Jesuit Louis Maimburg, carried the subtitle *sive de reformatione religionis ductu D. Martini Lutheri in magna Germaniae parte aliisque regionibus, & speciatim in Saxonia recepta & stabilita.* [23] The reformation represented the "purification of the condition of the church." This development among the Lutheran church historians, centurions of the seventeenth century, coincided with the articulation by the general historians of the three great ages of the world, ancient, medieval, and modern. The Reformation as a historical movement was now slipped into place as one of the twin sources of the third or modern period of world history.

The consciousness of the Reformation as a distinctive period developed in the Calvinist tradition in the West in a way analogous to that within the Lutheran area. Like Luther, Calvin was engaged in a reform of the church, not in leading a separatist movement as such. In his *Reply to Cardinal Sadoleto* (1539), he laid out the reasons for the necessity of a reform and claimed for his reformation continuity with the reformation of Martin Luther. [24] In his treatise *On the Necessity for Reforming the Church* (1543), Calvin depicted Luther as a prophet who proclaimed the gospel and struggled against the apostasy of the times. For Calvin as for Luther reformation meant the rediscovery and proclamation of the gospel.

Zwingli's emphasis differed from that of Luther and Calvin. Taking his cue from Erasmus's vision of a "renaissance of Christendom," Zwingli worked for a "restoration of Christendom," with social as well as purely spiritual implications. With the union of the reformed churches, this Zwinglian conception gained ground in the Calvinist tradition. In 1580 Calvin's successor as leader and spokesman of the movement, Theodore Beza, in his history of the church wrote of the "renaissance and growth" of the reformed churches. The Anabaptists, by way of contrast, sought withdrawal from the state and commonwealth in order to establish reformed congregations of saints patterned after the original apostolic community. The historians of the "reformed" churches in the Swiss tradition dated the Reformation from the year 1516 and played up Zwingli as the "first of all to reform the church." [25] Only gradually did the concept of the Reformation as a historical period evolve in reformed historiography.

By the middle of the eighteenth century the church historians of the Enlightenment quite generally acknowledged the Reformation as an independent and separable period of Western history. The so-called "father of modern church history," Johann Lorenz Mosheim, in his highly influential handbook of church history, the *Institutiones historiae ecclesiasticae antiquae et recentioris* (1755), viewed Luther as the restorer of the true Christian doctrine and initiator of a new period in church history. He saw the Reformation as a general European development.[26] A decade earlier Daniel Gerdes, a professor at Groningen, in his *Introductio in Historiam evangelii seculo XVI . . .* (Groningen, 1744), also presented the Reformation as a European movement which was transconfessional in nature. The *Aufklärung* historians constantly cited Luther as an authority and believed Luther to be the shield bearer of the movement. "Reformation" was one of their favorite words, and they called for a "reformation" of dogmatism, jurisprudence, orthography, the book trade, hymnbooks, and even of Lutheranism itself. In the *Frankfurter gelehrten Anzeiger* (1772), Goethe mocked the iconoclastic zeal of the "enlightened reformers" of his day. This pan-European approach gave way during the nineteenth century to the pressures of the rising nationalism, so that many, if not most, historians reverted to treating the Reformation merely in its French, German, or English aspects. But with the growth of secularism during the eighteenth and nineteenth centuries, the Reformation as a historical period was broadened to include the social, political, and cultural as well as the ecclesiastical and religious dimensions.

American historiography of the Reformation has contributed distinctively in two special ways, through a sense of detachment and objectivity and by restoring a pan-European view of the Reformation, thus contributing to the general acceptance of the Reformation as a distinct period of Western history. Moreover, since the most influential Reformation histories have been written by Protestants working in a university setting, the linking of Renaissance and Reformation as the twin cradles of modernity has been the natural assumption in most of these works.[27]

The Marxist conception of the Reformation is a product of a mixture of secular and enlightened traditions, with an understanding of revolution derived basically from the French Revolution. Marxists place stress upon the Peasants' revolt and the leadership of Thomas Müntzer, taking their cue from Friedrich Engels's *Der deutsche Bauernkrieg* (1850) which was so heavily dependent upon the work of Wilhelm Zimmermann, a disillusioned and untrustworthy author of a three-volume *Allgemeine Geschichte des Grossen Bauernkrieges* (Stuttgart, 1841–43). In orthodox Marxism the religious core of the Reformation is pushed into the background and the era is described as the time of the early bourgeois revolution. Although scholarship has moved beyond the mid-nineteenth-century assumptions which form the nexus of the Marxist interpretation, the Marxist focus upon the sixteenth century as a critical turning point and important phase in Western historical development has tended to reemphasize the Renaissance and the Reformation as a significant historical period.[28]

Taking a broad look at the entire course of Western history, we may venture to conclude that during the New Testament and patristic period renewal elements were very powerful, combined with ideas of personal reform. During the medieval and Renaissance periods the renewal motif was very powerful. In the late medieval and Reformation era the drive toward individual salvation and restoration and the drive to reform the Christian church and communities emerged in strength. In more recent centuries the reform of society has become a basic concern of Western man in the liberal traditions. The very concepts Renaissance and Reformation bring with them, then, not merely a dictionary definition to be applied in some positivistic, linguistic way, but they can be understood only historically, for they bring with them a long record of special usage as they were employed in varying modalities by many parties through the millennia of history. The development of Renaissance and Reformation from history as past actuality to their enshrinement as a period of history in historical interpretation was long, gradual, and enduring.[29]

2. *Interior Cohesiveness*

The coordinating conjunction in the standard pairing of Renaissance *and* Reformation requires justification. If the copulative belongs there, the case for period identification is strengthened. But it is precisely the appropriateness of this linkage that has been fiercely controverted since early in the twentieth century. The classic formulation of the issues took shape in the great debate between Wilhelm Dilthey, the father of the modern *Geisteswissenschaften*, and Ernst Troeltsch, one of the few major figures in religious sociology. It was quite standard in the nineteenth century, given a Whiggish interpretation of history which was by no means limited to Protestant, progressive, and liberal England, to interpret the Reformation as the German expression of the Renaissance cultural phenomenon. A variation of that theme described the two as national movements which differed in character in accord with the genius of the two peoples, the Italians being sensuous and outward, and the Germans being deeply inward and religious, and with each making its special contribution to the modern world. Dilthey saw both movements as parts of a general

European struggle for intellectual liberty. He traced their common origins to the ascendancy of urban life, the progress of commerce and growth of industry, the rise of the bourgeoisie, and the formation of modern states, for it was an age of princes and kings. Taking his cue from the young German humanists of Luther's day who saw the Reformation as the renewal of the last and highest of the disciplines, theology, he held that in Germany the rediscovery of the world and of man took the form of a new depth in religion and the demand for ecclesiastical reform. The Reformation freed man from the domination of the medieval hierarchy, built inner liberty and interior strength into individual men for their struggle against the power of the external environment, and directed man's moral energy toward his economic and political life. Thus in breaking with the medieval world, it decisively reinforced the contribution of the Renaissance to the rise of modernity.[30]

Ernst Troeltsch, embittered and disillusioned with the church-state culture of Wilhelmine Germany, took the precise opposite tack in his analysis and became the central figure in a controversy which has not yet completely subsided. He argued that the Reformation, while splitting up the unity of Christendom, established essentially an authoritarian ecclesiastical culture analogous to that of the medieval church. In its most important aspects, he argued, it was more religious than secular, more supernaturalist than this-worldly, more transcendent than immanent, more spiritual than material. The Reformation represented a religious throwback, countered the cultural values of the worldly Renaissance, and made no significant contribution to the rise of the modern world. It is fascinating to note the easy acceptance of the Burckhardtian picture of the Renaissance on the one hand and the old Protestant view of the Reformation on the other. The problem has gotten tremendously more complex since their day.[31]

A deeper look below surface phenomena of both the Renaissance and Reformation centuries reveals underlying affinities and connections which support the thesis of their interior cohesiveness and genuine togetherness. At the same time there is in the matter of religious concern an essential difference which proves the impossibility of completely identifying the two.

If one approaches the Renaissance and Reformation as an age in European history, one finds a basic similarity in the economic, social, and political trends and a striking sameness in the situations, although there were differences sometimes of decades in the arrival at a similar situation in various parts of Europe. As for the economy, there was throughout three centuries a continuous move away from an agricultural base, village life at near subsistence level, to an urban life nourished by commerce. Commercial capitalism and urban growth are characteristics of economic life in these centuries. The importance of the Italian city-states and especially the free republic as the urban base of Renaissance culture has long been recognized. But only now has the critical importance of the cities for the growth and spread of the Reformation been fully appreciated. In the course of the sixteenth century, fifty of the sixty-five imperial cities officially recognized the Reformation either permanently or periodically and either as a majority or minority movement. Protestantism was strong in nearly all of the some two hundred towns and cities with populations of one thousand and over, with many of the largest such as Augsburg, Nuremberg, Strasbourg, Lübeck, and Ulm becoming overwhelmingly Protestant. Like Renaissance culture, Reformation religion was at first urban centered.[32]

As for political life, there was a move away from the universal, coupled with local feudal control, toward a particularism of mid-range states. In Italy this took the form of city-states and princedoms. In the Holy Roman Empire it assumed a pattern of free imperial cities and territorial princedoms. In Switzerland it spelled Zurich and Geneva. In western Europe it meant the further rise of kings and national dynasties, with some particularist interests represented by lesser political entities. The importance of particularism for the success of the Reformation can be brought home by the mention of just one name—Elector Frederick the Wise.

The social experience of the city-dweller earning a living by his wit in a game in which he did not control the rules nor fully understand them was qualitatively different from that of the agricultural life. The eternal return of the seasons, the tie to a natural reality which seemed in some sense to be regular, the assumptions about natural hierarchy which seemed properly to be reflected in the feudal and ecclesiastical structure, all that gave way to a world of calculation, energetic action, initiative, practical ingenuity, wit, aggressiveness. Minds moved away from the static cosmic order and great verities of scholastic philosophy, which paid it an Aristotelian tribute, to a humanist approach to reality which stressed moral philosphy as prudential virtue, history as change, poetry as an expression of feeling, and above all rhetoric as an articulation of thought in action and truth not merely convincing by logic but moving the will to action.[33]

The price paid was a deeply rooted anxiety and not infrequently a dark melancholy, resulting from the new independence, the broader horizons, the conflict of Christian and classical cultural values, the impact of late classical pessimistic literature. The new lay culture which saw nonclerics writing theology was far less secure in its answers than the clerical culture of the twelfth and thirteenth centuries had been, for all the strife and rivalry of those times. The Neoplatonic school of late fifteenth-century Florence really represented a deviation from the norm of humanist culture, almost a reversion to the medieval cosmic order and hierarchy, for Ficino was a priest and Pico a follower of Savonarola.[34]

Northern humanism was generically related to Italian humanism in its major emphases. The reformers seconded the humanists in their rejection of scholasticism, although Luther's relation to modernism and his Biblical grounds for its repudiation were at variance with the humanists' basis for objection. Albrecht Dürer felt that enormous anxiety which was such an important element in the psychic makeup of so many city dwellers and humanists. When Luther cited as his sole authorities John Wyclif and Lorenzo Valla, he was pointing to a profound truth lying beneath the surface of the debt he felt to Valla for his attack on the Donation of Constantine and the questioning of free will. Like Valla, he penetrated the hollow recesses of pretentious philosophy. Like Valla, he felt man's limitations and need for divine grace.[35] But unlike Valla, he could not pay tribute to Aquinas or make his peace with Pelagianism. His rediscovery of the gospel was a total breakthrough. The young humanists, together with youthful renegade members of the regular clergy, became the chief carriers, the archers, and hoplites of the Reformation. The cities accepted the Reformation first, with patrician city councils bowing to the will of the bourgeoisie. Only from 1530 on were there enough evangelical preachers to man the country pulpits and instruct the peasants in the new gospel way. "Thank God," cried Dürer, "at last I have found certainty."

Dilthey's position was correct, but in a much more religiously profound way than he imagined. The Reformation was not the theological facet of an enlightened Renaissance culture. It was an answer to an aching question. Dilthey is not to be faulted, for since his day we have learned so much more about the darker vision of the Renaissance and about the existential depths of Luther's theology. Troeltsch's position was correct, but not merely in terms of that pejorative judgment which he passed on the Reformation. The Reformation was antithetical to the theological formulations of humanism, those of Erasmus as well as those of Petrarch or Ficino, but it was in a response to basic questions that persisted from the fourteenth into the sixteenth century, and it posed those questions in a far sharper and more consequential manner. The answer was not medieval, but ancient, and some would say, timeless. In terms of humanism, higher culture, and religion, the Renaissance and Reformation do belong together and are bound by interior bands of great strength. Humanism entered the Reformation, and the Reformation carried humanism into the seventeenth century.[36]

The Renaissance cannot stand alone as a period of history. Nor was it merely an age of transition, as Symonds once told the world and Wallace K. Ferguson is telling us once again, nor even merely an age of accelerated transition, an episode, a crisis age, or even merely a critical turning point in history.[37] The Renaissance cannot stand alone, Clio balanced on one foot. The Renaissance and the Reformation together constitute a period of history justified by interior cohesion, by characteristics distinct from those of the periods preceding and following, and by a cultural content (in Malinowski's as well as Cassirer's sense of the word culture) whose meaning is adequately expressed by the terms which historians use to identify them.

3. *Appropriate Chronological Limits*

By resorting to a mercifully foreshortened eschatology, the final two parts of this paper will be summary, suggestive, and very brief. The problem of periodization is usually reduced to haggling over terminal dates, *a quo* and *ad quem*, rather than directed to the more profound questions at the heart of the problem.

A look at some of the chronological limits offered by leading scholars will suggest the bewildering variety of possibilities. Arnold J. Toynbee proposed a period for the Renaissance from the fourteenth or fifteenth centuries to the nineteenth European century. He calls the period from 1475 to 1875 the Italistic age.[38] For Georg von Below the terminal date of the Renaissance had to be the traditional 1500. Wallace K. Ferguson sees the thirteenth to the fifteenth century as the period of transition characterized by the growth of a money economy and the consolidation of national dynasties, and sees the great historical transformation of the seventeenth, eighteenth, and nineteenth centuries as growing directly from it.[39] Unlike Ferguson, to whom economic and social criteria are paramount, Oscar Halecki values political events above all, and in his *The Limits and Divisions of European History* he offered an elaborate argument that the Middle Ages ended late in the fourteenth century (about 1378) and that the Renaissance ended in the last decades of the sixteenth century. But like Ferguson's "age of transition," Halecki's "age of crisis" is essentially a negative definition in contrast to the positive proposal of a unity based upon the intellectual and religious culture of those centuries.[40] Denys Hay, stressing economic and juridical considerations, has polemicized against the traditional 1492 or 1500 termination date for the Renaissance and proposes a period from 1300 to 1700. He urges that the old twofold division of European history (medieval and modern) should be replaced by a threefold division (medieval, the new period, modern).[41] H. R. Trevor-Roper would run the European Renaissance from 1500 through to 1620, a proposal of some merit.[42] Delio Cantimori is more daring and less specific, for he would vary the terminal date according to the various aspects of the society being considered. Thus he would run the history of the church from the Great Schism to secularization; in economic and social history he would go from the commune through mercantile precapitalism; and in political history he would join all from the death of Charles IV to the French Revolution. But with all the possible variations, internal contradictions, antecedents and subsequent developments, he nevertheless sees the Renaissance, Reformation, and Catholic Reformation as a unique period.[43]

It would be very gratifying, if it were possible, simply to argue that the Renaissance and Reformation period bracketed within such approximate dates as 1300 to 1650 coincided conveniently either with a Braudelian *conjoncture,* a short-term reality which as conspicuous history holds our attention by its uniqueness and continuous dramatic changes, or with a *structure*, a long-term reality which as submerged history, almost silent and always discreet, is virtually untouched by the obstinate erosion of time. But unfortunately our three and a half centuries are too long to be classified as *conjoncture* and far too brief to constitute a basic *structure*. We have argued that in the period 1300–1650 one finds a basic similarity in the economic, social, and political trends and a striking sameness in the situations in various parts of Europe, although on different time schedules. These are centuries during which society moved steadily away from the agrarian life characteristic of the earlier medieval period toward the growth of urban life nourished by commerce and industry. One can, of course, stretch the roots of city life back to the twelfth century and earlier, but the trend gains strength and characterizes these three and a half centuries over a larger part of Europe. Moreover, after the devastations of the mid-fourteenth century, the struggle to recoup population losses during the fifteenth century and the demographic upsurge during the sixteenth century into the seventeenth gave a basic unity to the central two centuries of the period that should be convincing to those who prefer studying history from the bottom up.

The sixteenth century especially laid the platform from which the Vital Revolution of the eighteenth century was to spring. Politically, the formation of states and development of monarchies was an ongoing process that lends a further element of unity to the entire period. The latest challenge to the concept of a "crisis of the seventeenth century" made by Theodore K. Rabb in his *The Struggle for Stability in Early Modern Europe* (New York: Oxford University Press, 1975) lends further support to the mid-seventeenth century as the *terminus ad quem* for the Renaissance and especially the Reformation period. From the early sixteenth through the mid-seventeenth century, Western man struggled to overcome the discord and disruption produced by the Reformation, overseas expansion, price revolution, demographic upsurge, and the consolidation of central governments. Not until after the Thirty Years War was stability achieved and a measure of assurance regained. In terms of basic economic, political, demographic, and social considerations, then, a good case can be made for the unity and cohesion of the period from the fourteenth to the mid-seventeenth centuries.

Moreover, if one focuses upon specifically higher culture, the arts, rhetoric, moral philosophy, humanism, religious thought, the cohesion of the fourteenth into the seventeenth century is very striking. The contrasts to scholastic, ecclesiastical culture, characteristic of the medieval period on the one hand and to the scientific and rationalistic emphases of the dominant modes of late-seventeenth and eighteenth-century thought on the other hand, tend to lend greater credence to the unity of Renaissance and Reformation culture. Contrasts set off the humanist cultural and evangelical religious mind sets like a two-toned cameo clearly distinguishable from their historical setting in the centuries preceding and succeeding them. Northern humanism provides the essential coupling.

It would take a sizable book to argue the case in detail. All that is possible here is to state my position clearly and to suggest why it is not necessarily an impossible opinion. *Quot homines, tot opiniones*, said the Romans. Nietzsche was quite right when he penned in *Thus Spake Zarathustra*: "Beware of the scholars! They hate you, for they are sterile. They have cold, dried-up eyes; before them every bird lies unplumed."

4. *Present Trends and Future Possibilities*

That master of understatement Sir Winston Churchill wrote: "History with its flickering lamp stumbles along the trail of the past, trying to reconstruct its scenes, to revive its echoes, and to kindle with pale gleams the passion of former days." Historians are still exploring new facets and dimensions of the Renaissance and Reformation movements, and our final assignment is to suggest whether the new directions in research are likely to force a reassessment of our periodization. It will be possible to allude only to the very major areas of advance and that in a most cursory fashion.

Extensive research is now being done on humanism in the Reformation. The net effect of this research is to document very explicitly the tremendous continuity of humanist culture and particularly the rhetorical emphasis and education. The Renaissance and Reformation did not constitute a clear and evident separation of European culture into its classical pagan or secular and Christian religious components. Through humanism the Renaissance lived on into and beyond the Reformation. Not only were humanist impulses widespread horizontally on a European scale, but they extended downward vertically through the Reformation to a broader range of the population and through the centuries toward modern times. The evangelical humanists in the learned tradition felt a strong sense of continuity of the classical tradition from the Italian through the northern Renaissance to themselves. Northern humanism during the Reformation decades fused with a great variety of religious positions from Luther to Zwingli, most successfully perhaps in Melanchthon. Humanism is the strongest cultural bond tying the Renaissance and Reformation movements together.[44]

The newly awakened interest in the Catholic Reformation has brought out more clearly the fact that it was not merely a Counter-Protestant reaction but that it antedated Luther and carried much Renaissance cultural good with it. This complicates a revisionist suggestion that the Counter-Reformation did not destroy the Renaissance but that the weakening of the Renaissance in Italy made the Counter-Reformation possible. The Catholic humanists, like most evangelicals, assumed that there was a natural connection between classical learning and religious faith. They drew on the resources of the moral philosophy of antiquity as the scholastics had used Aristotelian dialectic. Jesuit education became a major vehicle for the transmission of classical culture in ecclesiastical garb.[45]

The Neo-Orthodox revival in theology made possible an empathic reading of the problems of the humanists and the existential theology of the reformers. See, for example, Karl Barth's essay, "Reformation als Entscheidung," in his "Der Götze Wackelt."[46] We have rediscovered an old truth once pronounced as a dictum by Thomas Carlyle in his *Essays*: "What is all knowledge too but recorded experience, and a product of history; of which, therefore, reasoning and belief, no less than action and passion, are essential materials?" Thus we progress sideways in history. This emphasis underlines the validity of seeking epochal unity also in the realm of the spirit.

The Marxist historiography of both Renaissance and Reformation is directed in the main toward scientific heroes such as Leonardo or Bruno, toward social revolts and economic history. It is distinctly less impressive in its Renaissance aspects, understandable for the Russians, and it constitutes a curious blend of Burckhardtian and Marxian clichés. In part it reinforces some Western economic determinists, or they play into Marxists' hands, by emphasizing the rise of merchant capitalism and the transition to second-stage capitalism as the critical determinant. Monographic research on agriculture, mining, revolts, and all are of value, but no persuasive case has been made against our periodization.[47]

The psychoanalytical and social psychological approaches have contributed new insights into the history makers, individuals and crowds, offering a welcome relief to the abstractions and impersonal factors of the economic determinists. They remind us of the truth of Professor Lewis Namier's statement that "fifty men do not make one centipede." They add authenticity to criteria for periodization based upon feelings and ideas as the springboard for action of real men.[48]

New research into the impact of the intellectual and theological world of the Renaissance and Reformation upon the later idealist and anthropological realist views of man lengthened their lines of influence into the modern period. It reinforces the contention that the ideas and intellectual culture of a period are an essential subject determining the peculiar dynamic of the era. But perhaps there are developments historical in nature transpiring in our day which will eventually do more than the verbal gymnastics of historians in forcing a reperiodization of history against our most judicious opinion. The oil crisis may further subsume European history under Asian categories. Clonal reproduction, cybernetics, space exploration, the fanciful flights "at the edge of history" (William Thompson) may alter human life in such a way as to tie Henry Ford to Leonardo, and Paul VI to Paul II, as part of the second and final phase of medieval history.

Let us summarize briefly the results of these reflections on the problem of periodization in history as it concerns the Renaissance and Reformation. The classical tripartite division of European history into ancient, medieval, and modern should give way to a scheme which better reflects the historical reality to be characterized. Thus the period of the barbarian invasions and early Germanic kingdoms should either be annexed to the late ancient world or treated as a separate period but not absorbed into an overarching medieval age of a thousand years. From the time of Europe's recovery in the eleventh and twelfth centuries down to the eighteenth century, European civilization as a Christian culture displays a striking cohesion and continuity. Those eight centuries may justly be called old Europe. Within that continuum the Renaissance and Reformation era constitute a subperiod. They are not merely transitional but are *sui generis*. The natural development of the concepts during those very centuries and their entrance into the historiographical tradition argues for the legitimacy of their use to identify this subperiod. Renaissance and Reformation are bound together by many lines of interior cohesion. The effect of recent research, whether in the intellectual, social, political, or economic areas, has been to underscore the essential unity and the great continuity of those centuries. The traditional termini 1300–1650, allowing for flexibility at both ends of the period, are logical and defensible in terms of history as past actuality.

History grew out of myths, and it may well be, as the Argentine poet and essayist George Luis Borges declares, that universal history is the history of the different intonations given a handful of metaphors. The metaphors of rebirth and reformation are imbedded very deeply in the subconscious of Western man. The heroic age of Renaissance and Reformation will for that reason always have a place in his heart. These thoughts on Clio's periods do not pretend to give definitive answers to such questions of great magnitude. We may draw comfort from the modest demurrer of Thomas Carlyle, who wrote: "Listening from the distance of centuries across the death chasms and howling kingdoms of decay, it is not easy to catch everything."

NOTES

1. Fernand Braudel, *The Mediterranean and the Mediterranean World in the Age of Philip II*, 2 vols. (New York: Harper & Row, 1973); and his "Qu'est-ce que le XVIe siècle?" *Annales, Économies, Sociétés, Civilisations* 7, no. 1 (January–March 1953):69–73.

2. Dietrich Gerhard, "Periodization in European History," *American Historical Review* 61, no. 4 (July 1956):901, n. 3, 902. Wallace K. Ferguson, *The Renaissance in Historical Thought: Five Centuries of Interpretation* (Boston: Houghton Mifflin, 1948). See Karl Heussi, *Altertum, Mittelalter und Neuzeit in der Kirchengeschichte: ein Beitrag zum Problem der historischen Periodisierung* (Tübingen: J. C. B. Mohr [P. Siebeck], 1921); and H. Spangenberg, "Die Perioden der Weltgeschichte," *Historische Zeitschrift* 127 (1923): 1–49. Oscar Halecki, *The Limits and Divisions of European History* (South Bend, Ind.: University of Notre Dame Press, 1962), p. 153ff., argues that the Middle Ages ended in

the late fourteenth century (c. 1378) and that the Renaissance continued into the last part of the sixteenth century.

3. Gerhard, "European History," pp. 903–04. Similarly George M. Trevelyan, *English Social History* (London: Longmans, Green, 1944), p. 96, saw a clear continuity from the Middle Ages through the eighteenth century, holding that the industrial revolution altered human life much more radically than either the Renaissance or the great political revolutions.

4. Delio Cantimori, "La periodizzazione dell'età del Rinascimento," in *Storici e storia* (Turin: Einaudi, 1971), p. 553. Cantimori considered the period from Petrarch to Goethe and the rule of Charles IV to the French Revolution as an identifiable epoch of history. See also Federico Chabod, "The Concept of the Renaissance," in *Machiavelli and the Renaissance* (New York: Harper & Row, 1965), pp. 149–200; Denys Hay, "The Renaissance as a Period in European History," in *The Italian Renaissance in its Historical Background* (Cambridge: At the University Press, 1961), pp. 11–25; and Karl H. Dannenfeldt, ed., *The Renaissance: Basic Interpretations*, 2d ed. (Lexington, Mass.: Heath, 1974). A recent publication contains two lectures bearing on the question of the periodization of the Renaissance: A. G. Dickens et al, *Background to the English Renaissance* (London: Gray-Mills, 1974). E. H. Gombrich, "The Renaissance—Period or Movement?" pp. 9–30, argues that the Renaissance was not so much an "age" as it was a movement. J. R. Hale, "The Renaissance Label," pp. 31–42, cautions us to treat the Renaissance as no more than an informal, easy way of referring in one word to many years including many strands of thought and action, and he urges us to suspend our belief above all in the chronological limits it has come to enshrine and to be cautious about any qualities of the human spirit that it purports to monopolize.

5. Martial, *Epigrams*, V, 7, cited in *Zu Begriff und Problem der Renaissance*, ed. August Buck (Darmstadt: Wissenschaftliche Buchgesellschaft, 1969), p. 2. Vergil, *Eclogues*, IV, 4–6:

> Magnus ab integro saeclorum nascitur ordo iam redit et virgo, redeunt Saturnia regna; iam nova progenies caelo dimittitur alto.

6. On the concept of rebirth in the early Middle Ages, see Eugenio Anagnine, *Il concetto di rinascita attraverso il Medio Evo (V-X sec.)* (Milan: R. Ricciardi, 1958), cited in *Zu Begriff und Problem der Renaissance*, ed. Buck, p. 1, n. 6.

7. Niccolò Machiavelli, *History of Florence and of the Affairs of Italy* (New York: M. Walter Dunne, Publisher, 1901), bk. 1, chap. 6, p. 37.

8. Giovanni Boccaccio, *The Decameron*, trans. Richard Aldington (New York: Dell, 1971), Sixth Day, Fifth Tale, p. 387.

9. Aeneas Silvius Piccolomini, *Opera* (Basel, 1571), Ep. CXIX, p. 646: "Post Petrarcham emerserunt literae. Post Jotum surrexere picturam manus, utramque ad summam iam videmus artem pervenisse." Cited in *Zu Begriff und Problem der Renaissance*, ed. Buck, p. 5.

10. Cited in *Zu Begriff und Problem der Renaissance*, p. 5.

11. Marsilio Ficino, *Opera* (Basel, 1576), I, 944, cited in August Buck, *Das Geschichtsdenken der Renaissance* (Krefeld: Scherpe-Verlag, 1957), p. 14, n. 27. Buck argues that the feeling of living in a new time was the characteristic mark of the Renaissance. He concludes that the medieval view of history was static, with man in a fixed position, whereas the Renaissance view of history was dynamic, with man's place changing to the extent that man is himself active. Despite the obvious oversimplification, this formula is basically sound. On the battle as to the superiority of the ancients or moderns, see the articles by Hans Baron, "The 'Querelle' of the Ancients and Moderns as a Problem for Renaissance Scholarship," *Journal of the History of Ideas* 20 (1959):3–22;

and by August Buck, "Aus der Vorgeschichte der 'Querelle des anciens et des modernes' im Mittelalter und Renaissance," *Bibliothèque d'Humanisme et Renaissance* 20 (1958): 527–41.

12. Denys Hay, "The Reception of the Renaissance in the North," in *The Italian Renaissance in its Historical Background*, pp. 179–203. Jean Plattard assembled the many terms and expressions used for the Renaissance by the French humanists in the sixteenth century, "Restitution des bonnes lettres" and "Renaissance," in *Mélanges offerts par ses amis et ses élèves à M. Gustave Lanson* (Paris: Hachette, 1922), p. 128. Although Plattard said that the word Renaissance itself was not used in the sixteenth century, Lynn Thorndike, "Renaissance or Prerenaissance?" *Journal of the History of Ideas* 5 (1943):65–74, discovered an instance of its use by the naturalist Pierre Belon, referred to above.

13. For a summary assessment of the concept of the Renaissance in Marxist literature, see the article by Abraham Friesen, "Renaissance," in *Sowjetsystem und demokratische Gesellschaft: Eine vergleichende Enzyklopädie*, ed. C. D. Kernig (Freiburg: Herder, 1966), cols. 648–57; and M. Goukowsky, "La renaissance italienne dans les travaux des historiens de l'URSS," in *Bibliothèque d'Humanisme et Renaissance* 18 (1956):306–15.

14. The great work on the renewal and reform ideologies in the early centuries of the Christian era is Gerhart B. Ladner, *The Idea of Reform: Its Impact on Christian Thought and Action in the Age of the Fathers* (Cambridge: Harvard University Press, 1959). See especially pp. 9–35, 39–44, 63–107, and 133–42, where he develops the four categories of renewal ideologies and sketches the history of the concept in the early centuries.

15. Mircea Eliade, *Le mythe de l'éternel retour: Archétypes et répétition* (Paris: Gallimard, 1949).

16. Heiko A. Oberman, ed., *Forerunners of the Reformation: The Shape of Late Medieval Thought, illustrated by key documents* (New York: Holt, Rinehart, Winston, 1966), has reverted to a concept of prereformers familiar in the nineteenth century from such books as Ullmann, *Reformatoren vor der Reformation*. The nineteenth-century bourgeois mind, it has been suggested, did not feel comfortable with sudden emergences such as Luther's strong personality and program and preferred gradualism and shades of gray. With Oberman's recasting of the concept its utility has been restored.

17. See Martin Schmidt, "Who Reforms the Church?" in *Ecumenical Dialogue at Harvard*, ed. Samuel H. Miller and G. E. Wright (Cambridge: Belknap Press, 1964), pp. 191–206.

18. Heinrich Koller, ed., *Reformation Kaiser Sigismunds* (Stuttgart: A. Hiersemann, 1964), pp. 4–5.

19. See Wilhelm Maurer, "Reformation," in *Die Religion in Geschichte und Gegenwart* (Tübingen, 1961), V, cols. 857–73, 861–63.

20. *Luthers Werke*, Weimar Ausgabe I, 627, lines 27ff.

21. Philipp Melanchthon, "Funeral Oration over Luther," in *The Protestant Reformation*, ed. Lewis W. Spitz (Englewood Cliffs, N.J.: Prentice-Hall, 1966), pp. 68–76. How comprehensive this view of the Reformation within the sweep of church history became can be seen in the ecumenical study in history by Glanmor Williams, *Reformation Views of Church History* (Richmond: John Knox Press, 1970).

22. Maurer, "Reformation," cols. 861–63.

23. Lewis W. Spitz, Sr., *A Critical Evaluation of Veit Ludwig von Seckendorf as a Church Historian* (Ph.D. dissertation, University of Chicago, 1943), p. 53.

24. Brian A. Gerrish, "John Calvin on Luther," in *Interpreters of Luther*, ed. Jaroslav Pelikan (Philadelphia: Fortress Press, 1968), pp. 67–96, 86. John C. Olin, ed., *John Calvin and Jacopo Sadoleto. A Reformation Debate. Sadoleto's Letter to the Germans and Calvin's Reply* (New York: Harper & Row, 1966).

25. Gottfried W. Locher, *Huldrych Zwingli in neuer Sicht* (Zurich: Zwingli-Verlag, 1969), pp. 137–71: "Die Wandlung des Zwingli-Bildes in der neueren Forschung." Locher regrets the widespread tendency to view Luther as normative for the other reformers and to overlook the variations in the many different reformatory efforts of that period.

26. Lewis W. Spitz, "Johann Lorenz Mosheim's Philosophy of History," *Concordia Theological Monthly* 20, no. 5 (May 1949):321–39.

27. Lewis W. Spitz, "The Lutheran Reformation in American Historiography," in *The Maturing of American Lutheranism*, ed. Herbert T. Neve and Benjamin A. Johnson (Minneapolis: Augsburg Publishing House, 1968), pp. 93–123, 240–46.

28. Friesen, "Renaissance," in *Sowjetsystem und demokratische Gesellschaft*, ed. Kernig, cols. 562–73. See also Abraham Friesen, *Reformation and Utopia: The Marxist Interpretation of the Reformation and Its Antecedents* (Wiesbaden: F. Steiner, 1974), a most thorough study of the Reformation in Marxist historical thought.

29. For a fuller account of this history of the religious idea of Reformation, see Lewis W. Spitz, "Reformation," in *Dictionary of the History of Ideas: Studies of Selected Pivotal Ideas*, ed. Philip P. Wiener (New York: Scribner, 1973), 4:60–69.

30. Hanns Rückert, "Die geistesgeschichtliche Einordnung der Reformation," *Zeitschrift für Theologie und Kirche* 52 (1955):43–64, discusses the nineteenth-century *opinio communis* that the Reformation marked the breakthrough of modernity and overcoming of the Middle Ages. But he believes that the secret of that truth which Luther perceived in the mathematical point of his faith is forever old and forever new, and this prevents the positioning of the Reformation on the historical table relative to medieval and modern. Cantimori, *Storici e storia*, pp. 624–56, offers a thumbnail sketch of interpretations of the Reformation from John Sleidan and Sebastian Franck to Max Weber and R. H. Tawney.

31. For a translation of the key statements of the respective positions of Dilthey and Troeltsch, see Lewis W. Spitz, ed., *The Reformation—Basic Interpretations* (Lexington, Mass.: Heath, 1972). A companion volume in this series is Karl H. Dannenfeldt, ed., *The Renaissance—Basic Interpretations* (1974), which contains representative selections from the entire spectrum of Burckhardtian and revisionist historians.

32. Steven E. Ozment, *The Reformation in the Cities: An Essay on the Appeal of Protestant Ideas to Sixteenth-Century Society* (New Haven: Yale University Press, 1975), introduction; and Bernd Moeller, *Imperial Cities and the Reformation: Three Essays* (Philadelphia: Fortress Press, 1972), pp. 41–115. Moeller points to Cologne as the only major imperial city to remain Catholic, p. 57. Working at the Institut für Spätmittelalter und Reformation in Tübingen, Hans-Christoph Rublack is heading a task force which is assembling an inventory of archival materials in the Southwest German cities relating to the introduction of the Reformation. Rublack is the author of an excellent monograph which might well serve as a model for such investigations, *Die Einführung der Reformation in Konstanz von den Anfängen bis zum Abschluss 1531* (Gütersloh: Gerd Mohn, 1971). A valuable recent monograph on Augsburg just before the Reformation is Rolf Kiessling, *Bürgerliche Gesellschaft und Kirche in Augsburg im Spätmittelalter: Ein Beitrag zur Strukturanalyse der oberdeutschen Reichsstadt* (Augsburg: Mühlberger, 1971). G. Benecke, *Society and Politics in Germany, 1500–1750* (Toronto: University of Toronto Press, 1975), a study based upon documentary materials largely in Northwestern Germany, investigates the effectiveness of the Empire's loose federal system as a form of government for that time and comes to a positive conclusion.

33. William J. Bouwsma, "Renaissance and Reformation: An Essay in Their Affinities and Connections," in *Luther and the Dawn of the Modern Era*, ed. Heiko A. Oberman

(Leiden: Brill, 1974), pp. 127–49. Bouwsma emphasizes the unity and cohesion of Renaissance and Reformation, stressing the continuity of rhetoric as a key unifying cultural force. It is true that Luther's word differed from the humanists' words, but on a cultural level the point stands. Though cast in broad general terms, Bouwsma's argument is sound and convincing. In his University of California Sather Lecture, 1975, Bouwsma explored the subject of "Culture and Anxiety in the Age of the Renaissance." He sought to show how all-pervasive the phenomenon of anxiety was during the Renaissance, and that the city was a particular locus of anxiety. This feeling of insecurity, apprehension, and anxiety was characteristic of urban life in the North as well as in Italy and provided one social psychological precondition for the success of the evangelical movement in German cities. Natalie Z. Davis, *Society and Culture in Early Modern France* (Stanford: Stanford University Press, 1975), in Parts I and II considers the context of the Protestant Reformation in terms of religion in its urban setting and the relation of religious rites and riots.

34. A title representative of recent studies emphasizing the stress, anxiety, melancholy, and dark underside of the Renaissance is Robert S. Kinsman, ed., *The Darker Vision of the Renaissance Beyond the Fields of Reason* (Berkeley and Los Angeles: University of California Press, 1974), which explores nonrational, irrational, and suprarational events between the years 1300 and 1670.

35. See Salvatore I. Camporeale, *Lorenzo Valla: Umanesimo e teologia* (Florence: Nella sede dell'Istituto nazionale di studi sul Rinascimento, 1972), for some deeper aspects of Valla's thought.

36. This conclusion runs counter to the traditional view articulated by Paul Joachimsen and older distinguished scholars, who believed that by 1550 or 1560 humanism had spent its force and was subordinated to and thoroughly absorbed by the religious reformation movement.

37. Wallace K. Ferguson, "The Interpretation of the Renaissance: Suggestions for a Synthesis," *Journal of the History of Ideas* 12 (1951): 483–95. It is Ferguson's contribution that the period from about the beginning of the fourteenth century to the end of the sixteenth witnessed the transition from medieval to modern civilization, that is, the gradual shift from one type of civilization to another, radically different in almost every respect. See his *Europe in Transition, 1300–1520* (Boston: Houghton Mifflin, 1962), p. vii.

38. Arnold J. Toynbee, *A Study of History*, abridgment of vols. 1–4 by D. C. Somervell (London: Oxford University Press, 1948), p. 312.

39. Wallace K. Ferguson, "Recent Trends in the Economic Historiography of the Renaissance," *Studies in the Renaissance* 7 (1960): 7–26.

40. Oscar Halecki, *The Limits and Divisions of European History* (Notre Dame, Ind.: University of Notre Dame Press, 1962), chap. 8: The Chronological Divisions: (a) The Middle Ages and the Renaissance,pp. 145–61; chap. 9: The Chronological Divisions: (b) Modern and Contemporary History, pp. 165–82.

41. Denys Hay, "The Renaissance as a Period in European History," in *The Italian Renaissance in its Historical Background*, pp. 10–25.

42. H. R. Trevor-Roper, *The European Witch-Craze of the Sixteenth and Seventeenth Centuries and Other Essays* (New York: Harper & Row, 1969), pp. 1–45: "Religion, the Reformation and Social Change." Page 1: "If we were to summarize the whole period we could say that the first long period, the 120 years 1500–1620, was the age of the European Renaissance, an age in which the economic and intellectual leadership of Europe is, or seems to be, in the south, in Italy and Spain; the period 1620–60 we could describe as the period of revolution; and the second long period, the period 1660–1800, would be the age of the Enlightenment, an age in which the great achievements of the

Renaissance are resumed and continued to new heights, but from a new basis."

43. Delio Cantimori, "La periodizzazione dell'età del Rinascimento," *Relazioni del X Congresso Internazionale di Scienze Storiche* 4 (Rome, 1955), and republished in his *Storici e storia*, pp. 553–77.

44. Consult the bibliography referred to in the annotations of the following articles: Lewis W. Spitz, "Humanism in the Reformation," in *Renaissance Studies in Honor of Hans Baron*, ed. Anthony Molho and John A. Tedeschi (Dekalb, Ill.: Northern Illinois University Press, 1971), pp. 641–62; his "Humanism and the Reformation," in *Transition and Revolution: Problems and Issues of European Renaissance and Reformation History*, ed. Robert M. Kingdon (Minneapolis: Burgess, 1974), pp. 153–88; and his "The Course of German Humanism," in *Itinerarium Italicum (Festschrift for Paul Oskar Kristeller)*, ed. Heiko Oberman and Thomas A. Brady (Leiden: Brill, 1975), pp. 361–426. See the brilliant article by Heinz Liebing, "Die Ausgänge des europäischen Humanismus," in *Geist und Geschichte der Reformation: Festgabe Hanns Rückert*, ed. Heinz Liebing and Klaus Scholder (Berlin: de Gruyter, 1966), pp. 357–76.

45. The new tone in writing about a Catholic Reformation which drew on pre-Protestant sources such as humanism rather than merely a negative Counter-Reformation is evident in such works as A. G. Dickens, *The Counter Reformation* (New York: Harcourt, World, Brace, 1969), whose title belies the tone; or the introduction to John C. Olin, ed., *The Catholic Reformation: Savonarola to Ignatius Loyola. Reform in the Church 1495–1540* (New York: Harper & Row, 1969). The new book in the Langer "Rise of Modern Europe" series does less than it could have in this regard: Marvin R. O'Connell, *The Counter Reformation 1559–1610* (New York: Harper & Row, 1974).

46. Karl Barth, "Reformation als Entscheidung," in his *"Der Götze Wackelt": Zeitkritische Aufsätze, Reden und Briefe von 1930 bis 1960* (Berlin: K. Vogt, 1961), pp. 71–86.

47. The great comprehensive work on the Marxist interpretation is that of Abraham Friesen, *Reformation and Utopia* (cf. n. 28 supra). A radical condensation of this study is his article, "The Marxist Interpretation of the Reformation," *Archive for Reformation History* 64 (1973):34–54.

48. The literature on psychohistory has burgeoned beyond belief in recent years. The most notable book dealing with a Reformation subject is no doubt Erik H. Erikson, *Young Man Luther: A Study in Psychoanalysis and History* (New York: W. W. Norton, 1958), appraised in various articles, among them, Lewis W. Spitz, "Psychohistory and History: The Case of Young Man Luther," and George A. Lindbeck, "Erikson's Young Man Luther: A Historical and Theological Reappraisal," *Soundings: An Interdisciplinary Journal* 56, no. 2 (1973):182–209, 210–27.

10

Contemporary History in the Contemporary Age

Gordon Wright

Of all the topics that make up this symposium on "The Future of History," "contemporary history" strikes me as the most problematical. Indeed, I suspect that it may verge on being a nonsubject—for reasons that will appear in the course of this essay. True, many of us do spend much of our time teaching and writing about the very recent past; so perhaps it is worth reflecting on the nature of that enterprise and on its peculiar problems, if any. In the end, however, we are likely to find that those problems really are not so peculiar and that the contemporary historian is, and should be, simply a historian *tout court*.

"Contemporary history" is an imprecise concept and therefore difficult to grapple with. Historians disagree even about the meaning of the term, as well as about its chronological limits. The French have long used it to denote the period since 1789—which stretches the concept of "contemporary" almost to the point of rupture. The London based quarterly called *Journal of Contemporary History* stakes out the twentieth century as its proper domain.[1] The British historian Geoffrey Barraclough contends that the contemporary age dates from only a few years ago, somewhere around 1960.[2] The relativism of these judgments calls to mind the teenage girl who was asked recently when, from her viewpoint, modern times began. "When John Kennedy was assassinated and the Beatles started," was her answer. When did they begin for your parents? she was then asked; to which she replied, "They haven't started for them yet."[3]

Delimiting the field in time isn't the only controversial issue. Some people doubt that anything called contemporary history can actually exist at all. Recently one of my students refused to answer an examination question that contained the phrase on the ground that the concept is patently absurd: "contemporary," he declared, means the present and "history" means the past. This artful dodge raised such complex philosophical questions that I'm still not sure whether the student deserved an A or an F. But if we put aside the logical difficulties and posit that something called contemporary history may in fact exist, and that its practitioners address themselves to roughly the last fifty years, this still doesn't bring historians much closer to consensus. *Should* it exist? And if so, on what terms and conditions? Is it a reputable or a degenerate form of our discipline? Is it fraught with greater difficulties and dangers than other kinds of history? Should it be practiced by only the most mature and sophisticated members of our craft, or rather by those marginal types who have no higher ambition than to write what C. L. Mowat calls "provisional" history, a kind of "historical journalism?"[4] Should its devotees be required to develop a new set of methods, techniques, and rules, as precise and specialized as those of the medievalists? Can the end product —contemporary history as written and taught—offer us anything more than the most tentative and superficial insights into the mysteries of human behavior and the processes of social change?

In the time of our fathers and grandfathers, the skeptics and denigrators were in the saddle. From the mid-nineteenth century almost to the mid-twentieth, historians were taught to scorn the record of the recent past, which was seen as the proper realm of the journalists, the political scientists, and other lesser breeds without the law. To be sure, that was more clearly the case in Europe than in America; our American bent toward pragmatism partially countered the prevailing current. But on both sides of the Atlantic historians were dominated by what has been described as "the fetishism of documents"[5] and "the superstition of historical distance."[6] History was a science, objectivity its creed. True history could not be written, or taught, so long as many of its secrets lay locked in the archives and so long as its subject matter might engage the historian's own values, prejudices, and emotions.

This lengthy eclipse of contemporary history as a reputable enterprise was part of the price paid for the professionalizing of the discipline. Throughout the ages prior to the mid-nineteenth century, when the writing of history had been an amateur sport, men had addressed themselves to the recent past without embarrassment or excuse. Some of them, in fact, had argued that contemporary history was the only kind that could stand serious scrutiny. Thucydides held that one could write with confidence only about events that he himself had experienced; the more distant past was necessarily wreathed in myth and mystery. Many medieval monks wrote something that passed for history and that dealt with what they had seen or known at first hand. Pascal went so far as to assert that "all history that is not contemporary is suspect."[7] As late as the mid-nineteenth century, contemporary history was being written by such authors as Paul Thureau-Dangin, Louis Blanc, Harriet Martineau, and Karl Marx; and their work still offers rewards to those who read it today. But by the 1870s, the great freeze had set in. The newly founded historical quarterlies of Britain, France, and Germany took a solemn vow against accepting articles with contemporary content or overtones. At Oxford, courses in English history came to a full stop with the accession of Queen Victoria in 1837 and continued to be stuck in that rut as late as 1914. The British governing class of the Victorian and Edwardian age, Llewellyn Woodward later remarked, knew more about ancient Greece and Rome than about their own world and that of their immediate forebears.[8] Continental historians were no different. Before the Second World War, no doctoral candidate at the Sorbonne was allowed to embark on a thesis subject for which the archival sources were closed—a denial which ruled out, in practice, virtually any topic since the Franco-Prussian War. The Sorbonne remained uncontaminated at least until 1960, when I heard its leading modern historian, Pierre Renouvin, make an eloquent plea to guard the ramparts against the assault of contemporaneity.

Today, of course, all that is (as the saying goes) ancient history. The change since the Second World War has been noticeable in the United States but really dramatic (though more recent) in Europe. In France, for example, contemporary history has invaded the school curriculum at every level. The revised lycée program established in the 1960s devotes the final year's history course entirely to the twentieth century. In the universities an adventuresome Ministry of Education created the first chair in contemporary history and directed that the first year of study toward the *licence d'histoire* be devoted to the recent past. Even in those rock-ribbed strongholds of tradition, the *agrégation* and the École Normale Supérieure, the competitive examinations now include questions on the interwar years.[9] Aspirants to the doctorate have registered such a flood of thesis topics dealing with twentieth-century events that it threatens to drown out some of the older fields.[10] In the French publishing world the trend has been even more striking. History comes to us smoking hot off the griddle; one popular series is brassily entitled "L'Histoire

Immédiate."[11] After the Paris quasi revolution of May 1968, thirteen books about the events of May were on sale within three weeks; the first one broke all records by being written, printed, bound, and delivered to the bookstalls just one week after the events it described. True, few of these masterpieces of instant history are the work of professional historians, who are quite understandably inclined to be sniffy about them. But the professionals no longer fear ostracism if they venture, somewhat more deliberately, into the quicksands of contemporary history, either in print or via a course offering on a subject so vividly present and emotionally charged as the Vichy era.

All this, of course, doesn't prove that really reputable contemporary history *can* be written or taught or that anybody should try to do so. The possibility remains that the effort is misguided and the product inferior. Cries of anguish from the defenders of tradition are heard from time to time, and occasionally these protests are thoughtful and well reasoned. The case for the prosecution has recently been put with his customary force and verve by one of our most learned scholars, Frank E. Manuel of New York University:

> Contemporaneity, a latter-day faith, is the old pragmatic idol in a new disguise. There is every likelihood that professional activity will be increasingly concentrated on contemporary or recent history. The illusion is widespread that recent history is somehow more relevant than ancient history, that the ills which beset us are inherited from the more immediate past and that studying these events might lead to the discovery of sovereign remedies. . . . Shrinking the whole past into the just-become past and compressing the future into an exercise in graphed extrapolation is nothing but another form of bondage to the present. These are shriveled, spurious pasts and futures, so limited in scope that they imprison us in immediacy. . . . The growing preference for recent history as a field of study is really a copping-out from the historical.[12]

To the extent that contemporary history is in fact displacing the longer view in the minds of teachers, students, and citizens, Professor Manuel's jeremiad is surely justified. Exposure to a foreshortened past that runs back only to 1945, 1929, or even 1914 is likely to produce a shallow understanding of where we find ourselves today and of how we got there. One can find occasional signs that what Manuel calls "shrinking the whole past into the just-become past" has been happening in this country, in response to the cry for "relevance" and the understandable urge in the high schools to save history from total curricular extinction. But I believe that I see some recent indications of an opposite trend as well, in certain universities at least (including my own)—indications of a resurgent student interest in the longer-range past, of a moderate swing away from courses such as the one that students at Harvard, I am told, used to call in their local patois "The News in Depth." Perhaps this trend represents nothing more than a kind of escapism—a desire to turn away from a foreboding future, an uncertain present, and a distasteful recent past. One prefers to hope that it stems rather from a healthy urge to look for deeper roots and to understand more fully both the present and the recent past.

There is, nevertheless, a potential danger in these current signs of distaste toward a recent past that is viewed in Hobbesian spirit as nasty and brutish as well as short.[13] It does not take long for the historical content of a recent period to be erased from the minds of a new generation that was born too late to experience it directly but soon enough to share its elders' feeling of revulsion. We forget all too easily, writes a British reviewer, ". . . how ignorant the young are of the immediate past. The years immediately preceding their own birth are a non-period, the biggest blank in the long dateless night [of the past]."[14] And C. Vann Woodward adds this warning: "The twilight zone that lies between living memory and written history is one of the favorite breeding places of mythology."[15] Neglect of the recent past could quickly produce a significant vacuum, a gap in the record, a short circuit in that understanding of the human condition to which historical study is supposed to contribute.

Thus far I have not attempted to deal with the more traditional challenges to contemporary history. They can be summed up in three phrases: inadequate sources, excessive subjectivity, stunted perspective. All three criticisms are too weighty to be ignored. But since a number of historians have already formulated answers, there is not much new to be said, so I shall be brief.

Obviously, some secrets remain locked for a time in the archives or in private papers that living persons hesitate to release. In normal circumstances, to take a dramatic example, the White House tapes would at best have remained under seal for two or three decades, and historians would have been able to produce only a truncated version of the Nixon years until their release. It would be foolhardy to discount the importance of these materials that escape the clutches of the contemporary historian. Nevertheless, as René Rémond observes, "the religion of the document must not be degraded into a superstition."[16] In the vast outpouring of information that marks our age and the proliferation of sources to which the present-day historian can turn, the public archives play a relatively less important role than used to be the case. Indeed, such secrets as remain sequestered under a twenty- or a fifty-year closure rule are, for the most part, of secondary or marginal importance. The contemporary historian's problem is, on the whole, an excess rather than a shortage of documentation; his challenge is to select intelligently from a wide diversity of sources and to interpret them according to standards that may vary from one type of source to another. For what one might call the contemporary contemporary historian (as opposed to the contemporary historian of Thucydides' time, or even of the early nineteenth century), the range of choice is further broadened by changes in the conception of history itself; for once we move beyond politics and diplomacy narrowly conceived, archival restrictions are much less likely to block the road. Furthermore, nobody can doubt the most obvious advantage enjoyed by the contemporary historian—that of access to some of the actors in his drama. Oral testimony, when checked against other evidence, can clarify many dark corners that may remain permanently dark after the death of the participants in an action. There is of course the correlative disadvantage that live subjects can talk back; unlike Cotton Mather or Napoleon, they may read what you say about them and seize their pens to denounce your frivolity and blindness (or, worse still, file a suit for libel). Perhaps this was the danger Raymond Sontag had in mind when he wrote some years ago: "Undoubtedly it is a thankless task to rewrite the history of the recent past: 'He who follows truth too closely at the heels may have his brains kicked out.' "[17] Still, the contemporary historian feels a certain smug compassion for his colleagues who must try to guess what Lincoln or Ivan the Terrible or Alexander the Great thought (or even did) at a given moment, or who must try to gauge the temper of the public in an era bereft of opinion polls.

Excessive subjectivity is another risk we run, or are alleged to run, when we deal with the recent past. "Deep, emotional personal involvement," writes an American scholar in a late issue of the *American Historical Review*, "is, unfortunately, a characteristic among historians of contemporary history."[18] The risk is doubtless real, though its gravity is more relative than absolute; the contemporary historian is likely to reply with the polite equivalent of "you're another." Few historians any longer cling to the illusion of pure objectivity in the writing of any kind of history, unless the subject happens to be so distant in emotional terms as to breed total indifference in both the historian and his readers. Indeed, many scholars doubt that the scientist's objectivity, even if achievable, would be a desirable goal. If it is true, as E. H. Carr puts it, that history is "a continuous process of interaction between the historian and his facts,"[19] any effort to transmute the living, breathing historian into an ambulatory computer is not so much impossible as misguided. Benedetto Croce was getting at the same point when he coined that famous phrase that has become a cliché: all history is contemporary history. He meant simply that the historian, contemporary or otherwise, cannot and should not shake loose from the concerns of his own time. This fact of life cannot, of course, justify loading the dice in support of the historian's personal biases. But if contemporary historians are especially susceptible to such a risk, all kinds of historians need to be on their guard.

The third accusation, that of stunted perspective, is a more compelling one. No historian can escape the fact that it is his business to view events in the perspective of time, and that view is unavoidably foreshortened when he writes about the very recent past. Sometimes the process he is analyzing has not yet reached its culmination (assuming, that is, that sequences of events or processes ever have a culmination); and judgments must be highly tentative when the outcome is not yet known. It would be foolish, therefore, to write or teach contemporary history without a full meed of that humility which ought properly to mark every good historian of whatever epoch. Yet here again there is a partial but persuasive rebuttal to be made. Historical distance from the object of study is by no means a sure guarantee of understanding; in fact, it may produce exactly the opposite effect. As the past recedes, meanings and context become blurred; there is a serious loss in our capacity to make qualitative judgments. We have a "feel" for what we have actually seen and experienced; we seek it conscientiously when we explore distant times and places, but we may seek it in vain. "Within ten years of a great historical event," Sir Herbert Butterfield once wrote, "you get the essence of the truth. Then, as the archives are opened, and as more information is available, there is an *absolute* decline in the quality of historical knowledge."[20] The "superstition of historical distance" (again I borrow a phrase from René Rémond) can blind us to the fact that the contemporary historian may produce a more faithful account than his later successor, who will possess a fuller documentary record plus the blessings of long perspective but who will suffer from the astigmatism caused by the distortions of time.

This symposium is supposed to attack the question of the future. "Future" is a word that frightens most historians; it seems to imply prediction, and experience suggests that historians are not much better at it than anybody else. Perhaps, however, what the symposium organizers had in mind was not prediction but prescription: if contemporary history continues to be taught and written, what *should* its practitioners set out to do in the next generation? The most sensible portmanteau answer is, I think, that their general goal should be exactly the same as that of historians concerned with any other past epoch. Here I remind you of my earlier suggestion that contemporary history may be a nonsubject; save for some peculiarities, I see it as simply a part of historical scholarship in general and not a thing apart. Perhaps contemporary historians ought to make a more sustained effort than they have so far done to develop special techniques, tests of evidence, and ethical standards adapted to the materials they use.[21] More than other historians, for example, they rely on the press for factual data and for contemporary opinion about the facts, and I suspect that they have shortchanged the problems involved in using it effectively and the risks involved in its slovenly use. No doubt most of us need to refine our interviewing and questionnaire techniques, drawing on the cumulative experience of other disciplines but adapting these devices to our own particular needs. Certainly we need to reflect on such questions of professional ethics as the use or withholding of evidence, from oral testimony or private papers, that has come to us "off the record" or on condition of confidentiality. Probably we should be less reluctant to learn and use the new quantifying techniques that have spread like a prairie fire through some earlier fields of study but that have found few exponents among contemporary historians. The case for psychohistory needs less urging, since in that realm the historians who deal with recent times are out ahead of the pack. But the history of recent developments in science lies largely untouched (due, no doubt, to our lack of real expertise); and most of us must also admit to a superficial grasp of economics, which for the contemporary historian is likely to be a peculiarly crippling weakness.

At the end of this meandering journey in search of a subject, two questions of a general nature may be worth at least brief comment. The first has to do with the effect on contemporary history of that group of French historians known as the *Annales* school. No other new force (except, perhaps, for Marxism) has been so influential in reshaping what historians in the Western world do and how they go about doing it. The *Annales* school has been inclined to treat contemporary historians with disparagement or even contempt—an attitude that carries something of the aura of excommunication by the Pope. Its founders, Lucien Febvre and Marc Bloch, preached the need for a total history, for a study of underlying structures, and for what Febvre called *la longue durée* as opposed to an older tradition that he branded *"histoire événementielle."* "Eventish" history—the study of isolated episodes or individuals torn out of their long-range context—they passionately rejected; they advocated instead vast frescoes that cover centuries of time and that deal with the slow processes of social change and with such slippery concepts as "collective mentalities."

The new truth preached by the *Annales* school has profoundly affected the writing of early modern history, from the late Middle Ages to the French Revolution; and its impact can also be seen on nineteenth-century studies. But contemporary history, locked into a brief period of some fifty years, scarcely lends itself to the concept of *longue durée*, unless one sees it as merely a brief and tentative postscript to a glacial process of change. The contemporary historian, more perhaps than any other, has been and is likely to be tempted into "eventish" history of the more traditional sort; he lacks the temporal elbowroom of the early-modern specialist, and if he seeks to do something like "total" history or to get at underlying structures, he is likely to sink without trace in the morass of available evidence.

Happily, there are some recent signs that the *Annales* school is growing more tolerant and no longer consigns all contemporary historians forever to the outer darkness. At the same time, some contemporary historians have taken the *Annales* criticism to heart and are attempting to profit by it. "Eventish" history, says one of them, can be reconciled with the demands of structural analysis and *longue durée*; the careful analysis of a single event in either the distant or the recent past can have real value, for an event is sometimes "a prodigious revealer of phenomena arising from the depths of time . . . and an accelerator . . . that permits the transition from one structure to another."[22] What the contemporary historian must do, if he is to be admitted to the inner sanctum, is to keep steadily in mind the dialectic between the event and the structures that underly it;[23] he must "stress the non-eventish aspects of the event."[24] This means, I take it, a stricture against viewing episodes and individuals as isolated or unique and a resolve to focus on those events that crystallize a process of social change. Such prescriptive guides are surely reasonable ones, more likely to improve than to cripple the work of the contemporary historian.

A second general question that confronts contemporary history has been posed by the British scholar Geoffrey Barraclough. In his widely read and provocative book *An Introduction to Contemporary History*, Barraclough argues that the contemporary age into which we have entered since about 1960 (after a long transitional period that began in the 1890s) differs sharply from all preceding eras in being universal in scope. A Europe-centered or Atlantic-centered history of our time, he contends, is no longer useful or even intellectually honest; those who write or teach contemporary history today and henceforward are obligated to think in global terms and to put particular stress on the neglected regions of the Third World if they wish to be read and heard. Such a constraint, if we take it seriously and literally, would be even more restrictive than the *Annales* school's insistence on *la longue durée*. It would rule out most of the limited topics that normally attract contemporary historians and would leave the field to those few who possess the erudition of a Barraclough, a Toynbee, or a William McNeill, who can take a stratospheric view or who can range comfortably through a vast sector of the Third World.

No one is likely to question the sharply increased importance of global concerns in our age or the partial nature of a Europe-centered or an Atlantic-centered perspective. But it would be self-defeating, I believe, to preach the Barraclough gospel as the only path to salvation. I can see no reason why sound and useful history cannot continue to be written about a selected part of the world, even though that part may not be the dominating center of the world or a microcosm of all mankind. Most written history is, and has to be, focused on part of a greater whole; it is by necessity partial rather than total in both space and time. To strive for a grasp of totality is of course an admirable goal; and historians, whose sprawling enterprise requires them to synthesize as well as analyze, probably have a special obligation to keep the idea of totality alive—to see the life of mankind whole even as they work on one of its dissected parts. Still, as they cling to that almost-impossible dream and seek, within the limits imposed by human frailty, to make it a reality, they ought not despair of making partial contributions along the way. A branch of the profession that can look to a Thucydides and a Tacitus and that has produced in our own time a whole cluster of impressive works has good reason to believe that it has a future.

NOTES

1. *Journal of Contemporary History* 1 (1968): iv.

2. Geoffrey Barraclough, *An Introduction to Contemporary History* (New York: Basic Books, 1964), p. 29.

3. John B. Poster, "The Birth of the Past: Childrens' Perceptions of Historical Time," *The History Teacher* 6 (1973): 598.

4. C. L. Mowat, *Great Britain Since 1914* (Ithaca, N.Y.: Cornell University Press, 1971), p. 17. James Ford Rhodes, in his presidential address to the American Historical Association in 1899, told his colleagues that the historians of the classical age had written "superior history" in part because "no extraordinary ability [is] required to

write contemporary history" (*Annual Report of the American Historical Association for the Year 1899* [Washington: Government Printing Office, 1900], 1: 59).

5. E. H. Carr, *What Is History?* (New York: Alfred A. Knopf, 1963), p. 15.

6. René Rémond, "L'histoire, science du présent," *Revue de l'Enseignement Supérieur*, no. 44–45 (1969), p. 94.

7. Quoted by Pierre Nora in *Le Figaro* (Paris), May 4, 1974.

8. Sir Llewellyn Woodward, "The Study of Contemporary History," *Journal of Contemporary History* 1 (1966): 1–2.

9. Rémond, "L'histoire, science," pp. 90–91.

10. In France the new interest in contemporary topics for doctoral theses resembles the Klondike gold rush. During the half decade 1963–68, there were only 20 thèses d'État in progress on the post-1914 period, as compared to 75 on the nineteenth century and 21 on the Revolutionary-Napoleonic era. But during the half decade 1968–73, contemporary topics surged into the lead with 74, outpacing the nineteenth century (68) and the Revolutionary-Napoleonic epoch (20) (Association des professeurs d'histoire contemporaine, *Liste des thèses d'histoire contemporaine déposés dans les universités françaises* [mimeographed: Metz, 1973]). In the United States during 1967–70, 47 percent of the dissertations registered in American history dealt with contemporary topics, as did 30 percent of the dissertations in postmedieval European history (*List of Doctoral Dissertations in History in Progress in the United States*, May 1967–May 1970 [Washington: American Historical Association, 1970]). The British have remained more traditional; only 15 percent of their theses on postmedieval British history deal with twentieth-century topics (University of London, Institute of Historical Research, *Historical Research for University Degrees in the United Kingdom: Theses in Progress 1974* [London, 1974]).

11. *Le Monde* (Paris), April 26, 1969. The phrase is used in another and quite different sense by the Belgian sociologist Benoît Verhaegen in his recent *Introduction à l'histoire immédiate* (Gembloux: Duculot, 1974). Verhaegen describes "immediate history" as a new discipline "at the junction of history, anthropology and sociology"; its object is to study present-day societies that are in process of rapid change, and its method is "based on the greatest possible identification between object and subject" (pp. 188–89). Verhaegen, who looks to Marx and many others for inspiration, has been trying out his experiment on the history of Zaïre from 1950 to 1965.

12. Frank E. Manuel, *Freedom From History* (New York: New York University Press, 1971), p. 14.

13. T. S. Eliot a generation ago anticipated this disabused mood when he wrote of "the immense panorama of futility and anarchy which is contemporary history."

14. *Times Literary Supplement* (London), February 25, 1972, p. 221.

15. C. Vann Woodward, *The Strange Career of Jim Crow*, 2d rev. ed. (New York: Oxford University Press, 1966), p. xii.

16. Rémond, "L'histoire, science," p. 92.

17. Raymond J. Sontag, "The Democracies and the Dictators Since 1933," *American Philosophical Society Proceedings* 98 (1954):317.

18. Warren F. Kimball in *American Historical Review* 79, no. 4 (October 1974): 1135.

19. Carr, *What Is History?* p. 35.

20. Quoted by A. J. P. Taylor in *The Observer* (London), July 28, 1974.

21. G. R. Elton contends that "it is one of the shortcomings of more recent history that its practitioners, overwhelmed by the task of mere study, have done almost nothing so far to work out proper rules of this kind" (*The Practice of History* [London: Collins-Fontana, 1969], p. 24). C. R. Mowat, on the other hand, holds that "recent history . . . is really conventional history, when it comes to sources and standards," so that conven-

tional rules and techniques are on the whole quite adequate (Mowat, *Great Britain Since 1914*, p. 17). It may be worth adding that Professor Mowat, unlike Professor Elton, was a "practitioner" of contemporary history.

22. Jean-Marie Mayeur in *Le Monde*, May 3, 1974.

23. Jacques Julliard in *Faire l'histoire*, ed. Jacques Le Goff and Pierre Nora (Paris: Gallimard, 1974), 2: 240.

24. Mayeur, *Le Monde*, May 3, 1974.

11

The History of
United States Foreign Policy:
Past, Present, and Future

Richard W. Leopold

For this lecture in the Centennial Symposium on "The Future of History," it was suggested that I speak on "The New Diplomatic History." That title did not fully cover the thoughts I wished to convey; for although I shall deal with current trends in teaching and research, I do not wish to emphasize newness. To be sure, recent years have brought changes in the field, yet there is more continuity and less novelty today than many of the younger specialists believe. Hence it is helpful, in seeking to illuminate the problems of the present and to predict the shape of things to come, to focus on 1938, the year in which I backed into the field—the year in which, without previous training in or familiarity with American diplomatic history, I was told as an instructor at a major university to teach an undergraduate-graduate lecture course and a graduate research seminar.

The year 1938 was an exciting one for diplomatic historians. Events abroad had led to congressional attempts to legislate neutrality, and these aroused bitter debates on college campuses. Teachers in the field were coming to regard theirs as an identifiable specialty within United States history.[1] As to research, the new National Archives building was in full use, servicing efficiently the State Department records to August 1906. In 1939 the files were opened on a restricted basis through 1918—a pleasant contrast to England and France, whose foreign office papers were closed beyond 1885 and 1871 respectively. In December 1938 Franklin D. Roosevelt announced plans for the first presidential library, while the completion of the new Library of Congress Annex enabled the Manuscript Division to move from cramped quarters in the main building early in 1939.

In 1938 a program of government documentary publication was in full swing. The *Foreign Relations* series, which since 1861 had printed in one or more annual volumes selected papers from the State Department, had reached 1923, save for the proceedings of the Paris Peace Conference, and—more important—was being acclaimed for its scholarly standards. The same could be said for Hunter Miller's editing of *Treaties and Other International Acts of the United States*, which provided not only texts with scrupulous accuracy but also archival materials bearing upon treaty negotiations. Begun in 1931, this project numbered five volumes and had reached the year 1852. Also valuable to diplomatic historians were Clarence E. Carter's compilation of the *Territorial Papers of the United States*, of which six volumes had been published since 1934, and the seven volumes of *Naval Documents Related to the Quasi-War between the United States and France*, prepared in the Navy Department under the supervision of Captain Dudley W. Knox.[2] Abroad, the late belligerents were issuing gargantuan collections dealing with the period 1871–1914. The Germans and the British had completed their series by 1938—the former in fifty-four volumes, the latter (who had started with 1898) in thirteen. By 1938, the French had released twenty-seven volumes with many more still to come for the years 1891 to 1901 and 1906 to 1911.

More important for the novice were the guides, textbooks, and standard works. In 1935 the Library of Congress had published a *Guide to the Diplomatic History of the United States, 1775–1921*, compiled by Samuel Flagg Bemis and Grace Gardner Griffin—the former an outstanding historian, the latter an expert bibliographer. No other specialty in United States history possessed so valuable a manual, one that appraised judiciously the secondary literature and described fully the primary sources, printed and manuscript. This thousand-page tome cost $2.50 and was thus, even in those depression years, within the means of indigent instructors. It was my bible for many years to come. Equally influential was Bemis's *A Diplomatic History of the United States*, which had appeared in 1936 and rendered obsolete the textbooks by Carl Russell Fish, Randolph G. Adams, John H. Latané, and Louis M. Sears. Based upon a masterly control of monographs and articles and a firsthand knowledge of source materials for the half century after 1775, the Bemis text stressed diplomacy and required close reading. Not until 1940 was it challenged by a different and more popular type of textbook, Thomas A. Bailey's *A Diplomatic History of the American People*.

, A quick survey of the best secondary works available in 1938 reveals those topics and areas that attracted the leading practitioners of the day. The emphasis was on the years before 1900, on the Western Hemisphere and Western Europe, and on bilateral negotiations. The chief methodological advances were two: multiarchival research —that is, the examination of foreign office records of all relevant nations—and the use of unprinted personal papers of participants to supplement official records. Those engaged in multiarchival research and drawing on private papers had to concentrate on the early period of the republic. The most satisfactory books of those years—ones not entirely superseded even today—were by three men, all of whom had taken the doctorate at Harvard: Samuel F. Bemis under Edward Channing, Arthur P. Whitaker under Frederick J. Turner, and Dexter Perkins under Archibald Cary Coolidge. Also deserving of mention are Julius W. Pratt, who studied under William E. Dodd at Chicago; Charles C. Tansill, a protégé of John H. Latané at Johns Hopkins; and J. Fred Rippy, a disciple of Herbert E. Bolton at California.[3]

What were the major challenges facing diplomatic historians in 1938? First, the twentieth century beckoned. The decades from 1901 to 1921 could be explored as never before now that the State Department's archives were open fully to 1906 and on a restricted basis to 1918; now that the *Foreign Relations* series was nearing the mid-1920s; and now that the personal papers of Theodore Roosevelt, John Hay, Elihu Root, Philander C. Knox, William Jennings Bryan, Robert Lansing, and Edward M. House were available. Given the fears of a new European war that swept the country after 1935, it is not surprising that the experience of 1914 to 1917 should be among the foremost concerns of diplomatic historians.

A second challenge was to extend the geographic limits of the field. In 1938 almost no specialist in American foreign policy dealt with Eastern Europe, the Middle East, Africa, or South and Southeast Asia. Neither diplomats nor scholars paid much heed to Greece, Palestine, the Congo, Indochina, or Korea. An ability to read French, German, and Spanish was sufficient when the focus was on Western Europe and the Western Hemisphere. Slavic and East Asian area studies did not exist in 1938. With one or two exceptions, the few writers on Russo-American relations could not read Russian. The leading diplomatic historian on Japan, Payson J. Treat, and his counterpart for China, Paul H. Clyde, used only Western-language sources. A. Whitney Griswold, whose *The Far Eastern Policy of the United States* was the most influential book in the field of 1938, was not trained in foreign policy or East Asia and could not read Chinese or Japanese. In this area the future belonged to younger men like John K. Fairbank, who spent four years after 1932 doing research in China, and Edwin O. Reischauer, who had been reared in Tokyo and had devoted five years after 1933 to study in Europe, Japan, Korea, and China.

A third challenge was to enlarge the concerns of diplomatic historians. To be sure, the ablest had never been content, as some critics charged, to summarize negotiations as if statesmen played chess in insulated chambers. In his account of the Jefferson and Madison administrations, Henry Adams had woven foreign affairs into the total national experience.[4] Bemis and Whitaker tied diplomacy to commercial rivalry and the moving frontier. The growing vogue of intellectual and social history in the 1930s encouraged attention to the role of ideas—national pride, ethnic prejudices, religious antipathies, racial theories—in shaping the actions of individuals, groups, and governments. Such a work was Albert K. Weinberg's *Manifest Destiny: A Study of Nationalist Expansionism in American History*, published in 1935. In 1938, as I moved from my original specialty to diplomatic history, I planned as my next book a comparable analysis of the influence of Anglophobia on United States foreign policy. It is one of several books I never finished, but I should add that no one else has yet written such a volume.

A fourth challenge for diplomatic historians in 1938 was one facing every generation—interpretation. Could the record of American foreign policy be explained by the character of the people, the genius of their institutions, the vigor of their economy, the advantage of their location, the nature of their society? Bemis attributed many diplomatic successes of the first half century to rivalries and wars among the transatlantic powers, or, as he put it, Europe's distress became America's advantage. Pratt and Weinberg dissected the arguments for expansion to determine whether the ideas they contained were the cause or rationale of the drive for new lands. Griswold offered a cyclical theory of advance and retreat for the Open Door in China. But for many in 1938, as today, the most satisfying interpretation was to view foreign policy as the product of capitalist pressures. Attacks in the 1920s on protectorates in the Caribbean led to a series of books on dollar diplomacy, while critics of American intervention in 1917 increasingly blamed the business and financial community for influencing Wilson's course on the Great War.[5] The most ambitious effort was a collaborative investigation, headed by Charles A. Beard and supported by the Social Science Research Council. Author of *An Economic Interpretation of the Constitution* in 1913 and *Economic Origins of Jeffersonian Democracy* in 1915, Beard had stressed the material factors shaping foreign policy in *The Rise of American Civilization*, written in 1927 with his wife. In 1934 he published *The Idea of National Interest* and *The Open Door at Home*. The thrust of these volumes was that the phrase "national interest," as used by diplomats, was a self-contradictory catchall and that the open-door policy, as pursued by the United States, was an imprudent exercise of government power that eventuated in the Great Depression.

Finally, a word about teaching diplomatic history in 1938. Very few colleges or universities had a specialist in the field, and not many offered a full-year course for undergraduates. Those that did gave over the first semester to the period before 1865. There was a reluctance to go beyond 1921 at the end of the second semester. My first effort in 1938, a one-semester course, covered the years 1775 to 1898. Four years later I regarded myself as daring for dividing a two-semester course at 1898.

It is now time to turn to the present—to evaluate the state of American diplomatic history today. We should keep in mind that foreign policy now plays a more central role for the nation than it did in 1938. Then men believed we had the option of keeping aloof from international crises; since 1941 few have felt that luxury existed. Foreign affairs are now global and total. This fact can be seen in the expansion of the powers of the president, especially in his control of the armed forces, and in the emergence of the military as a constant element in shaping foreign policy. Rivals to the State Department have proliferated: the Department of Defense, the National Security Council, the Joint Chiefs of Staff, the Central Intelligence Agency, the President's Special Assistant for National Security Affairs. These bodies did not exist in 1938.

Today there are probably twenty persons teaching American diplomatic history for every one in 1938.[6] College courses have multiplied along with textbooks and source readings. The literature, primary and secondary, has become so extensive that a proposal to replace the Bemis-Griffin guide of 1935 envisages five volumes, twenty-four editors, and a computerized bibliographical retrieval system.[7] In 1967 specialists formed a Society for Historians of American Foreign Relations, which since 1969 has arranged sessions at meetings of the major historical associations, published a newsletter, compiled a directory of members and their research projects, and listened to annual presidential addresses. With a membership of over 400, it held its own two-day meeting in 1975 and is launching its own journal.[8]

Today's diplomatic historians, like today's diplomats, deal with areas ignored in 1938. The need for language skills is acute—not only Russian, Chinese, and Japanese but also Arabic, Korean, and numerous dialects of Africa and Asia. Since 1945 many universities have adopted a regional approach—Harvard's East Asian Research Center, Columbia's Russian Institute, Northwestern's Program of African Studies, California's Center for Japanese and Korean Studies. Their presses have created series to carry monographs. Since most graduates of these area programs tended to specialize in the internal or external history of a particular country, the need remained for training that would combine knowledge of a foreign nation and its language with expertise in American foreign policy. An experimental program in American–East Asian Relations was launched in 1967 with the blessings of the American Historical Association and a grant from the Ford Foundation. It has sponsored three summer language institutes, offered a limited number of fellowships, held two research conferences, and published an historiographical volume.[9]

Diplomatic historians find their sources more scattered today than in the past. The geographic extension of the field compels travel abroad undreamed of in 1938. For those with topics manageable within the United States, it is no longer sufficient to settle in Washington with occasional trips to major repositories along both seaboards. Anyone working in the years after 1921 must be prepared to visit presidential archives in West Branch, Iowa; Hyde Park, New York; Independence, Missouri; Abilene, Kansas; Waltham, Massachusetts; and Austin, Texas. The National Archives, having long ago outgrown the building completed in 1935, has established fifteen federal records centers from Seattle to Atlanta. Fortunately, a generous resort to microfilm and electrophotography can eliminate some travel, while burgeoning finding aids help locate specific private papers and public records. The National Archives and Records Service has published a host of registers and inventories, including those for presidential libraries. The Library of Congress merits praise for sponsoring the indispensable *National Union Catalog of Manuscript Collections* and for microfilming, with every item indexed, its holdings of the personal papers of twenty-three presidents.

In gaining access to diplomatic archives, the scholar is better off today than he was in 1938. The United States' records are available through 1949, Britain's through 1945, France's through 1929, and —thanks to wartime capture and postwar microfilming—Germany's and Japan's through 1945. Thus the lag has been cut from thirty-two years to twenty-seven for the Americans, from fifty-three to twenty-nine for the British, from sixty-seven to thirty-five for the French, and from fifty-eight to twenty-nine for the Germans. Still, these gains do not satisfy most historians. The archives of the Soviet Union remain closed. During and after the Second World War some key documents never reached the State Department but were retained by the president or the military. Although almost all of Roosevelt's papers and those of the Joint Chiefs through 1945 have been declassified, those of Truman dealing with diplomatic and strategic matters are still under lock. Most diplomatic historians believe that all records should be open after twenty years; some argue for ten.[10]

The same delight and disappointment exist over documentary publications. The years since 1945 have witnessed ambitious programs of printing source materials, much of it relevant to foreign policy. I refer to the new editions of the papers of Benjamin Franklin, Thomas Jefferson, the Adams family, Alexander Hamilton, James Madison, John C. Calhoun, Henry Clay, James K. Polk, Andrew Johnson, Ulysses S. Grant, Theodore Roosevelt, Woodrow Wilson, Dwight D. Eisenhower, and Adlai E. Stevenson. I have in mind, too, the comprehensive *Public Papers of the Presidents*, beginning with Truman and prepared by the Office of the Federal Register, which include verbatim reports of all press conferences.[11] Other governments undertook after 1945 compilations of diplomatic documents for the years since 1919. None is finished. The British have reached 1939 with many gaps to fill; the same is true of the French who have gotten to 1938, the Italians to 1940, and the Germans to 1942. The highly selective annual Soviet volume is at 1936. The United States has done much better. The superbly edited seven-volume subseries of *Foreign Relations*, dealing with the top-level wartime conferences, is complete, while four of the nine volumes for 1949 have been released.

These achievements do not meet the expectations of today's historians. They deplore linking access to the State Department's files to issuance of the *Foreign Relations* volumes. They note that the interval between the date of the documents and the date of their publication has lengthened from fifteen years in 1938 to twenty-seven in 1976. Steps to ameliorate the situation have become a casualty of Watergate. In March 1972, President Nixon directed the Secretary of State to reduce the time lag to twenty years by 1975. Executive Order 11652 was designed to speed up and simplify the declassification of federal records.[12] The operation was entrusted to Donald Young under John Ehrlichman. Alas, that pair had been engaged nine months earlier in a clearly nonhistorical program in the office of a now famous West Coast psychiatrist; by June 1972, following an incident along the Potomac, the White House team seemed more intent on concealing evidence than divulging it. Frustrated scholars are again discussing two steps which I deem unwise. One is to curtail the scope of the *Foreign Relations* series, even abolish it, in order to hasten opening the State Department's archives. The other is to permit a select group of specialists to work in restricted records so as to produce for government use monographs that might, at an early date, be made public.[13]

So much for general problems confronting diplomatic historians today. Let us now examine some trends in writings on American foreign policy but without a long list of titles or invidious comparisons. First, the four challenges of 1938 are being faced, even if not fully overcome. Today scholars are working in the twentieth century, perhaps too much so. They have broadened their geographic horizons but are hampered in some areas by language obstacles and archival restrictions. Specialists are more concerned than previously with the domestic background of foreign policy—ideologies, institutions, interest groups, the economy. Nor is there any lack of search for interpretations to explain the record from George Washington to Richard Nixon.

Second, the most popular period for research is that of the Second World War and the onset of the Cold War. There is where the action is. There is where is available the largest number of untapped sources —official and private, printed and manuscript, written and oral. There are the decisions that shaped the course of American foreign policy for three decades—to those born in the 1930s, their entire life. To this age group, the decade after 1939 offers the excitement and challenge that many in 1938 found in the First World War and the Paris Peace Conference.

One consequence of this enthusiasm for the 1940s has been a decline in major works dealing with the years before 1865. When Norman A. Graebner questioned members of the Society for Historians of American Foreign Relations in 1972, he discovered that only five out of about 250 respondents put their primary interest before 1800, while fifty marked the Second World War and the Cold War as theirs.[14] Except for biographies, I can think of only about ten books on the period 1775–1865, published in the last decade, that are essential reading for teachers of United States foreign policy. There is more of value for the years 1865 to 1900, particularly with respect to overseas ambitions and activities.

The best accounts of United States policy outside the Western Hemisphere and Europe by American diplomatic historians deal with East Asia and the Middle East. Properly researched volumes on relations with Africa or South and Southeast Asia are few. In the last decade several excellent studies on the Middle East, one of distinction, have appeared, all based on a wide array of sources but none using materials in Arabic or Turkish. For the Far East, the record is better, though usually the Oriental languages are handled by area specialists, not diplomatic historians. One exception meriting identification is Akira Iriye. Born in Tokyo, trained in the United States, and fluent in Japanese, Chinese, Russian, French, and German, he has dealt perceptively with American–East Asian relations in three time periods—1897–1911, 1921–1931, and 1941–1951.[15]

A fourth trend in writing on American foreign policy is the attempt—not always successful—to analyze the domestic forces that shape external relations. There is a laudable concern for ideas, institutions, and groups. Foremost under ideas is the view Americans have of themselves and of the role they should play in world affairs. This view embraces attitudes toward other peoples and cultures and raises questions of racism and ethnocentrism. It also subsumes popular notions on the use of thermonuclear weapons, the utility of the United Nations, and the obligations of international law. Some effort has been made to grapple with the murky problem of public opinion and to set standards for measuring its influence, but more needs to be done.

Greater progress has marked the study of institutions and the decision-making process. The traditional struggle between president and Congress to control foreign policy—especially the Senate's action on treaties—had been the subject of several books before 1938. With the relative decline in treaties as an irritant in this struggle, the president's role as commander-in-chief came to the fore. More attention is being paid to military-legislative contacts and to interservice rivalries. Scholars are also assessing the influence of departments other than State—Defense, Treasury, Commerce, Agriculture—and where possible, of such new bodies as the National Security Council, the Atomic Energy Commission, and the Central Intelligence Agency. There is ample opportunity in this area for diplomatic historians who lack linguistic skills to test the validity of, and then push beyond, theories about the irrational in decision making, the impact of bureaucratic politics, and the emergence of an elite now termed the national security managers.

Similar opportunities beckon with regard to private groups seeking to shape foreign policy. The peace movement is being reexamined by a generation for whom the draft was a reality and Vietnam a nightmare. The misnamed military-industrial complex is being debated by scholars as well as by polemicists. Pressure from the business, financial, and agrarian communities is a prominent theme in monographs. There is a new interest in how missionaries have operated and what scientists have recommended. The impact of groups like the Council on Foreign Relations and the Institute of Pacific Relations is undergoing scrutiny.

I come, finally, to the current debate over revisionism, over categorizing diplomatic historians, and over generalizing about American foreign policy. Some of you may have expected me to reach these topics much earlier in the hour; a younger person, I suspect, might have devoted most of the lecture to them. Frankly, all this talk about revisionism leaves me with a sense of déjà vu. Revisionism is the essence of the historian's trade. His initial account of an event or decision is based inevitably on incomplete sources and inadequate perspective. In foreign affairs this version is often favorable to the government because it relies on official records. As time passes, scholars gain access to the private papers of participants and the archives of foreign governments. They can also see what consequences have followed the event or decision. Small wonder that later authors revise and improve upon their predecessors. But since revisionists are frequently too eager to win fame by advancing new interpretations and too affected by their own day to re-create fairly the earlier period, they are in turn revised by later revisionists. In my academic lifetime I have witnessed this cycle of revisionism on such topics as Wilson's neutrality from 1914 to 1917, the peacemaking at Paris in 1919, the road to Pearl Harbor, the origins of the Cold War, and now the diplomacy of John F. Kennedy. I suggest as required reading for all graduate students in the field, and their mentors too, Arthur P. Whitaker's witty address before the Society for Historians of American Foreign Relations in April 1973, entitled "Aren't We All Revisionists?"[16]

I find misleading, if not self-serving, the vogue of labeling diplomatic historians. A questionnaire in 1972, designed to construct a profile of specialists, asked respondents to define their interpretations as either "traditional" or "radical." Are those pejorative terms the only options? Does it help to call someone "orthodox" or "conventional" because he has reservations about the theses of William Appleman Williams or about the often one-sided criticism of United States policy toward the Soviet Union after the Second World War? Such labels suggest a closed mind and allegiance to past judgments that run counter to the canons of our craft. Does it help to divide practitioners into "realists" and "idealists"? Who would want to be termed an idealist if it meant he did not cultivate a skepticism that lies at the heart of historical inquiry? Does it help to identify oneself as an "eclectic"? Is it not the task of our guild to draw upon all sources and employ all concepts?[17] Equally unsatisfactory are attempts to label types of revisionists. One writer divides them into "soft" and "hard"; another, into "left-liberal" and "radical." Still a third uses "moderate revisionists" to separate them from those of the New Left.[18] That last tag also needs defining. In sum, it is more important to know what a historian has to say and how he handles his materials than to worry about the school he represents.[19]

I am equally leery of attempts to fit all American foreign policy since 1775 into one of two interpretations. The realist-idealist dichotomy, so popular a decade ago, does not make sense for most of the nineteenth century or the years after 1939. George F. Kennan and Hans J. Morgenthau provided helpful insights for specific time periods and topics, but neither they nor others have dealt systematically with our entire history. The concept of empire, so attractive to many today, will not withstand semantic analysis or case-by-case study.[20] It is the legitimate function of government to promote the economic well-being of its citizens overseas, one that goes back to the beginning of the republic; but the current version of "open-door diplomacy" contains too many internal contradictions to make it acceptable to me.

Let me not be misunderstood. I am not implying that historians have failed to benefit from the contributions of those scholars who won their doctorates in the late 1950s or early 1960s and who because of their criticism of past policies and past histories have been lumped together as revisionists. Walter LaFeber, Gabriel Kolko, Lloyd C. Gardner, Barton J. Bernstein, and Thomas G. Paterson—to name a few—have by diligent research and imaginative thinking compelled older hands to reconsider long-held views. If I do not find novel or convincing the imperialist theme—I heard a lot about it in 1938—it has been useful to be reminded that empires can be informal as well as formal. If I reject the open-door thesis as imprecise, I concede that for too long most works on the period 1914–1950 paid too much attention to efforts to make the world safe for American political institutions and too little to efforts to make the world safe for American business enterprise. If I am not persuaded by attempts to denigrate Roosevelt's role in the diplomacy of the Second World War, I agree that the problem of the revolutionary Left and of the colonial world merit more space than they received in the 1950s. We can learn much from both Professor Williams and his followers and from the critics of Harry S. Truman. But we must also heed another group of able young men —John L. Gaddis, George C. Herring, Lisle A. Rose, Alfred A. Eckes, and Melvyn P. Leffler, again to name only a few—who are providing sound alternative accounts of the years from 1941 to 1947 or revealing case studies of the open-door thesis.[21]

And now to the crystal ball.[22] What can we reasonably predict to be the future course of American diplomatic history? First, we will discard that title. Future scholars will talk less about the diplomacy of ambassadors and foreign secretaries and more about the shaping of foreign policy, the ramifications of foreign relations, and the nature of international affairs. Foreign policy is the goals set by governments to promote the nation's interests and welfare abroad. Foreign relations are the sum total of all connections—official, private, commercial, and cultural—with other countries and peoples. International affairs involve a completely global approach to dealings among nation-states.

Second, I foresee a continued emphasis, apparent in recent years, on the domestic forces that affect foreign policy and influence foreign relations. For decision making, historians will focus on individuals and institutions in Washington. With the current reaction against the imperial presidency, we can expect every occupant of the White House to be scrutinized anew and the record of Congress to be judged critically. I anticipate that more attention will be paid to the armed forces and that we shall have better balanced studies of military planning and administration. For nongovernmental forces, there will be a more sophisticated analysis of public opinion and a deeper probing of elites and interest groups. Future scholars will view foreign policy as a product of not only the domestic economy but also the political scene. The link between foreign policy and political survival, suggested by some writers in recent years, was underscored by the events leading to the resignation of President Nixon.

Third, I predict a greater use of the comparative approach in the study of foreign policy. The experience of not one but many other nations on the problems faced by the United States will offer a better perspective, especially for the period when the republic became a great power. A major flaw in all books on the origins of the Cold War is their one-dimensional view, their failure to describe the pressures and perceptions that molded policy making not only in Moscow but also in London, Paris, and other capitals. A comparative approach should throw light on the pre-1941 paralysis of the victors of Versailles and on the post-1945 developments in the Middle East, Indochina, and Korea. Some progress has already been made in delineating American perceptions of other peoples and governments; now historians must show how the United States was perceived by potential friends and foes. They must also consider how American actions abroad—official and private—affected other societies.

Will these new concerns require a methodological revolution? I think not. Students of foreign policy will continue to draw, as they have been doing, on the other social sciences, especially as they explore bureaucratic functioning, popular perceptions, and seemingly irrational behavior. Quantification will help, mostly for roll calls in legislative bodies, such as Congress and the United Nations, and for profiles of key groups, such as the Foreign Service or the Council on Foreign Relations. Language skills will be more essential than ever before, for both research and keeping up with the best foreign scholarship. For example, there are many valuable works on events in East Asia between the two World Wars, but they can be exploited only by those who read Japanese. To a lesser extent the same thing can be said about recent books in German for the period before, during, and after the Great War of 1914–1918. Finally, there will be a renewed dedication to basic research. The last few years have seen too many superficial accounts of the Eisenhower, Kennedy, and Johnson regimes, ones that rest on the published recollections of participants, on the oral comments of persons who wish to remain unidentified, and on the columns of the *New York Times*. We cannot be content with judgments based on such sources if the standards set by Bemis, Whitaker, and Perkins in the 1920s are to be maintained. We must return to multinational research in not simply the files of foreign offices but also the personal papers of all who contribute to the decision-making process.

The difficulties, obviously, are enormous, given the number of collections to search, at home and abroad, and the plethora of documents to read. The field is not one for the faint-hearted or those intent on instant finds. But it is one that has an honorable past, an exciting present, and a challenging future.

NOTES

1. Charles E. Neu, "The Changing Interpretive Structure of American Foreign Policy," in *Twentieth-Century American Foreign Policy*, eds. John Braeman, Robert H. Bremner, and David Brody (Columbus: Ohio State University Press, 1971), p. 2, n. 3, citing the recollections in 1968–69 of Samuel F. Bemis and Thomas A. Bailey.

2. Knox was also responsible for *Naval Documents Related to the United States Wars with the Barbary Pirates: Naval Operations Including Diplomatic Background from 1785*

through 1807, 7 vols. (Washington: Government Printing Office, 1939–46). The Carnegie Endowment for International Peace continued its program, under the editorship of William R. Manning, of publishing unprinted State Department records in its twelve volumes of *Diplomatic Correspondence of the United States: Inter-American Affairs, 1831–1860* between 1932 and 1939, and its four volumes of *Diplomatic Correspondence of the United States: Canadian Relations, 1784–1860* between 1940 and 1945.

3. Samuel Flagg Bemis, *Jay's Treaty: A Study in Commerce and Diplomacy* (New York: The Macmillan Company, 1923); *Pinckney's Treaty: A Study of America's Advantage from Europe's Distress, 1783–1800* (Baltimore: The Johns Hopkins Press, 1926); *The Diplomacy of the American Revolution* (New York: D. Appleton-Century Company, 1935). Arthur Preston Whitaker, *The Spanish-American Frontier, 1783–1795: The Westward Movement and the Spanish Retreat in the Mississippi Valley* (Boston: Houghton Mifflin Company, 1926) and *The Mississippi Question, 1795–1803: A Study in Trade, Politics, and Diplomacy* (New York: D. Appleton-Century Company, 1934). Dexter Perkins, *The Monroe Doctrine, 1823–1826* (Cambridge: Harvard University Press, 1927); *The Monroe Doctrine, 1826–1867* (Baltimore: The Johns Hopkins Press, 1933); *The Monroe Doctrine, 1867–1907* (Baltimore: The Johns Hopkins Press, 1937). Julius W. Pratt, *Expansionists of 1812* (New York: The Macmillan Company, 1925) and *Expansionists of 1898: The Acquisition of Hawaii and the Spanish Islands* (Baltimore: The Johns Hopkins Press, 1936). Charles Callan Tansill, *The Canadian Reciprocity Treaty of 1854* (Baltimore: The Johns Hopkins Press, 1922); *The Purchase of the Danish West Indies* (Baltimore: The Johns Hopkins Press, 1932); *The United States and Santo Domingo, 1798–1873* (Baltimore: The Johns Hopkins Press, 1938); *America Goes to War* (Boston: Little, Brown and Company, 1938). J. Fred Rippy, *The United States and Mexico* (New York: Alfred A. Knopf, Inc., 1926); *Rivalry of the United States and Great Britain over Latin America, 1808–1830* (Baltimore: The Johns Hopkins Press, 1929); *Joel R. Poinsett: Versatile American* (Durham: Duke University Press, 1935).

4. Henry Adams, *The History of the United States of America during the Administrations of Jefferson and Madison*, 9 vols. (New York: Charles Scribner's Sons, 1889–91).

5. Scott Nearing and Joseph Freeman, *Dollar Diplomacy: A Study in American Imperialism* (New York: Viking Press, 1925); C. Hartley Grattan, *Why We Fought* (New York: Vanguard Press, 1929). See also the following *Studies in American Imperialism*, edited by Harry Elmer Barnes with the support of the American Fund for Public Service Studies in American Imperialism and published by Vanguard Press of New York: Melvin M. Knight, *The Americans in Santo Domingo* (1928); Margaret Alexander Marsh, *The Bankers in Bolivia: A Study in American Foreign Investment* (1928); Leland Hamilton Jenks, *Our Cuban Colony: A Study in Sugar* (1928); Bailey W. and Justine Whitfield Diffie, *Porto Rico: A Broken Pledge* (1931); J. Fred Rippy, *The Capitalists and Colombia* (1931); and Charles David Kepner, Jr., and Jay Henry Soothill, *The Banana Empire: A Case Study of Economic Imperialism* (1935).

6. Lawrence E. Gelfand, "Justification for a New Bibliographical Guide and a Retrieval System" [1973], p. 5. A copy of this unpublished essay is in the author's possession.

7. Lawrence E. Gelfand, "Bibliographical Guide and Retrieval System: A Statement of Method" [1973]. A copy of this unpublished essay is in the author's possession.

8. The growth of the society can be traced in the *SHAFR Newsletter*. The first three volumes, December 1969–May 1972, were edited by Gerald E. Wheeler and issued semiannually at San José State University. Beginning with Volume 4 in March 1973, it has been edited by Nolan Fowler and is issued quarterly at Tennessee Technological University.

9. Ernest R. May and James C. Thomson, Jr., eds., *American–East Asian Relations: A Survey* (Cambridge: Harvard University Press, 1972). The work of the Committee on American–East Asian Relations is summarized in the annual reports of the American Historical Association.

10. James MacGregor Burns, "The Historian's Right to See," *New York Times Book Review*, November 8, 1970; and Richard W. Leopold, "A Crisis of Confidence: Foreign Policy Research and the Federal Government," *American Archivist* 34 (April 1971): 139–55.

11. Since the first volume in this series appeared in 1958, the presidencies of Harry S. Truman, Dwight D. Eisenhower, John F. Kennedy, and Lyndon B. Johnson have been completed. The last of the volumes published thus far of Richard M. Nixon, the one for 1972, was released in 1974. The first volumes of Herbert Hoover were issued in 1974. It is assumed that the administration of Franklin D. Roosevelt will eventually be covered.

12. *Department of State Bulletin* 66 (April 3, 1972): 518–22; *Federal Register* (March 10, 1972), pp. 5209–18. See also Richard W. Leopold, "The *Foreign Relations* Series Revisited: One Hundred Plus Ten," *Journal of American History* 59 (March 1973): 935–57.

13. Ernest R. May, "A Case for 'Court Historians,' " *Perspectives in American History* 3 (1969): 413–32, and *"Lessons" of the Past: The Use and Misuse of History in American Foreign Policy* (New York: Oxford University Press, 1973), pp. 172–90. See also a proposal drafted by Henry Owen, Director of the Foreign Policy Studies Program of the Brookings Institution, enclosed in May to Leopold, January 21, 1974.

14. Norman A. Graebner, "The State of Diplomatic History," *SHAFR Newsletter* 4 (March 1973): 4.

15. *Pacific Estrangement: Japanese and American Expansionism, 1897–1911* (Cambridge: Harvard University Press, 1972); *After Imperialism: The Search for a New Order in the Far East, 1921–1931* (Cambridge: Harvard University Press, 1965); and *The Cold War in Asia: A Historical Introduction* (Englewood Cliffs, N.J.: Prentice-Hall, Inc., 1974).

16. *SHAFR Newsletter* 4 (June 1973): 2–10.

17. Sandra Caruthers Thomson and Clayton A. Coppin, Jr., "Texts and Teaching: A Profile of Historians of American Foreign Relations in 1972," *SHAFR Newsletter* 4 (September 1973): 4–23; and Graebner, "The State of Diplomatic History," *SHAFR Newsletter* 4 (March 1973): 2–12.

18. Robert James Maddox, *The New Left and the Origins of the Cold War* (Princeton: Princeton University Press, 1973), pp. 4–6; Barton J. Bernstein, "Commentary," in *The Truman Period as a Research Field: A Reappraisal, 1972*, ed. Richard S. Kirkendall (Columbia: University of Missouri Press, 1974), pp. 162–66; and Joseph M. Siracusa, *New Left Diplomatic History and Historians: The American Revisionists* (Port Washington, N.Y.: Kennikat Press, 1973), pp. 76–79.

19. Recent appraisals which focus on problems and issues, not personalities, are Charles S. Maier, "Revisionism and the Interpretations of Cold War Origins," *Perspectives in American History* 4 (1970): 313–47, and J. L. Richardson, "Cold-War Revisionism: A Critique," *World Politics* 24 (July 1972): 579–612.

20. The notion of empire has been set forth most importantly by William Appleman Williams in *The Tragedy of American Diplomacy* (Cleveland: World Publishing Company, 1959; rev. eds., 1962 and 1972, by Dell Publishing Company) and in *The Roots of the Modern American Empire: A Study of the Growth and Shaping of Social Consciousness in a Marketplace Society* (New York: Random House, 1969). See also Williams, ed., *From Colony to Empire: Essays in the History of American Foreign Relations* (New York: John Wiley & Sons, 1972); Walter LaFeber, *The New Empire: An Interpretation of American Expansion, 1860–1898* (Ithaca: Cornell University Press, 1963); Lloyd C. Gardner, *Eco-*

nomic Aspects of New Deal Diplomacy (Madison: University of Wisconsin Press, 1964); Thomas J. McCormick, *China Market: America's Quest for Informal Empire, 1893–1901* (Chicago: Quadrangle Books, 1967); and Lloyd C. Gardner, Walter LaFeber, and Thomas J. McCormick, *Creation of the American Empire: U.S. Diplomatic History* (Chicago: Rand McNally & Company, 1973). For excellent appraisals, see J. A. Thompson, "William Appleman Williams and the 'American Empire,' " *Journal of American Studies* 7 (April 1973): 91–104; Arthur Schlesinger, Jr., "America II," *Partisan Review* 37, no. 4 (1970): 505–19; and Robert Zevin, "An Interpretation of American Imperialism," *Journal of Economic History* 33 (March 1972): 316–60.

21. Melvyn P. Leffler, "The Origins of Republican War Debt Policy, 1921–1933: A Case Study in the Applicability of the Open Door Interpretation," *Journal of American History* 59 (December 1972): 585–601; and Alfred E. Eckes, Jr., "Open Door Expansionism Reconsidered: The World War II Experience," *Journal of American History* 59 (March 1973): 909–24, indicate how the open-door thesis may be tested.

22. I have benefited from ideas contained in the following diagnoses of and prescriptions for the field: Thomas J. McCormick, "The State of American Diplomatic History," and Lawrence Evans, "The Dangers of Diplomatic History," in *The State of American History*, ed. Herbert J. Bass (Chicago: Quadrangle Books, 1970), pp. 119–41, 142–56; Alexander DeConde, "What's Wrong with American Diplomatic History," *SHAFR Newsletter* 1 (May 1970): 1–16; Ernest R. May, "The Decline of Diplomatic History," in *American History: Retrospect and Prospect*, ed. George Athan Billias and Gerald N. Grob (New York: The Free Press, 1971), pp. 399–430; and Norman A. Graebner, "The State of Diplomatic History," *SHAFR Newsletter* 4 (March 1973): 2–12.

NOTES ON THE CONTRIBUTORS

WOODROW BORAH (b. 1912), Abraham D. Shepard Professor of History at the University of California at Berkeley, is a specialist in the demographic and economic history of Mexico and Latin America. Born in Mississippi, he earned the A.B. and M.A. degrees at UCLA and the Ph.D. (1940) in History and Geography at the University of California at Berkeley. He is the author or coauthor of nine monographs and more than three dozen articles. Among his most noteworthy publications are *New Spain's Century of Depression* (1951); *Early Trade and Navigation between Mexico and Peru* (1954); *Aboriginal Population of Central Mexico on the Eve of the Spanish Conquest* (1963); and the two-volume *Essays on the History of Population: Mexico and the Caribbean* (1971-74).

I. BERNARD COHEN (b. 1914), Professor of the History of Science at Harvard University, is a specialist in the history of scientific ideas. Born in New York City, he earned the B.S. cum laude and Ph.D. (1947) degrees from Harvard University. He served for seven years as editor of the History of Science Society's journal, *Isis*, succeeding its founder, George Sarton. He was active in the emerging field of general education at Harvard University, but his dominant concern has been the growth of physical thought of the seventeenth and eighteenth centuries and the rise of science in the United States. His three-volume critical edition of Isaac Newton's *Principia* (undertaken with the late Alexandre Koyré) appeared in 1972-73. His earlier studies of American eighteenth-century science include *Benjamin Franklin: His Contributions to the American Tradition* (1953); and *Franklin and Newton* (1956). At the modern end of the historical spectrum, Professor Cohen is engaged in exploring the implications of more immediate twentieth-century issues: the history of the computers, the relations between concepts and theories of the natural and physical sciences and the rise of the social and behavioral sciences; the fate of the individual in an age of numbers.

PAUL K. CONKIN (b. 1929), Professor of History at the University of Wisconsin in Madison, is a specialist in American intellectual history. A native of Tennessee, he holds the M.A. and Ph.D. (1957) degrees from Vanderbilt University. His first book, *Tomorrow a New World: The New Deal Community Program* (1959), won the Albert J. Beveridge Award from the American Historical Association. In intellectual history Conkin is best known for *Puritans and Pragmatists: Eight Eminent American Thinkers* (1968). With Roland Stromberg he has written *The Heritage and Challenge of History* (1971). Conkin's wide-ranging interests are revealed in his other books: *Two Paths to Utopia* (1964), a study of the Hutterites and of a socialist colony in California and Louisiana; *FDR and the Origins of the Welfare State* (1967); *Self-Evident Truths* (1974), analyzing the development of popular sovereignty, natural rights, and the balance and separation of powers in American government; and, with David Burner, *A History of Recent America* (1974).

CHARLES F. DELZELL (b. 1920), Professor of History at Vanderbilt University, is a specialist in modern European history. Born in Oregon, he received the B.S. degree from the University of Oregon, and the A.M. and Ph.D. (1951) from Stanford University. He also studied at the Istituto Italiano per gli Studi Storici in Naples. Prior to his appointment to the Vanderbilt faculty in 1952, he taught history at the Universities of Hawaii and Oregon and was Curator of Mediterranean Collections in the Hoover Institution at Stanford. He was elected President, European History Section, Southern Historical Association (1963–64); President, Society for Italian Historical Studies (1968–69); Chairman, American Committee on the History of the Second World War (1973–75); and member of the Council of the American Historical Association (1974–76). He has held Fulbright and NEH Senior fellowships. His books include *Mussolini's Enemies: The Italian Anti-Fascist Resistance* (1961; reprint, 1974), which received the George Louis Beer Prize of the A.H.A. and the Borden Award of the Hoover Institution; and *Italy in Modern Times* (1964). He is coauthor of *The Meaning of Yalta* (1956), and *Historians of Modern Europe* (1971). He has edited *The Unification of Italy, 1859–1861* (1965); *Mediterranean Fascism, 1919–1945* (1970); and *The Papacy and Totalitarianism Between the Two World Wars* (1974).

JOHN W. HALL (b. 1916), A. Whitney Griswold Professor and Chairman of the Department of History at Yale University, is a specialist in Japanese history. Born in Tokyo, he received the B.A. degree from Amherst College and the Ph.D. (1950) from Harvard University. He has spent many years in the Far East. From 1948 until 1961 he was on the faculty of the University of Michigan–Ann Arbor, serving also as Director of its Center for Japanese Studies for several years. In 1961 he became the first incumbent of the A. Whitney Griswold chair of history at Yale University. In 1967–68 he was elected President of the Association of Asian Studies. He is the author and coauthor of numerous books, including *Japanese History: A Guide to Japanese Research and Reference Materials* (1954); *Tanuma Okitsugu, Forerunner of Modern Japan* (1955); *Twelve Doors to Japan* (1965); the prize-winning study, *Government and Local Power in Japan, 500–1700* (1966); *Studies in the Institutional History of Early Modern Japan* (1968);

Japan from Pre-History to Modern Times (1970); and (with Jeffrey P. Mass) *Medieval Japan: Essays in Institutional History* (1974).

RICHARD W. LEOPOLD (b. 1912), William Smith Mason Professor of American History at Northwestern University, is a specialist in the history of United States foreign policy with a secondary interest in the history of the presidency and the armed forces. He holds the A.B. from Princeton University and the A.M. and Ph.D. (1938) from Harvard University. He has served on advisory committees concerned with the *Foreign Relations of the United States* series, the *Papers of Woodrow Wilson*, and official government histories. His publications include *Robert Dale Owen* (1940), which received the John H. Dunning Prize of the American Historical Association; *Elihu Root and the Conservative Tradition* (1954); *The Growth of American Foreign Policy* (1962); and essays dealing with historical writing and research, American–East Asian relations, and governmental historical activities. He was President of the Society for Historians of American Foreign Relations in 1970, and his election in 1975 as Vice President of the Organization of American Historians places him in the line of succession to the presidency in 1976–77.

KENNETH A. LOCKRIDGE (b. 1940), is a specialist in early American social history. He is also interested in the comparative study of Anglo-American social and cultural history in the seventeenth and eighteenth centuries. A native of Los Angeles, he earned the B.A. degree at Yale University and the M.A. and Ph.D. (1965) degrees at Princeton University. Professor Lockridge formerly taught at the University of Illinois at Chicago Circle. He helped to set up the Newberry Library Center for the Study of the Family in Historical Perspective. In 1974 he was Fulbright lecturer at the University of Umeå in Sweden. He now lives in Ann Arbor, Michigan. He has published two books: *A New England Town: The First Hundred Years* (1970); and *Literacy in Colonial New England: A Study of the Social Context of Literacy in the Pre-Modern West* (1974).

LEWIS W. SPITZ (b. 1922), William R. Kenan Professor of History and Associate Dean of the School of Humanities and Science at Stanford University, is a specialist in Renaissance and Reformation history. Born in Nebraska, he received the A.B. degree from Concordia College, the M.Div. from Concordia Seminary, the M.A. from the University of Missouri, and the Ph.D. (1954) from Harvard University. He taught at the University of Missouri before moving to Stanford University in 1961. He is a former President of the American Society for Reformation Research and is the American Managing Editor of the *Archive for Reformation History*. Among his books are *Conrad Celtis: The German Arch-Humanist* (1957); *The Religious Renaissance of the German Humanists* (1963); *Life in Two Worlds: A Biography of William Sihler* (1967); and *The Renaissance and*

Reformation Movements (1971). He has also edited or coedited *Major Crises in Western Civilization* (1965); *The Protestant Reformation* (1966); *The Reformation: Basic Interpretations* (1972); and *The Northern Renaissance* (1972).

LAWRENCE STONE (b. 1919), Dodge Professor of History and Director of the Shelby Cullom Davis Center for Historical Studies at Princeton University, is a specialist in early modern British social history. A native of England, he studied at the Sorbonne and at Christ Church, Oxford, where he received the M.A. degree in 1946. From 1946 to 1950 he was Lecturer at University College, Oxford, and from 1950 to 1962 was a Fellow of Wadham College, Oxford. In 1955 he received the Leverhulme Award for Research and in 1960–61 was a member of the Institute for Advanced Study in Princeton. He was appointed to the Princeton University faculty in 1963 as Dodge Professor of History and was Chairman of the Department of History in 1967–69. His books include *The Crisis of the Aristocracy, 1558–1641* (1965); *An Elizabethan: Sir Horatio Palavicino* (1956); *The Causes of the English Revolution, 1529–1642* (1972); *Family and Fortune: Studies in Aristocratic Finance in the Sixteenth and Seventeenth Centuries* (1973). Also an authority on English sculpture and architecture, he is the author of *Sculpture in Britain: The Middle Ages* (1955). In 1965 he edited *Social Change and Revolution in Seventeenth-Century England*. He is a member of the Editorial Board of *Past and Present*.

STEPHAN THERNSTROM (b. 1934), Professor of History at Harvard University, is a specialist in the history of American population and social structure. A native of Michigan, he earned the B.S. degree with highest honors at Northwestern University, and the A.M. and Ph.D. (1962) degrees at Harvard University. He has taught at Brandeis University and UCLA. His most recent book, *The Other Bostonians: Poverty and Progress in the American Metropolis, 1880–1970* (1973), won the Bancroft Prize for History (1974) as well as the Harvard University Press Faculty Prize. His earlier books were *Poverty and Progress: Social Mobility in a 19th-Century City* (1964); and *Poverty, Planning and Politics in the New Boston* (1969). He has coedited *Nineteenth-Century Cities: Essays in the New Urban History* (1969). He serves on the Editorial Boards of the *Journal of Inter-disciplinary History;* the *Journal of Urban History; Labor History;* and *The Family in Historical Perspective.* He is also Series Editor, The Harvard Studies in Urban History, Harvard University Press.

C. VANN WOODWARD (b. 1908), Sterling Professor of History at Yale University, is a specialist in the history of the American South. A native of Arkansas, he holds the Ph.B. degree from Emory, the M.A. from Columbia, and the Ph.D. (1937) from the University of North Carolina at Chapel Hill. Before his appointment to Yale in 1961, he taught at Johns

Hopkins, Scripps College, University of Virginia, University of Florida, and Georgia Institute of Technology. He has also held visiting appointments at Oxford, the University of London, and the University of Tokyo, and in 1975 was awarded an honorary D.Litt. by Cambridge University. He has been elected to the presidency of the Southern Historical Association (1951–52), the Organization of American Historians (1967–68), and the American Historical Association (1969). His books include *Tom Watson: Agrarian Rebel* (1938); *Reunion and Reaction: The Compromise of 1877 and the End of Reconstruction* (1951); *Origins of the New South* (1951); *The Strange Career of Jim Crow* (1955); and *The Burden of Southern History* (1960). He is coauthor of *The National Experience* (1963); and editor and coauthor of *The Comparative Approach to American History* (1967); *American Counterpoint* (1971); and *Responses of the Presidents to Charges of Misconduct* (1974). He is coediting the eight-volume *Oxford History of the United States*. His publications have won for him the Bancroft Prize for History (1952), the Literary Award National Institute of Arts and Letters (1954), and the Charles S. Sydnor Prize for Southern History (1963).

GORDON WRIGHT (b. 1912), William H. Bonsall Professor of History at Stanford University, is a specialist in modern European history. A native of Washington, he received the A.B. degree from Whitman College, and the A.M. and Ph.D (1939) from Stanford University. Before returning to Stanford in 1957, he taught at the University of Oregon. He has also been a visiting professor at Columbia University, a member of the faculty of the National War College, and has held appointments to the Institute for Advanced Study and the Center for the Advanced Study of the Behavorial Sciences. He was a specialist in the U.S. Department of State, 1943–44, and a Foreign Service officer in the U.S. Embassy in France, 1945–47. He was Cultural Attaché there from 1967 to 1969. He was elected President of the Society for French Historical Studies in 1971–72, and President of the American Historical Association in 1975. He has also been named to the Ordre des Arts et des Lettres (France) and to the American Academy of Arts and Science. His books include *Raymond Poincaré and the French Presidency* (1942); *The Reshaping of French Democracy* (1948); *France in Modern Times* (1960; rev., 1974); *Rural Revolution in France* (1964); *France in the Twentieth Century* (1965); and *The Ordeal of Total War, 1939–1945* (1968). He is coauthor of *European Political Systems* (1953; 1959); *A History of World Civilization* (1957); coeditor of *An Age of Controversy* (1963; rev. 1973); and editor of *Jules Michelet's History of the French Revolution* (1967).

Index

DATE DUE

DISPLAY			
FEB 2 8 '78			
MAR 16 '79			
OCT 21 '80			
NOV 11 '80			
NOV 01 '80			
ILL 811013 2 wks use			
OCT 1 9 1981			
DEC 17 '91			
GAYLORD			PRINTED IN U.S.A.